RECORDING
GUITAR
AND BASS

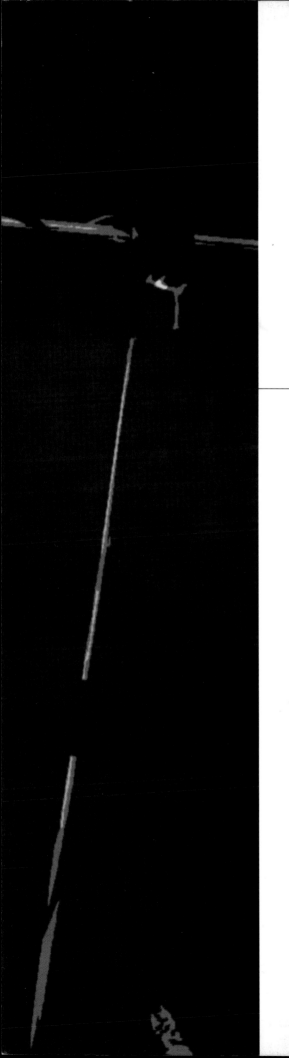

RECORDING
GUITAR
AND BASS

Getting a great sound
EVERY TIME YOU RECORD

by **HUW PRICE**

Backbeat
Books

RECORDING GUITAR AND BASS
by HUW PRICE

A BACKBEAT BOOK

First edition 2002

Published by Backbeat Books

600 Harrison Street,

San Francisco, CA 94107, US

www.backbeatbooks.com

An imprint of The Music Player Network United
Entertainment Media Inc.

Published for Backbeat Books by Outline Press Ltd,

115j Cleveland Street, London W1T 6PU, England

www.backbeatuk.com

ISBN 0-87930-730-7

Art Director: Nigel Osborne

Design: Paul Cooper

Editorial Director: Tony Bacon

Editor: Dave Hunter

Photography: Miki Slingsby

Production: Phil Richardson

Origination by Global Graphics (Czech Republic)

Print by Colorprint Offset Ltd (Hong Kong)

02 03 04 05 06 5 4 3 2 1

Contents

The Brave New World of Recording

It's a whole new world out there for the musician. Relying on your skills as a player or composer is no longer good enough: you need to be able to make yourself sound great on record, too. The recording industry has changed radically in recent years. The fan wouldn't necessarily notice it, but there has been a major revolution, which alters every aspiring career musician's role within the music business. Anyone with a decent computer and a good analog/digital interface – relatively inexpensive gear these days – can capture quality recordings that technically exceed the reproduction capabilities of the standard consumer audio CD. To the trained ear, however, such home-brewed sonics too often sound cold, flat, lacking in dynamics and, frankly, home-made. If you have tried recording your own music, you might be feeling frustration because your efforts never sound like the records your heroes make. The audio quality of your equipment is very high, but your guitar and bass sounds are often low grade. This is because the problem invariably originates at source.

To do yourself justice, you need to know how to make your guitar, bass or amplifier sound great. Before it even hits the tape or hard disk, that carefully honed sound has to be captured with precision and accuracy using microphones. This book is here to guide you: it's a compendium of sonic recipes and tonal tips for recording guitar and bass like the professionals, as it's done in the world's finest studios. The sonic virtue of a record is determined before you even hit the "record" button. It is easy to acquire top-notch gear these days, but without the knowledge and expertise to maximize that equipment's potential, your investment and best efforts might be in vain.

There are many guides to sound engineering available from bookshops, but these rarely contain more than a couple of paragraphs about guitars and bass. This book is directed specifically towards recording electric guitar, bass, and acoustic guitar. The information contained is based on my years of experience in professional recording studios working as a sound engineer and as a producer. You won't find this stuff in other textbooks because this goes beyond theory. I will be writing about the recording techniques (and tricks) that are actually used to create some of your favorite records.

As you will quickly gather as you read on, many aspects of recording are based on common sense and are actually quite simple. Taking a little science on board, however, will make you an even better recordist, so I hope you will bear with me when we get into the physics. It's probably far less painful than you think, and will enrich your musical life no end.

Reality And Illusion

It is important to discuss what we are actually trying to achieve through our recordings. In essence we are creating an illusion – a "sonic photograph." It is not and cannot be reality. Maybe this sounds overly philosophical, but the concept is crucial to understanding the purpose and limitations of recorded music. Consider a simple analogy from the visual arts. The subject of a photograph is generally recognizable, be it a face or a landscape, but nobody is fooled into thinking that it's the real thing. Accepting the limitations of the form, the photographer can enhance the image by choosing black and white, sepia or color. He can use filters to enhance or eliminate colors and he can change the balance of light and shade. Recording sound involves the same principles.

To extend the analogy, microphone selection is like choosing a lens for the camera. We deliberately use the characteristics of microphones to create desired effects. As with lenses, we often base our choice on a mike's inaccuracy rather than its accuracy. A specific mike – or lens – is used to "bend" reality in the direction we require to achieve specific results. The medium we record onto (like different brands of film) also has an influence on the end result. Analog tape is noisy but it has a warmth and musicality that many people claim is missing from digital media. On the other hand, digital hard-disc recording offers great flexibility and the opportunity to manipulate and control sound. Through this we can create music in new and exciting ways, which compensates for the supposed sonic deficiencies of the digital domain. The effects we use such as compression and equalisation correspond to the filters used by photographers. We can (and do) filter sound. Finally, the combination of all these elements to produce a final product, the mix, equates to the process of development.

Being Loud And Sounding Loud

What this actually means is that your 100W Marshall stack cranked up to "Patent Applied For" will sound different when it's coming out of two tiny hi-fi speakers than it does when you're standing in front of it in a room or on stage. That's inevitable but not necessarily a bad thing. As engineers and producers (recordists) it's part of our job to create the illusion of volume and power even when we're listening at low volume levels. Put another way, there's a difference between something being loud and sounding loud. I'll give you an example: have you noticed that some of your records sound great when the volume is turned up but they sound weak or thin when you're listening quietly? Other records sound great whatever the listening volume; these records appear to be loud even when they are played quietly. We call this "apparent volume."

The techniques used to achieve this illusion of loudness include compression, equalisation, multitracking, varispeeding the tape machine, and the good old-fashioned art of microphone placement. Digital effects such as sonic maximisation and audio energizing are also employed – often at the mastering stage.

The Purist Approach

Some genres of music – classical and acoustic jazz for example – demand a recorded sound that, as closely as possible, simulates reality. You might have noticed that some records in your collection create the impression that you could get out of your chair and walk into the room with the musicians. Every instrument in the mix seems to occupy a space all on its own and, on a really good hi-fi system, might even feel like a physical presence in the room.

This "purist" method is often accomplished using the simplest approach and a minimum (if any) of processing or effects. It does, however, require a solid grounding in recording technique, great sensitivity, plus a willingness to experiment and listen critically. Unfortunately this all takes time. Listen to Ry Cooder's soundtrack to *Paris, Texas*. The detail is incredible, with every knock of the slide, every scrape of the strings and every (behind the slide) ghost-tone harmonic clearly audible. If maximum "power" (depending on how you define it) and "loudness" are not your primary concerns then techniques from classical and jazz recording can be used. We will look at a variety of stereo microphone techniques, as well as ambient micing and multiple mikng of guitar cabinets. You might find this interesting if you like the type of approach that Ry Cooder, Steve Earle, Daniel Lanois or even Steve Albini brings to recorded guitar sound.

Experimental Techniques

At the other end of the spectrum, you might believe that, given the ultimate futility of trying to reproduce the "real" sound, you should abandon the effort altogether. Why not try to create sounds and textures that can only be achieved through processors and effects? After all, guitars and amps sound like guitars and amps and they always will. We can choose to celebrate the limitations of the form and repeat ourselves ad infinitum, or we can push back the envelope through the creative use of sonics. This is not necessarily breaking with tradition; processing has been with us ever since guitarists first started deliberately distorting their amplifiers. Think back to Brian Eno using his EMS synthesizer to treat Robert Fripp's E-Bowed guitar on *Heroes* by David Bowie. Listen to The Edge, Andy Summers, and Radiohead. Nowadays technology presents us with opportunities and possibilities that would have seemed like science fiction only ten years ago.

Sound Quality

When I started out as a sound engineer, I made the mistake of telling the indie superstar I was working with that we were getting a bad sound. "There's no such thing as 'bad' sound or 'good' sound," he said, "there is only sound." I have long since realized that he was right: sound quality is subjective – just like musical merit. Generally a consensus exists, and we use it to approach a definition of quality, but who's to say that the fuzzy "wasp in a tin can" sound produced by your 2x10 "Valvegrate" combo couldn't be the world's coolest guitar sound in the right context (arguably the city dump)?

If you listen to Chicago blues from the '50s, early rock'n'roll or rockabilly you are likely to hear some of the rawest sounds ever put to tape. Those records were made using the most basic, primitive equipment – but how many times have you heard people say that this music sounds "real?" On the other hand, think of an acoustic guitar recorded in a top studio in LA or Nashville – for example, Bruce Springsteen on *The Ghost Of Tom Joad*. It sounds pristine, even beautiful. You're certain it's an acoustic guitar but in your heart you know… acoustic guitars don't actually sound like that. If you're unconvinced, check out Bruce's acoustic guitar on *Nebraska*, which was recorded at home on a 4-track cassette machine. It sounds rough and brutal but somehow more truthful and compelling, and there's a world of difference between the two. Throughout the '90s there was a lot of talk about lo-fi music. It's odd, maybe a misnomer, because so much of what we call "hi-fi" actually sounds artificial and it is "lo-fi" that approaches the way music actually sounds when it is being performed right in front of you, by a band or a solo performer.

One night when I was doing concert sound, a visiting American engineer told me: "Studio stuff is boring, there's no danger in it. With live sound you only have one chance to get it right." At first I agreed, but as I thought more about it, I decided it was not true. When you make a record it is set in stone, and if you get it wrong, people will be listening to it for years to come. If you have a bad sounding gig, most people will have forgotten about it by the next day.

You should be prepared for some initial disappointments when you get serious about recording. The amp that you love so much for gigging will often sound unconvincing in the studio. The blend of effects pedals that sounds amazing to 500 moshing fans in a concert hall might sound like mush amid the other instruments in a studio mix, and so on. It's one of those being-loud vs. sounding-loud things again. Try to be realistic: you're not going to get an exact Jimi Hendrix tone out of the aforementioned 2x10 "Valvegrate" combo with your Korean Strat, however good the engineer is. Instead, what you might discover is your own sound. That is something that will be far more important to you in the long run.

From the age of 15 I studied every guitar magazine I could get my hands on. Later I devoured studio magazines too. I would recommend these magazines to anyone who is interested in sound recording. Amid those features and interviews lurks a wealth of knowledge. I knew which guitars and amps Stevie Ray Vaughan used a year before I first heard him play on *Let's Dance*, so do your research. The most distant and dimly remembered recording tip might spring to mind just when you need it most, to inspire the perfect sound for that sure-fire hit your band has been struggling all night to nail down.

Sound waves, Harmonics and distortion

The physics of sound, and how we can best capture it.

SOUND AND HEARING

There are three main elements involved in sound: generation, transmission, and detection. A loudspeaker, a plucked or bowed string, or the soundboard of an acoustic guitar generates sound through vibration. Their vibration causes the air molecules in front of them to compress and decompress. This is called compression and rarefaction, and it creates regions of pressure above and below atmospheric levels.

Sound is then transmitted by air particles bumping into one another, spreading away from the source. Sound travels at approximately 1,130 feet per second; thankfully, air molecules do not, otherwise we'd be in danger of being blown over if we stood in front of a bass drum.

Ears and microphones detect sound. When we record, we use microphones to detect acoustic energy and transform it into electrical energy. This information is then stored magnetically on analog tape or as digital data on digital tape or a hard-disc recorder. This enables us to send the stored information back into the air via a vibrating loudspeaker cone, to be detected by other ears in a different time and place.

The Ear

Ears and microphones are transducers, which means they convert one form of energy into another. The ear transforms acoustical energy into mechanical energy, then into electrical impulses that are sent to the brain. The information is then decoded to determine loudness, pitch and direction. The outer ear collects the sound and directs it through the ear canal. The sound waves hit the eardrum and are transferred mechanically across the middle ear by three small bones called the hammer, anvil, and stirrup. Inside the fluid filled inner ear is a coiled tube called the cochlea. Tiny hairs inside this tube respond to particular frequencies. When one of these is bent it fires a nerve impulse. A bundle of 4,000 fibers carry these electrical impulses to the brain via the auditory nerve.

Sound Waves

Sound is a disturbance that propagates through air. This disturbance is caused by something vibrating, for example a speaker or a plucked guitar string. When acoustic guitar tops or speakers vibrate they compress and release the surrounding air particles, causing them to radiate outwards. You can imagine this as a pebble hitting a pond, causing waves to spread out in a circle around the point of impact. Sound waves, however, radiate in three dimensions, creating a continually expanding sphere around the source.

The simplest form of sound wave is called a sine wave. The frequency of a sound – measured in Hertz (Hz) – is defined as the number of complete waves, or cycles, occurring per second (or, as discussed earlier, the number of times it moves from rarefaction to compression and back again). Musically we can equate high frequencies with high pitch and low frequencies with low pitch. If the sine wave in the diagram (right) completes its cycle from point A to point B once every second, its frequency is 1 Hertz (Hz). In reality we would not be able to hear this sound. Human hearing has a lower limit of around 20Hz and an upper limit at best of 20,000Hz (20kHz). Our upper limit drops as we get older – especially if we run our amps too loud on a regular basis. Interestingly, women's hearing is generally better than men's.

The physical distance traveled by a sound as it moves through one complete 360-degree cycle is known as its "wavelength," as shown in **diagram A**. Frequency and wavelength are related and can be calculated as Wavelength = Speed Of Sound divided by Frequency.

High frequency sounds have short wavelengths and low frequency sounds have long wavelengths. The wavelength of a 20kHz frequency is around half an inch long, and the wavelength of a 20Hz signal is around 56 feet. As temperature rises, the speed of sound increases. This can cause tuning problems, because if wavelength stays constant but the speed of sound increases, there is a corresponding increase in pitch.

COMPLEX WAVEFORMS AND HARMONICS

A sine wave has a very pure sound. For example, the noise produced by a tuning fork is a sine wave. So why does a tuning fork producing an A note (440Hz) sound different to an A played on your guitar? The reason is that your guitar creates a much more complex waveform. The tuning fork only produces one frequency, the fundamental, but the guitar produces the fundamental plus a series of harmonics. It is the balance or ratio of the harmonics with the fundamental frequency that shapes the timbre, or tone, of the instrument.

Now pick up your guitar and play the A string open. The note you hear is the fundamental frequency, in this case 440Hz. The point half way along the string is the point of maximum vibration amplitude; this is called an antinode. There is no vibration at each end of the string – the saddle and the nut – and these points are called nodes. (See **diagram B** on the following page.)

When the distance between the nodes is halved, the frequency of the note is doubled. Play a harmonic exactly half way along the same string to test this out; this happens to be directly above the 12th fret unless, like me, you own a Gretsch… in which case it'll be around there somewhere.

This produces the first harmonic, which is an octave above the fundamental and double its frequency, 880Hz (**diagram C**, overleaf). Note that there are now two antinodes and three nodes. If you pluck a harmonic one third of the way along the string – above the 7th or 19th fret – you will produce the second harmonic (**diagram D**, overleaf). The 5th fret marks one quarter of the string's length, and the harmonic at that point is the third harmonic (**diagram E**, overleaf).

You will find more high harmonics bunched closely together at ever-decreasing volume between the 4th fret and the nut. Place your finger lightly on the string at the 5th fret and move it slowly towards the nut whilst you are picking. You will hear the harmonic series. For each higher harmonic, one more node is added, and for any harmonic the nodes are always an equal distance apart.

When we think of a Fender (as opposed to a Gibson) we imagine a guitar with a "bright" sound; that is, with a lot of high frequencies. This means that the materials

CD track 1: sine wave

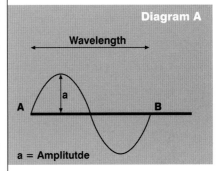

Diagram A
Wavelength
a
A   B
a = Amplitutde

WAVELENGTH

The distance a sound wave travels is called its wavelength. The relationship between wavelength and frequency is simple: low frequencies have long wavelengths and high frequencies have short wavelengths. Amplitude is the measure of a wave's intensity, which we perceive as volume.

CD track 2 harmonic series

HARMONICS

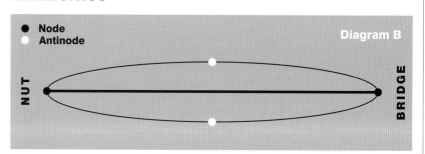

Diagram B

- ● Node
- ○ Antinode

NUT — BRIDGE

NODES AND ANTINODES

When an open guitar string is plucked, the bridge saddle and nut act as the nodes – the points at each end of the string where there is no vibration, as shown in diagram B above. Half way along the string, at the point of maximum vibration, we find the antinode.

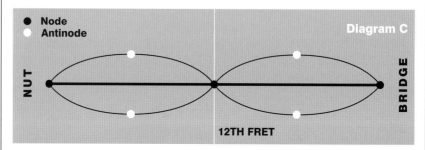

Diagram C

- ● Node
- ○ Antinode

NUT — BRIDGE

12TH FRET

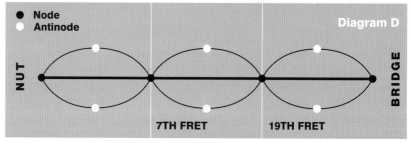

Diagram D

- ● Node
- ○ Antinode

NUT — BRIDGE

7TH FRET   19TH FRET

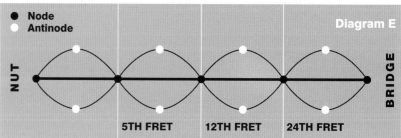

Diagram E

- ● Node
- ○ Antinode

NUT — BRIDGE

5TH FRET   12TH FRET   24TH FRET

FIRST, SECOND AND THIRD HARMONICS

Continue dividing the guitar string into halves, thirds and quarters to reveal the open note's first (C), second (D), and third harmonics (E). Most guitarists will already recognize these as the natural harmonics produces by lightly damping the string over the 12th, 7th and 5th frets respectively. When any open note is played – not necessarily a natural harmonic itself – the buildup of these harmonics contributes greatly to the guitar's timbre or tone.

used in its construction – the bolt-on maple neck, ash or alder body, and single-coil pickups – all combine to accentuate the upper harmonics in relation to the fundamental. At the other end of the spectrum, a carved-top Gibson jazz guitar like a Super 400 or a Tal Farlow is constructed to produce a warm, pure sound with more emphasis on the fundamental and the lower harmonics. The Jazz guys who use these also tend to favor flatwound strings and the neck pickup, both of which provide fewer high frequencies.

DISTORTION

Harmonic Distortion

At this point you might be wondering how all this talk about frequencies and harmonics relates to you as an electric guitar player. Well, it's not just the wood, pickups, and strings that determine the balance of harmonics in your sound (that is to say, your tone), it's also the circuitry in your amplifier. In theory the sole purpose of an amplifier is to take a quiet sound and make it louder.

In hi-fi terms, the waveform should remain completely unchanged by the amplification process. The late, great Mr. Leo Fender and his contemporaries, however, did not (thank God) set out to make hi-fi amplifiers. They were interested in producing high volume levels from simple circuits with the minimum number of components. Consequently their amplifiers tended to be non-linear. This means that as the guitarist turned up his amplifier, volume would increase in a linear fashion up to the point of the amplifier's maximum undistorted output level. Above this, any attempt to produce additional volume by turning the volume control higher or playing harder causes the top of the wave form to be chopped off. Distorted amplifiers shift the balance of the fundamental frequency and the upper harmonics that are present in the original signal. The distorted sound becomes saturated with harmonics. This is harmonic distortion – also known as *kerrchang!* We like that.

You have probably heard the term "clipping" or "square wave" used to describe distorted sounds. **Diagram F** (right) shows how a square wave can be built up by adding harmonics to a sine wave.

In the same way that instruments can be distinguished by their harmonics, so can amplifiers. The class A circuitry of a Vox AC30 amplifier, for example, has a softer, more harmonically complex distortion characteristic than a class A/B Fender or Marshall. For their own part, old Fenders and Marshalls tend to have more bite, edge and rawness. All of these characteristics are affected by the harmonic character of the individual amplifier as it goes into distortion.

Intermodular Distortion

To complicate matters even further, speakers designed for guitar amplifiers are also highly colored and exert a significant influence on sound. In fact, because it is the speaker that actually produces the acoustic energy, your precious tone is at its mercy. This is probably why very few guitarists choose to retrofit their Mesa/Boogie dual rectifier combos with Fane Crescendos. Mechanical and magnetic non-linearities can also cause speakers to exhibit harmonic distortion when they're pushed to their limit. Some players like this, and this is why many Americans choose to put Celestion speakers in Fender amps in order to emulate that famous "British Sound." It's reasonable to assume that a 12" speaker will sound different from a 10" speaker. The former is characterized by a long "ahh" sound and the latter by a long "eee;" again, this is due to harmonic coloration.

Speakers can also produce a less pleasing effect known as intermodular distortion. This occurs when a speaker is required to reproduce high and low frequencies simultaneously. The low frequencies modulate the highs due to the doppler effect. As the speaker cone moves forwards, the pitch of the high harmonics is slightly raised and as it moves back their pitch drops. This can

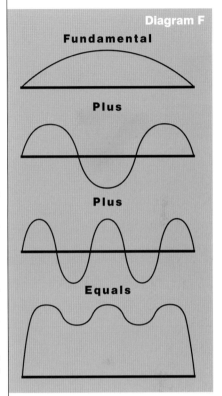

Diagram F
Fundamental
Plus
Plus
Equals

SQUARE WAVE DISTORTION

Adding further harmonics to a sine wave creates harmonic distortion, also known as "square wave" distortion. When the sound waves from the note's harmonics are added to the note, the otherwise pure sine wave becomes perceptively "squared off" – as in the diagram above – which explains the name.

produce strange, discordant results where the effect has no harmonic relationship to the fundamental frequency.

Frequency Distortion

The unevenness in frequency response that can occur even with undistorted amplifiers and speakers is known as "frequency distortion." Room acoustics and speaker placement can dramatically alter your tone by inducing this form of distortion. Hard, reflective surfaces can create a harsh, edgy sound, while soft furnishings and carpet can make things sound dull. If your speakers are placed next to a wall or in a corner, you will experience an increase in bottom end. This is why your amp can sound awesome one night and lifeless the next. It's also one of the reasons that you need tone controls. You can spend hours carefully honing your sound at home, but don't assume that it will automatically translate to the club, soundstage or studio.

Bottom Octave Deficiency

This form of distortion describes the situation where the lowest frequencies sound weak, or even disappear. Poor speakers and/or cabinet design generally cause this. If you send a 50Hz sine wave through a standard 4x12" cabinet the fundamental will disappear, but you will hear higher harmonics. Of course, these are actually distortion. We might not even notice the absent fundamental because our brains paste in the missing frequencies. This acoustic phenomenon is known as "synthetic bass."

To properly reproduce extremely low fundamental frequencies, large, air-tight (infinite baffle) speaker cabinets are needed with effective internal dampening. These things are needed to absorb and dissipate the sound waves emanating from the rear of the speakers, which can otherwise weaken the low-frequency reproduction through phase cancellation.

All of this might seem more like a high school physics class in acoustics than something you expect to find in a book about recording guitars. But to understand how guitars produce the rich, complex harmonic sounds we love so much – and how they differ from the pure tone of a tuning fork – makes us better able to record them. Understand where your sound comes from, and you might stand a chance of capturing it.

Microphones

The mics that are best suited to recording guitars, how they function, and how to use them.

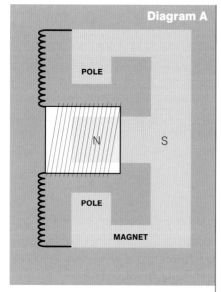

Diagram A

POLE

N

S

POLE

MAGNET

DYNAMIC MICROPHONE

The most basic and most common type of microphone in general use, the dynamic moving coil mic employs a coil moving within a magnetic field to convert sound to electrical energy.

CD track 4: **dynamic mike**

Now that we understand what a guitar sound actually is and what it consists of, we can think about recording it. Ultimately the electric guitar becomes an acoustic instrument because at the end of the sound chain it still just moves air, driving a speaker instead of a soundboard. So we need microphones to record acoustic and electric guitars. It could be argued that a recording microphone has only one purpose, and that is to make sound cross from the acoustic domain into the electrical domain with the minimum possible coloration. The performance quality of a microphone, based on this definition, is dependent on its design, its construction, and its constituent parts (components). Unfortunately, everything we have discussed so far about tone, coloration, and distortion also applies to microphones. The good news is that the recording engineer can use the technical "shortcomings" of microphones creatively, to enhance sound and achieve effects.

In a studio, or even a home recording setup, you are likely to encounter three basic types of microphone: dynamic moving coil, condenser (capacitor), and dynamic ribbon. Each has its advantages and disadvantages, but all three are used to record electric guitars.

DYNAMIC MOVING COIL

Construction

The dynamic moving coil microphone uses a light coil of wire wrapped around a cylindrical former attached to a diaphragm, as illustrated in **diagram A**. Sound pressure hitting the diaphragm causes the coil to move. The coil moves within a cylindrical magnetic field, and as it operates inside this field an AC voltage is generated in the coil. It is possible to wind many turns of wire onto the coil, and this can result in a microphone with a high output level (as with a powerful over-wound electric guitar pickup), but this can have disadvantages tonally.

These mikes tend to be very robust and can tolerate extremely high sound pressure levels (SPLs). This makes them ideal to place in front of guitar speakers. They are relatively affordable compared to other types of mikes, and ideally suited to live work. The problem with the average dynamic mike is that it tends to be inaccurate or colored and has a narrow frequency range. This is because the conversion process is indirect: the sound moves the diaphragm, which in turn moves the coil. The timbre of the sound is influenced both by the weight of the coil and by the mechanical coupling between the coil and the diaphragm. If the coil is heavy or the mechanical coupling stiff, sensitivity to high frequencies is reduced.

SHURE SM57

Transducer type – dynamic moving coil
Pickup pattern – cardioid
Frequency response – 40Hz – 15KHz
Impedance – 150 ohms (310 actual)

Dimensions – 6.125" x 1.25" (max.)
Weight – 10 oz (284g)
Case material – die cast steel

APPLICATIONS
General purpose mic for electric guitar, drums, percussion, vocals.

SHURE SM58

Transducer type – dynamic moving coil
Pickup pattern – cardioid
Frequency response – 50Hz – 15KHz
Impedance – 150 ohms (300 actual)

Dimensions – 6.375" x 2" (max.)
Weight – 10.5 oz (298g)
Case material – die cast steel

APPLICATIONS
General purpose mic for vocals, electric guitar, drums, percussion.

BEYER M201

Transducer type – dynamic moving coil
Pickup pattern – hypercardioid
Frequency response – 40Hz – 18KHz

Impedance – 200 Ohms
Dimensions – 6.3" x 0.9"
Weight – 7.75 oz (220g)
Case material – Brass

APPLICATIONS
Broadcast, speech, drums, percussion, electric guitar.

ELECTROVOICE RE20

Transducer type – dynamic moving coil
Pickup pattern – cardioid
Frequency response – 45Hz – 18kHz

Impedance – 150 Ohms
Dimensions – 8.53" x 2.14" (max.)
Weight – 1lb 10oz (737g)
Case material – steel

APPLICATIONS

Speech, broadcast, electric bass, electric guitar, brass, bass drums.

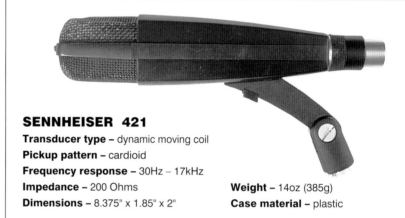

SENNHEISER 421

Transducer type – dynamic moving coil
Pickup pattern – cardioid
Frequency response – 30Hz – 17kHz
Impedance – 200 Ohms
Dimensions – 8.375" x 1.85" x 2"

Weight – 14oz (385g)
Case material – plastic

APPLICATIONS

Electric bass, drums, electric guitar, broadcast, brass.

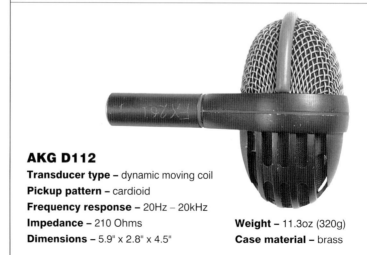

AKG D112

Transducer type – dynamic moving coil
Pickup pattern – cardioid
Frequency response – 20Hz – 20kHz
Impedance – 210 Ohms
Dimensions – 5.9" x 2.8" x 4.5"

Weight – 11.3oz (320g)
Case material – brass

APPLICATIONS

Strings, vocals, high hat, drum overheads, acoustic guitar, electric guitar.

In Use

My guess is that the majority of electric guitar sounds recorded during the last 35 years have been made with dynamic moving coil microphones. The most popular of these is the Shure Unidyne, later the SM57. Other dynamic microphones worthy of mention are the Sennheiser 421, the Shure SM58, the Beyer 201 and the Electrovoice RE20. The great thing about these mikes is that they tend to have a raised response in the upper mid frequency range. This accentuates the harmonic distortion so they are perfect for capturing that "cut" in your electric guitar sound. Many have a reduced low frequency response, which stops the sound becoming too boomy. On the other hand, their coloration and attenuated high frequency response make them unsuitable for some applications, such as recording acoustic guitar.

Studios generally have a limited supply of good microphones, which means that the sound engineer employs a hierarchical approach to microphone selection. The best microphones are reserved for the vocals; other high quality microphones will be placed over the drums, the piano or the acoustic guitar. Engineers probably started to use dynamic microphones on electric guitars because they were the only ones left in the cupboard! We are all now accustomed to their sound and they have become the industry standard. Think of the recorded sound of Metallica, Van Halen, Stevie Ray Vaughan and a host of others, and chances are you're recalling tones recorded through dynamic moving coil mikes. But it makes you wonder: why bother to spend all that money on your guitars and amps if your cherished tone ends up with a battered sixty-buck microphone as its route into rock'n'roll history?

CONDENSER MICROPHONES

Construction

There is an alternative to the dynamic mike's limited, colored capabilities, and it's called the condenser, or capacitor mike. These microphones are the most expensive in the recording studio. They are costly because they are complex to build and they have onboard amplifiers. They should capture all frequencies between the upper and lower limits of human hearing, and their response is less colored than that of dynamic mikes.

Instead of magnets and wire coils, the condenser microphone uses capacitance to convert sound waves in the air into an electrical signal. The capacitor is constructed using a solid backing plate and an ultra-thin plastic diaphragm coated

CD track 5 condenser mike

NEUMANN U87

Transducer type – capacitor (tube)
Pickup pattern – omni, cardioid, fig 8
Frequency response – 20Hz – 20kHz
Impedance – 200 Ohms

Dimensions – 7.8" x 2.2"
Weight – 1lb 1.7oz (500g)
Case material – metal

APPLICATIONS
Vocals, drum overheads, electric and acoustic guitar, room ambience, piano.

| *Microphones*

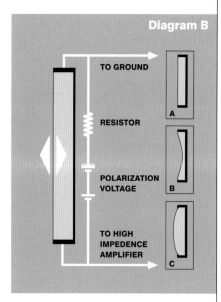

Diagram B

TO GROUND

RESISTOR

POLARIZATION
VOLTAGE

TO HIGH
IMPEDENCE
AMPLIFIER

with a microscopic layer of metal – usually gold. A high polarizing voltage is then fed to the diaphragm and the plate. When sound waves hit the diaphragm it moves relative to the plate, causing the capacitance to change. This results in a change in diaphragm voltage, which can then be amplified (**diagram B**).

Like moving coil microphones, there are mechanical factors that influence the response of the microphone. Capsule design is crucial, and some experts claim that the overall sound is 90 per cent dependant on the capsule. The tension of the plastic diaphragm strongly influences the sensitivity and high frequency response of the microphone. Over time this tension decreases – a bit like a drum skin – and the high frequency response falls off. Some engineers describe this as "warmth," others call it "dullness," but you can be certain of one thing: an original '50s Neumann or AKG condenser microphone will sound different today than it did when it left the factory.

Condenser microphones need to be supplied with power in order to polarize the capacitor and to run the onboard amplifier. We call this "phantom power" and it is generally supplied to the microphone by the mixing desk via the microphone cable at 48 volts. Condenser mikes have been around since the late '20s, and up until the mid-'60s they used tubes in their amplifier circuits. Yes, tubes, just like the orange glowing things in your guitar amplifier. In fact old tube condenser microphones have become extremely collectable and, consequently, expensive. Some engineers (myself included) have the same romantic feelings towards their tube mikes as vintage guitar fans have for their guitars.

CONDENSER CAPSULE

Remove the screen from a condenser microphone and the workings of its capsule are revealed, as in the photo above (Andy Lawrence Type B valve mike shown here). The round diaphragm is attached to a solid backplate, and together they form the capacitor which converts sound into electrical energy, as shown in diagram B at the top of the page.

ANDY LAWRENCE TYPE B

Transducer type – capacitor (tube)
Pickup pattern – cardioid
Frequency response – 20Hz – 20kHz
Impedance – 200 Ohms

Dimensions – 7.5" x 2"
Weight – N/A
Case material – brass

APPLICATIONS
Vocals, acoustic guitar, electric guitar, drum overheads, double bass, piano.

AKG C451 EB

Transducer type – capacitor
Pickup pattern – cardioid
Frequency response – 20Hz – 20kHz
Impedance – 200 Ohms

Dimensions – 6.3" x 0.75"
Weight – 4.4oz (125g)
Case material – metal

APPLICATIONS
Acoustic guitar, hi-hat, drum overheads, finger mike for double bass.

NEUMAN U47 FET

Transducer type – capacitor

Pickup pattern – cardioid

Frequency response – 20Hz – 20kHz

Impedance – 200 Ohms

Dimensions – N/A

Weight – N/A

Case material – metal

APPLICATIONS

Bass guitar, double bass, electric guitar, acoustic guitar, vocals.

AKG C414

Transducer type – capacitor

Pickup pattern – omni, cardioid, hypercardioid, fig 8

Frequency response – 20Hz – 20kHz

Impedance – 180 Ohms

Dimensions – 5.5" x 1.75" x 1.375"

Weight – 156g

Case material – brass

APPLICATIONS

Acoustic and electric guitar, drum overheads, snare, vocals, piano.

NEUMANN KM84I

Transducer type – capacitor

Pickup pattern – cardioid

Frequency response – 20Hz – 20kHz

Impedance – 50 Ohms

Dimensions – 3.7" x 0.8"

Weight – 2.82oz (80g)

Case material – metal

APPLICATIONS

Acoustic guitar, double bass, drum overheads, hi-hat, snare, piano.

PHANTOM POWER

Most modern solid state condenser microphones run on 48v phantom power, which can be supplied by most mixing desks down the mike's cable. Tube mikes, however, require higher voltages to operate. This necessitates the use of a dedicated power supply unit (PSU), such as that seen with the AKG C12 VR pictured right.

AKG C12 VR (with PSU)

Transducer type – capacitor (tube)
Pickup pattern – omni, cardioid, hypercardioid, fig 8
Frequency response – 30Hz – 20kHz

Impedance – 200 Ohms
Dimensions – 8" x 1.6"
Weight – 1lb 8oz (680g)
Case material – metal

APPLICATIONS
Electric and acoustic guitar, bass, double bass, drum overheads, vocals.

In Use

The drawback of condensers is that they tend to be more delicate than dynamic microphones, which can result in distortion from high SPLs. The advantage is that a good mike will capture more of your sound, with its subtleties and its nuances. The most common examples of condensers used for electric guitar include Neumann's U87, U89 and U47 and AKG's 414. I have also seen photographs of The Beatles using Neumann KM56s and U67s on their AC30s and the Byrds using AKG C12s.

The excellent frequency response and low distortion of condenser mikes is due to the very low mass of their diaphragms combined with the linear nature of their onboard preamps. All the major microphone manufacturers are now selling affordable condenser microphones; they've even started manufacturing tube microphones again. Neumann have reissued their U67 model and have two new models, the M47 and the M49. AKG have reissued their C12 (as the C12 VR) and introduced a budget (hybrid) model called the Solid Tube. Rode, Audio Technica, and Octava also produce tube and non-tube models at budget prices. You will almost certainly want to use a condenser microphone for your acoustic guitar.

DYNAMIC RIBBON

Construction

CD track 6: ribbon mike

Ribbon microphones have been around for a very long time; you have probably seen one being used by a television announcer in archive films from the '30s, or hanging in front of Elvis Presley on a classic album cover. They tended to be pretty large and were often suspended by springs or rubber mountings. Their construction is similar to the dynamic microphone because they both use electrodynamics. Instead of a wire coil, ribbon microphones use a very light aluminum foil suspended between the poles of a powerful magnet (**diagram C**). The tension on the foil is light, which enables it to move freely in response to sound waves. The velocity of the motion results in an alternating current being generated across the ends of the ribbon. A transformer then boosts the signal to produce a higher output voltage.

In Use

Ribbon microphones can be very accurate because, like condensers, their diaphragms have very low mass; but they really score versus dynamic moving coil mikes because the motion of the ribbon is converted directly into an electrical signal. The drawbacks are that the transformer has to be of extremely high quality to take advantage of this accuracy and that the foil ribbon has to be large to achieve sensitivity, which cuts off high frequencies. Some companies, such as Beyer and Octava, attempt to get around this problem by using two separate ribbons arranged in parallel. The low cut-off frequency is not a problem for recording electric guitars because there isn't much going on above 7kHz anyway. The big problem is that ribbon microphones are extremely fragile and high sound pressure levels can easily destroy the ribbon.

I'm a recent convert to ribbon mikes; a good one will sound incredibly real, smooth, and effortless. In fact they are everything condenser microphones pretend to be and usually cost a fraction of the price. The guitars on REM's *New Adventures In Hi-Fi* were recorded with a ribbon microphone placed about 12 inches away from the speaker, and you can hear the accuracy they have achieved there. Independently minded "alternative" producer Steve Albini is a big fan of ribbon mikes (as he notes in his interview in *Chapter 10*), as is alt-country maverick Steve Earle, who uses them for all his electric guitars, and more. Coles has reissued the classic BBC/STC 4038 model and it sounds awesome. Vintage RCA Ribbon mikes such as the Type 44 or Type 77 are highly sought after, and upscale copies are now being made by AEA. Royer makes a very robust ribbon microphone called the 121, which can withstand very high SPLs. Recently I've been using a Bang and Olufsen model and also a chunky Reslo that I found in a junk shop. Keep your eyes open, there are bargains to be found!

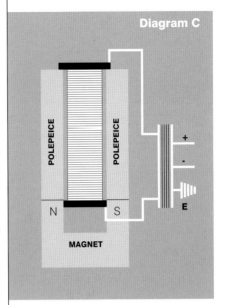

Diagram C

COLES 4038

Transducer type – dynamic ribbon
Pickup pattern – figure 8
Frequency response – 30Hz – 20kHz
Impedance – 300 Ohms

Dimensions – 7.25" x 3.25" x 2.25"
Weight – 2lb 6oz (1.077 Kg)
Case material – brass

APPLICATIONS

Electric guitar, double bass, drum overheads, vocals, strings, brass, piano.

RIBBON MIKES

Removing the screen from a ribbon microphone reveals the thin length of aluminum foil – or "ribbon" – stretched between two sturdy magnets, as on the vintage Reslo seen with case removed, above. This ultra-thin foil is the key to the mike's performance.

RESLO RBT

Transducer type – dynamic ribbon
Pickup pattern – figure 8
Frequency response – 40Hz – 15kHz
Impedance – switchable (by re-wiring):
30-50 ohm, 250 ohm, 600 ohm, Hi-Z

Dimensions – 2.75" x 1.5" (mike body)
Weight – 12oz (340g)
Case material – metal

APPLICATIONS
Strings, vocals, hi-hat, drum overheads, acoustic guitar, electric guitar.

BEYER M160

Transducer type – dual dynamic ribbon
Pickup pattern – hypercardioid
Frequency response – 40Hz – 18kHz
Impedance – 200 Ohms

Dimensions – 6.14" x 1.5"
Weight – 5.5oz (156g)
Case material – brass

APPLICATIONS
Electric and acoustic guitar, strings, vocals, drum overheads, hi-hat.

POSITIONING AND PHASE

Spillage And Separation

Over the years it has become standard studio practice to place guitar microphones very close to speaker cones. The reason we do this is to minimize spillage (also referred to as Steve Hillage). When recording groups live in the studio, one of the most common difficulties faced by studio engineers is that noise from drum kits, bass amps, and even vocals can leak or spill onto our guitar microphones. Placing the guitar microphone where the sound is loudest cannot eliminate spill, but it does ensure that the proportion of guitar captured in the microphone signal is as high as possible.

This is critical because any processing subsequently carried out on the recorded guitar sound will also be applied to the spillage. This means that adding a flanger to a guitar track with a lot of drum spill will result not only in a flanged guitar but also a flanged drum sound. Whilst this can be "groovy" or occasionally even "fab," nine times out of ten it will not be what you want. In other situations you will need to add high frequencies to a guitar track; this might improve the guitar sound but the cymbals in the mix could become overly bright. The point here is that spillage can seriously limit your options and create acute problems during the mixing process.

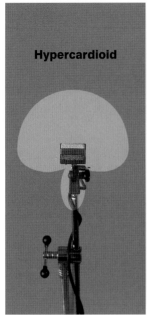
Hypercardioid

Cardioid

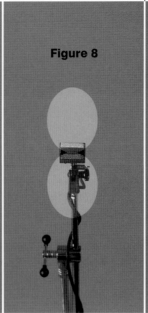
Figure 8

Omni

Diagram D

Pickup Patterns

Microphones have four distinct pickup patterns: hypercardioid, cardioid, figure 8, and omni (**diagram D**). In order to further reduce spillage and achieve good separation, recordists generally use microphones with cardioid or hypercardioid pickup patterns. This means that the microphone hears from its front and sides but rejects sound from its rear. As you might guess from the term cardioid, the pickup pattern is roughly heart shaped. Commonly used dynamic (moving coil) guitar microphones such as the Shure SM57, SM58, and Sennheiser 421 are fixed cardioid, which means you cannot alter the pickup pattern. They are also "end fire," which means you must point the microphone at the sound source.

Most condenser mikes offer a choice of pickup pattern, although many are fixed cardioid. Common choices for guitar – such as the Neumann U87 and U47 and the AKG 414 – allow you to select not only cardioid but also omni and figure 8. These microphones are "side fire," so the side of the microphone points towards the sound source.

With most end fire mikes, the direction in which you point them is obvious, but with some side fire microphones it's not so clear (**diagram E**). It's a good idea to

PICKUP PATTERNS

A microphone's pickup pattern – the most common variations of which are shown above – determines the width of its field of sound reception. In addition to this, mikes are made to be aimed straight at the sound source (end fire) or vertically face-on to it (side fire), below.

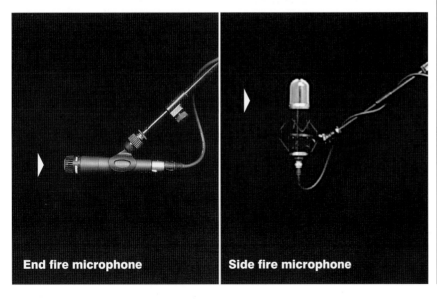
End fire microphone   **Side fire microphone**

| *Microphones*

make sure that you know which side is the "loud side." I have to confess that when I started out, I recorded my first two drum kits with the overhead mikes upside down. This is far more of an issue with condenser microphones, where the front and back often look extremely similar.

Close Mike Placement

The simplest and most common approach to recording electric guitars is to take a Shure SM57 and place it in the center of the speaker cone about half an inch away from the speaker cloth. This provides a good basic sound due to the inherent presence lift of the microphone plus good rejection of spill because of the pickup pattern.

CD tracks 7/8/9 **mike position**

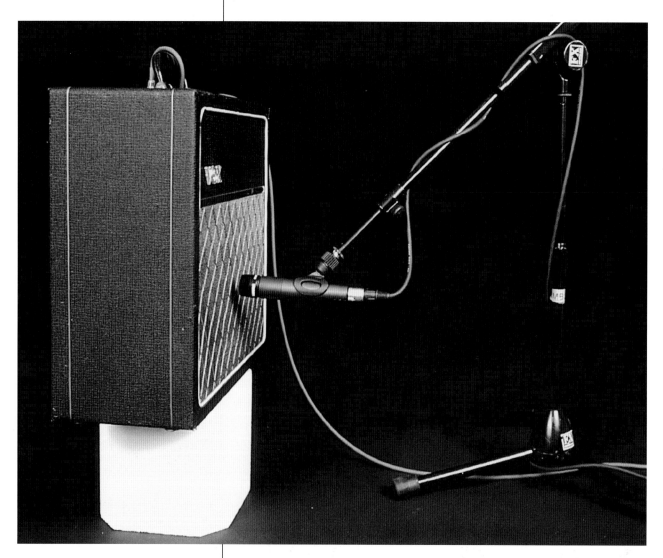

BASIC PLACEMENT

The technique of placing an SM57 close to the amp's grille cloth, directly in front of the speaker cone (as with the '61 Vox AC4 above), is probably responsible for more recorded guitar sounds than any other approach.

The section of speaker the microphone is pointed towards will profoundly affect the tone of your recorded guitar sound. A microphone firing directly into the dust cap (center) of the speaker will produce a trebly sound with a lot of bite. In other words, the high harmonics will dominate. As you move the microphone across the front of the speaker towards its outer edge, the sound becomes warmer and fatter but it starts to lose high frequencies. It is the job of the sound engineer to find a position for the microphone that reproduces the source sound as accurately as possible or enhances the sound to create a desired effect. Microphone placement is the essence of acoustic sound engineering.

CLOSE MIKING

Even most so-called "close mike" techniques involve leaving a little air between the microphone and the speaker cloth, as shown in the close-up, left. A gap of 1/4" to 1/2" is normal in such applications.

Proximity Effect

One potential problem you will encounter when close miking with cardioid microphones is tip-up, also known as the proximity effect. This occurs when the velocity exceeds the pressure component of the sound and causes a lift in the low and low-mid frequencies. We hear this as a boomy or muddy quality in our signal. This can be useful if you need to fatten up a thin sound; many vocalists exploit the proximity effect to add intimacy and weight to their performances. But more often than not you will need to overcome it.

The most obvious solution is to move the microphone further away from the

CORRECTING PROXIMITY EFFECT

The proximity effect can add a "boomy" or "muddy" quality to many condenser microphones when they are placed too close to the sound source. Moving the microphone back a few inches – as has been done with the Neumann U87 shown left – can make all the difference.

sound source or switch the pickup pattern to omni. Most condenser microphones have switchable high pass filters. This means that low frequencies (from 75Hz or 100Hz) can be filtered out. To my knowledge, only two dynamic microphones commonly found in studios – the Electrovoice RE20 and the Sennheiser 421 – provide this facility. A high pass filter enables you to reduce the proximity effect and maintain the position of the microphone where spillage is a potential problem. If spillage is not an issue you can move the microphone further away from the speaker or select an omni pickup pattern to counter it.

Using Headphones To Position The Microphone

CD track 10: cans & position

A good trick is to send the noise from your guitar amplifier back from the mixing desk into some headphones ("cans"). Sit next to your guitar amp with the headphones on and, without playing, slowly move the microphone across the front of the speaker. You will notice that the hiss and hum from your amp will change dramatically as the mike moves across it, sometimes over the space of an inch or so. If nothing else, this will demonstrate just how critical mike positioning can be.

You can use this technique to identify the optimum position for the microphone. Move the microphone until the balance of hiss and hum in the headphones matches the balance of hiss and hum coming out of the guitar speaker. Unplug the headphones, then walk back into the control room and take a listen. This will give you a great starting point in your quest for a killer guitar sound.

Ambient Sound

Spillage is not usually a problem when we're recording guitars because – more often than not – we'll be overdubbing, that is, playing along to pre-recorded rhythm tracks. Many engineers and producers, however, habitually use close microphones regardless. When a microphone is moved away from a speaker it will pick up the ambient sound of the guitar in the room as well as the direct sound from the amplifier. The further you move it from the source (i.e. the speaker), the more ambient and less punchy it becomes.

We generally try to avoid this because we might find ourselves stuck with a room acoustic that proves to be unsuitable in the context of the music. Often this only becomes apparent later in the production process. If a sound is recorded dry – with the minimum ambience – we can add reverb or delay later on, to create the illusion of a natural acoustic. The point is that engineers like to choose and control the character of that ambience.

Some genres of music – such as metal and contemporary rock – demand guitar sounds that are as dry and tight as possible. If you watch the video *A Year In The Life Of Metallica* you will see the producer building an acoustically dry environment from huge foam slabs and packing blankets to record the guitars. If a dry sound is the objective (and more often than not with electric guitars these days it is), you can achieve great results when recording at home by surrounding your amplifier with mattresses or covering it with a couple of quilts. Your neighbors will thank you for it too! If you try this, however, remember to make sure that the tubes have adequate ventilation or you could start a fire – or at least burn out those expensive matched RCA black plate 6L6s far sooner than you'd like.

Some engineers and producers take the opposite approach and deliberately exploit room acoustics to achieve natural and original sounds. As Jimi Hendrix's engineer Eddie Kramer puts it: "Distance equals depth." Materials used in the construction of rooms greatly influence their acoustic character. Recording areas in studios often have stone or wooden walls; wood and concrete floors are also common. These accentuate high frequencies, while carpet and soft furnishings soak them up. You can find interesting recording spaces at home in bathrooms, kitchens, or stairwells. Position a mike to achieve a balance of direct sound and ambience by moving it closer to or further away from the amplifier. To record in this way calls for courage, confidence, and plenty of experimentation because it is very hard, if not impossible, to dry out an ambient sound later in a production. You also need experience to know how much ambience to use and the type of ambience that will enhance the music rather than detract from it. If you get it right, you can produce music with individuality and personality. Also, you won't have to spend hours messing with digital effects, putting back in what you carefully took out. It forces you to make decisions as you go along rather than postponing them. This way the character of the music develops over time, rather than being manufactured in the last six to ten hours of the production process, during the mix.

Phase Cancellation

Before moving on to look at more advanced microphone techniques we need to talk about phase cancellation. Unfortunately this is not a new effects pedal from Electro-Harmonix; it is, however, one of the most serious hazards in sound engineering, and you need to understand it in order to make the best recordings. The **diagram F** shows two sound waves – A and B – of equal amplitude and frequency. These sounds are "in phase" with each other, and when they are added together the result is the arithmetic sum C. The sound gets louder.

In **diagram G**, signal A is 180 degrees out of phase with signal B. When these signals are combined, complete phase cancellation results – shown by C. The sound disappears into silence. If we are only using one close microphone on the amplifier then phase cancellation is not a concern. But if we choose to use two microphones – either next to each other or one on each speaker – we might experience it. If you want to hear what phase cancellation sounds like, try placing your hi-fi speakers side by side and reverse the positive and negative connections at the back of one of the speakers. Listening to your favorite records will be pretty unpleasant, with a noticeably "hollow," bass-light sound induced by the phase reversal. The effect will be even more obvious if you play a mono recording.

In the real world, sound waves are more complex than the sine waves shown in the diagrams in *Chapter 1*. Your out-of-phase signals will not completely cancel each other out. Instead they will sound thin and unnatural and might make you feel physically uncomfortable, even a little seasick after a while. A 180° phase shift is only found when the hot and cold connections in the microphone or mike cable have been incorrectly wired up.

I once took a chance on buying a vintage Vox AC10 amplifier for an extremely low price because it sounded thin and weedy; it turned out that the two speakers were out of phase. Twenty seconds with a soldering iron transformed it into the best Vox I have ever owned. This is why professional mixing desks have phase (polarity) flip buttons. Suspect mikes or phase relationships can quickly be checked with the press of a button.

Phase cancellation can also be caused by time delay. Engineers often use two microphones to record electric guitar: a close microphone is blended with an ambient microphone placed between 5 to 8 feet (1.5 to 2.5 meters) away from the amp. This offers a convenient way to control the degree of room ambience in the sound, but the benefits can be outweighed by phase cancellation. **Diagram H** shows how this can occur.

The signal from the close microphone A is combined with the signal from the ambient microphone B. The two signals are very similar – because they are both pointed at the same source – but because there is a physical gap between them, the ambient microphone B hears the sound later than the close microphone A. This delay causes a phase shift, which results in partial phase cancellation (shown in the shaded areas). As you begin to add the ambient sound to the close sound, the guitar becomes thinner, smaller, and less punchy rather than bigger and fatter. This is called "comb filtering," and unless you are specifically going for that flimsy sound or you are just completely insane you will want to avoid it. There are ways to add ambience to the sound without the compromises. In the next chapter, I'll show you some good ways to do so.

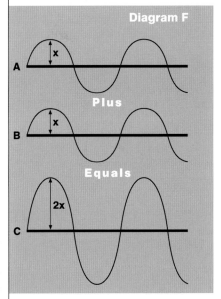

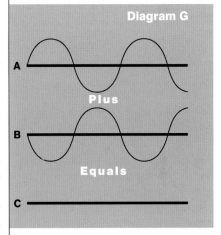

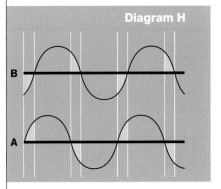

PHASE RELATIONSHIPS

Blend two sounds in phase (top), and you increase their volume. Out-of-phase signals cancel each other.

CD tracks 11-15: **close & ambient**

Advanced Microphone Techniques

Learn the art of mic positioning and you'll never have to fix it in the mix.

DIRECT AND REFLECTED SOUND

You can experience the effects of phase cancellation even when you are only using one mic. The diagram below shows how a timing difference can occur between a single mike's pickup of direct (D) and reflected (R) sound.

MINIMIZING PHASE CANCELLATION

Delay And Reflected Sound

Engineers often use the dual microphone approach to blend room ambience with a dry, close-miked signal. This technique is intended to achieve a more natural, open sound. But as we have already learned, phase cancellation can introduce problems. There are ways around this – the most obvious is to revert to one microphone and to place it relative to the speaker in order to balance the amount of ambience in the sound. Put simply, the dry sound of the close microphone will become more ambient as you move it away from the amplifier. Unfortunately phase cancellation can still result, even when we are using a single microphone.

Excepting polarity errors, phase shift in the studio is always caused by time delay. Although it is clear that a distant microphone will "hear" the sound later than the close mike, it is less obvious why this delay occurs when we are only using one microphone. The problems are caused by reflected sound.

The picture below shows a guitar amplifier with a microphone placed directly in line with the speaker. This setup would work very well if sound traveled only in

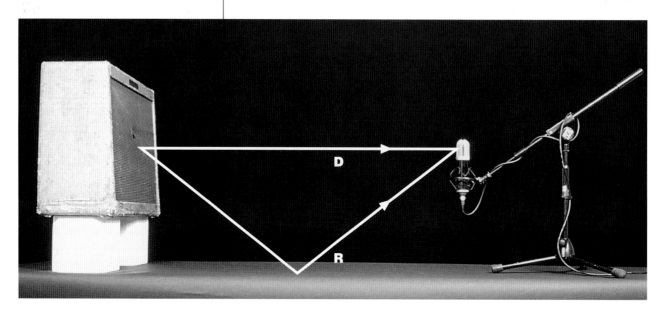

straight lines, but in reality loudspeakers radiate sound in all directions. This means that the microphone picks up the direct sound (D) and also the delayed sound reflected from the floor (R) that has traveled further.

At certain frequencies the extra path length will correspond to a 180 degree phase shift, causing phase cancellation. This will also occur if the amp is placed next to a wall, which will likewise reflect sound that the mike will pick up at a different time from the direct sound. The result is a series of evenly spaced nulls, resulting in an effect which is called "comb filtering." Many engineers and producers are using computer generated comb filter "plug in" effects in dance music. While this can sound "wicked" or "banging" on a drum loop, it might not be quite the ticket if you want to make your rock guitar track sound like Angus Young.

Placing Ambient Microphones

To find the ideal location for your ambient microphone in a big room, try standing in front of the amplifier while someone is playing through it, then very slowly move backwards. You should be able to hear that the sound becomes fatter and thinner in different locations. This happens because (at certain frequencies) the path length difference amounts to a multiple of a wavelength and the reflections are reinforcing the sound, rather than canceling each other. When you have found the "sweet spot," stand very still and place your microphone in exactly the same place as your ears. In other words, put your microphone where the sound is good!

The technique of moving your ears around an instrument to find the hot spot is incredibly useful and will always produce good results. I discovered this when I was making World Music recordings with instruments I had never even seen before. Often the best location for the microphone is not where you would expect.

AMBIENT MIKES

It takes a combination of skill and experience to mix ambient and close mikes. Many engineers begin with a distant mic 6' from the speaker, but usually you will need to try both this and the close mike in different positions to achieve the best balance of sound between the two. Below, a Reslo ribbon mike captures the close sound from a '59 tweed Fender Tremolux, while an Andy Lawrence tube condenser mike covers ambient duties.

Boundary Microphones

If space is limited but you still want to use ambient techniques you can use one of the great bargains of the audio world: the Pressure Zone Microphone or PZM.

This microphone was designed to be placed on flat surfaces, such as walls or floors, where it will not suffer from phase canceling reflections. PZM microphones could once be purchased at Radio Shack (Tandy in the U.K.) and were very reasonably priced. Thanks to their popularity in recording over recent years, other – generally more expensive – companies are now manufacturing PZMs too. We use PZMs, and sometimes condenser microphones, with a technique called "boundary miking." Simply place the microphone on the floor in front of the amp, and adjust the distance for the most desirable sound. Because the PZM is lying right on the floor – as it is designed to do (though they can be mounted on walls too, the versatile little fellows) – it is picking up direct, ambient sound, rather than any reflections from the floor.

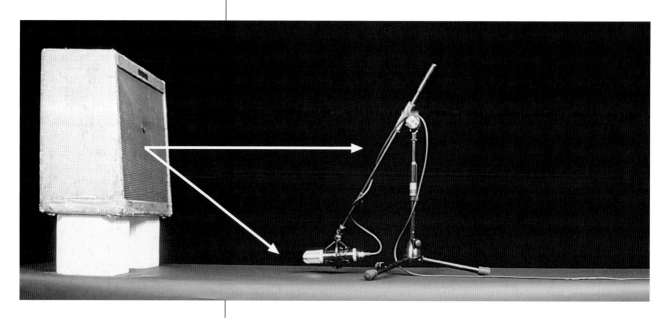

BOUNDARY MIKING

A useful technique for recording ambient sound while minimizing the hazards of phase cancellation, boundary miking can be achieved with an inexpensive PZM mike – which is specifically designed for the job – or with any good condenser mike. The latter is mounted to hover just above the floor, as above.

When condenser mikes are used for boundary miking, a similar principle applies. Mount the mike horizontally so it hovers parallel to the floor and just a short distance off it, with the capsule pointing toward the ceiling. From here, you can adjust the mike's distance from the cab to achieve the most desirable sound.

You could also try placing an ambient microphone at a distance directly in front of the speaker, then covering the floor with absorbent, sound-deadening material such as foam, carpet or a quilt. This should significantly reduce the high frequency content of the reflected sound. If you still want to use a close microphone combined with a distant mike you could even listen to the signal from both microphones wearing headphones, and then move the ambient mike to find the position that works best in combination with the close microphone.

Correcting Phase Shift On Hard Disc Recordings
If you are recording to a computer using a hard disc-based recording system, there is a simple way to correct phase shift. Make sure you record the signals from the close and ambient microphones onto separate tracks. After the part is recorded, move the sample region containing the ambient sound backwards in time – that is, towards the beginning of the arrangement – in very small increments, maybe a couple of samples at a time, while the two signals are playing. You will notice that the sound starts to thicken up as the signals move into phase then thin out if you move the region too far. Adjust the timing to achieve the thickest possible sound and adjust the balance of the two signals to taste. After this you could bounce this blend down to one track.

Figure 8 Side Rejection
Dynamic ribbon microphones are excellent for recording guitar. Due to their figure 8 pickup patterns, ribbons "hear" the direct sound and also the ambient sound (front and rear). In other words, they have a tight and narrow focus. My experience with ribbon mikes makes me suspect that the side rejection of the figure 8 pattern benefits the sound by ignoring signals reflected from side walls. Recently I switched a Neumann U67 from cardioid to fig 8 and discovered that its character became much closer to the ribbon mike I was using for comparison. This can help, especially when you are recording in an imperfect acoustic environment.

Using Multiple Microphones

In other chapters I described how engineers use the inherent coloration of microphones creatively. A classic example is the use of the Shure SM57 dynamic moving coil. This mike can be used very effectively on guitar amps because of its built in presence lift (at around 4kHz) and its tolerance of high SPLs. On the other hand it is not a particularly subtle or detailed microphone – characteristics more often associated with quality condenser mikes. This leads to an obvious question: why not use both types of microphone at the same time to get the best of both worlds?

When I am recording electric guitar I regularly use a condenser and a dynamic moving coil microphone. I take the signal from both mikes and mix them together to create the best overall sound before recording it onto a single track of my multitrack tape machine or hard disc. Quite often musicians ask why I don't record

CD track 16: close pair

MULTI-MIKING

Below, a Shure SM57 and a Neumann U87 team up to capture a vintage Vox AC10. To minimize phase cancellation, their capsules are kept as close together as possible, without touching.

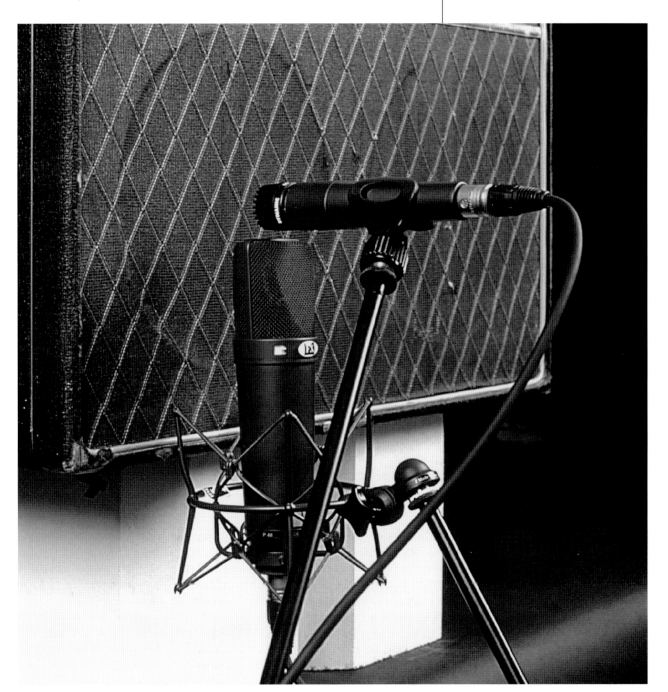

| *Advanced Microphone Techniques*

one mike on one track and the other mike on a separate track for "stereo." The point to remember is that the signal from the two microphones is not in stereo, it is essentially split mono. Panning the two microphone signals wide left and right will only result in a vague and unfocused sound.

Common combinations used by me and many other engineers are a Shure SM57 with a Neumann FET U47, U87 or U89 or an AKG 414. If I'm lucky enough to have access to tube microphones, I'm likely to use a Neumann U67 or a U47 or an AKG C12 or C12A. The dynamic mike will provide the cut, punch, and excitement. The condenser will capture the tone, subtlety, and nuance of the performance. It is important to remember what we learned earlier about phase cancellation occurring when we use more than one microphone. To minimize this, place the two mikes with their capsules as close together as possible without letting them touch. This minimizes any path-length differences.

MULTI-SPEAKER CABS

Great results can be had from miking separate speakers in multi-speaker cabs – as on the two 10s of the AC10 here.

CD track 17 **miking 2 speakers**

If you are using a 2x10", 2x12", 4x10" or 4x12" speaker cabinet, a slightly more sophisticated approach is to use two microphones and place one each on two different speakers. Note that the speakers nearest the floor will have more low end than the top speakers in a 4-speaker cabinet. Here's how you achieve the best results. Find the optimum position for the microphones, then set the mike gain for each microphone so that the level to tape or hard disc reads around –3 on the meter. After you have done this, reverse the polarity of microphone 1 (using the desk phase switch) and push the send-to-tape fader of mike 1 up to the 0 mark on the desk. Slowly push up the send-to-tape fader of microphone 2. The combined sound will get quieter, not louder, because the two signals are "out of phase" and are canceling each other out. When the sound is at its quietest point – where maximum phase cancellation is occurring – flick the phase switch again on mike 1 to put the two signals back "in phase." The sound should knock your head off!

Back-Of-Cabinet Miking

CD track 18-20 back-cab miking

Many combo amps, such as Fenders, Vox AC15s and AC30s, Mesa/Boogies, and others, have open-back speaker cabinets. Open-back cabs radiate sound from the front and the back of the cabinet (more of the tonal intricacies of speaker cabs are discussed in *Chapter 9: Speakers And Cabs*). This means that the sound we know and love when we are standing in the room with the amp cannot be captured accurately or faithfully using front microphones alone. One solution is to use a microphone placed in the rear of the cabinet. The rear microphone will pick up a sound with a throaty, low-frequency characteristic. The idea is to blend the rear

mike into the mix you have created for the front mikes; a rear microphone is the only way to capture the total sound in a close-miking situation. I love this trick and it always works for me. I like the sound of the rear mike so much that on occasion I have ended up using the rear mike on its own.

Remember that while the speaker is moving towards the front mikes it's moving away from the rear mike, so the rear mike will be out of phase with the front mikes, and you will have to correct this using the phase switch on the desk.

That's all I need to tell you about applying microphone techniques to guitar amps. There will be plenty more discussion elsewhere in this book about multi-amp setups, pro's tips and tricks, and ways to maximize the quality of your captured sounds. The best thing you can do is to experiment and find the approach that works for you, and you might even discover some tricks of your own. As I mentioned before, sound quality is subjective, so if it sounds good to you, use it! As a freelance sound engineer I work in many genres of music that require different techniques. Get your instrument sounding great, choose your microphones carefully, and place them where the sound is good. This is the essence of sound engineering and if you do that, you can't go too far wrong.

MIKING THE BACK OF A COMBO

Placing a mike at the back of an open-back combo is one of the only ways to capture the full sound of the amp.

UNDERSTANDING IMPEDANCE

In order to get the best out of our equipment, a basic understanding of impedance is essential. I won't pretend that this is an easy concept to grasp but it is not impossible, and undoubtedly worth tackling. Take your time; you might need to read this section more than once.

In a purely resistive circuit – where there are no capacitors or inductors – impedance and resistance are the same thing. Resistance is the property of a material that resists the flow of electricity by dissipating electrical energy as heat, and it is measured in ohms. Ohm's law shows the relationship between resistance (R), voltage (V) and current (I) and it can be expressed in three ways: $I = V/R$, $V = IxR$, or $R = V/I$.

If resistance is high, more voltage is needed to drive the current through the circuit. Impedance is also measured in ohms, and impedance remains constant regardless of frequency in a purely resistive circuit.

We need to look at two key areas: the impedance relationships between microphones and mike preamps, and between electric guitars and guitar amps.

Optimizing Microphone And Preamp Impedance

Output (source) impedance is related to how much current the source (e.g. a microphone) can supply, and input (load) impedance to the amount of current the circuit (e.g. the preamp) soaks up. The goal is to transfer the signal voltage from the microphone to the preamp with the smallest possible losses. We want fidelity, not power. If $V = RxI$ then 1 Volt = 10K x .0001 Amp

If load impedance (R) drops to 1K then current (I) will need to increase to maintain voltage (V). 1 Volt = 1K x .001 Amp.

In professional audio, the source (microphone) has the lowest workable impedance. This ensures that any high frequency roll-off due to cable capacitance is minimized. Also, any ambient interference (noise) is attempting to drive what is effectively a short circuit and cannot develop high voltages, therefore a good signal-to-noise ratio is maintained. The load impedance is set around ten times higher, to avoid excessive currents flowing and to allow more than one load to be placed across the microphone. You might wish to do this if you are using a mid and side pair or splitting the output of a microphone between a PA mixer and a recording setup.

A professional microphone will typically have an output impedance of less than 300 ohms. The microphone preamp should therefore have an input impedance of around 3K ohms. Some manufacturers, such as Thermionic Culture, Summit, and Avalon, include input impedance controls on their products. This enables the engineer to fine-tune the load impedance by ear to achieve the most pleasing result.

Some old ribbon microphones tend to provide very low source impedance – around 30 to 60 ohms. These microphones require a preamp with suitable load impedance (i.e. 300 to 600 ohms) or an impedance transformer to raise the source impedance to modern standards. Fortunately, these are readily available.

High impedance (Hi-Z) microphones, such as the old "bullet" models, are great for blues harp or distorted vocals but they are not generally useful for recording or live applications. They work well plugged straight into a guitar amp. If you try to plug them directly into the microphone input of a mixing desk, you will experience distortion and a loss of level.

There is no agreed standard for the output impedance of microphones or the input impedance of preamps. Commercial preamps generally have a preset input impedance to cover the widest possible range of microphones. When evaluating a microphone it is advisable to try it with a variety of preamps; the microphone might sound great with one and very ordinary with another. Much of this can be put down to differences in impedance.

Optimizing Guitar And Amplifier Input Impedance

Unlike a microphone, a guitar pickup has high source impedance – typically 6K to 10K. Let's examine the implications of connecting a 10K ohm pickup to three preamps with different input impedances. The calculation is simply a matter of taking the ratio of preamp impedance to total (source + preamp) impedance as follows in these three examples:

● 1K ohm input impedance. For every 10 volts that the pickup is trying to generate, 9 volts is lost in the guitar and 1 volt appears at the amp. We end up with only 10 per cent of our signal. (1:(10 + 1) = 1:11) = 10 per cent signal transfer.

● 10K ohm input impedance. For every 10 volts that the pickup is trying to generate 5 volts is lost and 5 volts appears at the amp. We end up with 50 per cent of our signal voltage. (10:20 = 1:2) = 50 per cent signal transfer.

● 100K ohm input impedance. For every 10 volts that the pickup is trying to generate, 1 volt is lost and 9 volts appears at the amp. We end up with 90 per cent of our signal. (100:110 = 10:11) = 90 per cent signal transfer.

You could also say that in c) we are "lightly loading" the guitar and so have a "higher fidelity" because of the much higher signal that this amp "sees." You might ask, "Why not go further and have 1Meg Ohm input impedance?" In this case, we would have a ratio of 100:101 = 99 per cent signal transfer. This is a good question, but there are two reasons why we don't. Firstly, the increase of input from 9 to 9.9 volts is a relatively small increase (only 10 per cent). Secondly, noise tends to be more volts than amps, so the higher the impedance of a preamp, the more of an effect noise will have. To summarize, if we compare a 1Meg ohm input preamp with a 100K ohm input we will find that we have 10 per cent more signal – but more than 10 per cent increase in noise, so that even though the signal level has increased, the signal to noise ratio has become worse.

If you want to combine guitar amplifiers, use a stereo effects pedal or dedicated splitter pedal as a buffer. That way, the output and the input are isolated and the load on the pedal does not affect the guitar. If you use a Y chord to connect two amplifiers simultaneously, the effective load impedance drops to 50K and signal loss is 20 per cent. If you combine three amplifiers this way it drops to 33K and your tone will suffer badly.

The term impedance is also used for resistance, capacitance, inductance, or any combination of these three. A circuit with capacitors and inductors is reactive and impedance in reactive circuits does not remain constant with frequency. An electric guitar pickup and a cable have all three elements. This often results in lower signal level and an uneven frequency response – particularly in the top end. A guitar pickup is both resistive and inductive while guitar cables are always capacitive. Resistors cannot store electrical energy but inductors and capacitors can.

Inductors are measured in Henrys (H) and capacitors in Farads (F), microfarads (mF) or picofarads (pF). Some electronic engineers call the last two muffs and puffs. As frequency increases, the impedance of a capacitor decreases and the impedance of an inductor increases.

If we place a 0.01 mF capacitor across the output of the guitar we create a low pass filter. Voltage remains constant to approximately 800Hz, where it begins to drop. It's all downhill from there! The lows get through, but the highs are blocked.

At around 2kHz it's down by 3dB and voltage will fall to around 50 per cent of its original value as capacitive impedance decreases. This is why long guitar cables cause a lack of bite and high harmonics. Cable capacitance is proportional to length, so try to keep your cables as short as possible.

| *Advanced Microphone Techniques*

Matters are further complicated by the inductance of the pickup. Resistance remains constant but inductive impedance increases with frequency, raising source impedance. As we have seen, high source impedance relative to load impedance leads to a loss of signal level. Increasing the number of wire coils on the bobbin creates "hot" pickups; this is called over-winding. The extra coils provide a higher signal voltage, but also increase inductance to around 8H. This results in a 3dB loss of signal voltage at 2kHz, increasing by 6dB per octave. This is why hot pickups often sound loud but also dull and lifeless – especially for clean sounds when we want clarity and sparkle. One partial solution is to change the load impedance of the amplifier to 200kHz. This shifts the 3dB point to 4kHz where the effect is less noticeable.

At this point you are probably wondering why you can't simply turn up the treble and presence controls on your amp to counteract the effect. You can, but you might make the situation worse. In a guitar set-up a resistive and inductive pickup feeds resistive and capacitive volume and tone controls. The signal passes through a capacitive cable where it meets a resistive and capacitive load impedance. The effect of all these factors is complex and difficult to predict. We can say that above a certain frequency (the cut-off frequency) the signal level will drop (**diagram A**, left). Resistance in the circuit produces a resonant peak around the cut-off frequency, which can sound very strange (**diagram B**, left). Your treble pot is more likely to be behaving as a resonance control and your guitar will be sounding more like a second-rate analog synthesizer.

Studio guys and musicians talk a lot of voodoo about magical microphone and preamp combinations or guitar and amp combinations. This is all great fun and part of our musical culture. It could be argued, however, that much of this stems from ignorance regarding the true effects of impedance on sound. A little science and study can help you to optimize your tone using the equipment you already have. You might also achieve significant improvements by spending peanuts instead of a week's wages.

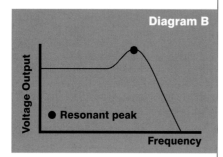

Diagram A

Voltage Output

Frequency

Diagram B

Voltage Output

● **Resonant peak**

Frequency

RESONANT PEAKS

The effect of a resistive and capacitive load impedence will induce a cut-off frequency in any signal (top diagram). Excessive resistance in the circuit, however, can induce an odd-sounding resonant peak before a sudden drop of frequency response.

Do's And Don'ts
● Try to keep your guitar cables as short as possible.
● Avoid driving multiple amplifiers using a splitter cable or Y plug.
● Always use a buffer or stereo effects box to split the signal.
● Never use an amplifier with less than 100k input impedance, unless your guitar or bass has low impedance pickups.
● Check the impedances of your existing amplifier and guitar to assess their compatibility. The manufacturer or distributor should be able to able to help you.
● Don't plug low impedance microphones directly into guitar amps. Use a high impedance microphone or run the low impedance microphone signal backwards through a DI box.

Studio Approach

Enter the studio like a pro, and get the best out of your recording efforts.

Gigs are gigs and recording is recording. While that might seem a statement of the obvious, it is important to understand that our considerations for gigging are not necessarily the same as for recording. A common mistake many musicians make is to assume that something which works in a live context will automatically translate to the studio environment. Extreme volume and poor room acoustics at gigs combine brilliantly to obscure any number of problems. Most guitarists experience shock when they first start playing in studios. It comes as a great surprise to discover just how sensitive studio microphones, preamps, and monitor speakers can be – and how many flaws, and just plain ugly tone, they are capable of picking up.

This is the moment our aspiring guitar hero discovers that the handles on his speaker cabinet vibrate like a pneumatic drill every time he plays an A note, the microphonic tinkling of his brand new Chinese tubes adds a pretty Yuletide atmosphere to his Pantera-like chugs, and the "harmonically interesting" jazz-fusion bass line he had been enjoying was actually being played by his filter cap. Generally this comes as a disappointment.

Intonation
As a rule – in addition to all of the above – guitars are also found to be out of tune. During a gig you probably won't even notice this because:
● You can't hear yourself
● You can't hear anyone else, or…
● You can hear the other guys, but they are out of tune too!
Of course I'm talking about intonation. In the studio this problem will quickly reveal itself through the most humble of microphones. It is rare in my experience to record a guitar without having to set it up for the session – usually on the studio pool table. On one album I set up two basses and at least five guitars in a single week. In fact the Gretsch I took to the recording was the most accurate of the lot. Believe me, you know you're in trouble if a Gretsch is your most in-tune guitar.

I'm sure there are dozens of articles published in guitar magazines every year that tell you how to intonate your guitar, and there are certainly plenty of good books out there that do the same. I think it's an essential skill for any serious guitar player to be able to maintain their instrument and perform running repairs. If you can't afford to have it done professionally, then please learn to do it yourself – it's not rocket science. The pro guys will probably do a more accurate job with their strobe tuners, but even if you have to use your Boss stage tuner and your ears, it's better than nothing. You should also check your intonation regularly because any guitar's set-up moves around a lot due to temperature fluctuations, atmospheric conditions, and just carting it to the gig and back day in and day out. Quite often the positioning of the bridge saddles is fine; the problem is that the neck needs adjustment. You might find that your tuning difficulties vanish with a quarter turn of the truss rod. The magnetic field from guitar pickups (especially Fender-style single-coil ones, and the neck pickup in particular) set close to the bass strings will inhibit string vibration. This pulls the bass notes flat above the 12th fret. When you adjust your intonation, do it with the pickups moved away from the strings. You can raise them back up when you have finished but you should stop at the point where it begins to affect tuning. You'll get better tone this way too, even if you do have to work harder.

The last thing I want to say about tuning (I promise) is that even the most carefully set up guitar will always sound slightly out of tune. This is unavoidable on any fretted instrument. The trouble originates in the fact that "equal-tempered" tuning used on guitars involves some unavoidable compromises in intonation. In the studio, the best way to combat this is to tune up while fretting the notes in the area of the neck where you are actually playing for that particular song, not with open strings or 12th fret harmonics. If you are using a capo, tune up with the capo mounted on the guitar. One possible exception to this is for guitars equipped with the Buzz Feiten tuning system, which employs a compensated nut to help eliminate the inevitable minor imperfections introduced by equal-tempered tuning. I haven't had a whole lot of direct experience with such guitars myself, and with some critics the jury is still out, but I know plenty of techs and players who swear by the intonation improvements that the Feiten system brings, and many high-end guitar builders are now employing it on their instruments.

Equipment

Speaker cabinets generally have to endure years of suffering on the end of ridiculously overpowered guitar amplifiers. The vibrations caused by these extreme volume levels will eventually shake loose screws, bolts and even glue joints. This means that your guitar cabinets are continually falling apart. The rattling and vibrating noises produced by these loose fixings can be a huge obstacle in the studio. Often they will be more noticeable when using a clean sound than they will be with distortion.

During studio recording, problems cost money. It is the guitar player's job to ensure that their equipment is working properly before it is taken into the studio. You owe this to the studio staff and also to your own bandmates. Getting rid of these noises in the studio can take hours of work with duct (gaffer) tape and bubble wrap. The studio clock will be ticking all the time, and studio time is money. It is not something the engineer can fix by "trying a different microphone" or "putting the microphone somewhere else" – however tempting the second suggestion might be for the poor engineer. Listen closely for any stray noises emanating from any part of your gear prior to entering the studio, and sort it out before it becomes a frustrating and potentially expensive problem. Remember: these problems are your problems, and therefore your responsibility.

Tube Noises

Tubes can also produce unwanted noises. These usually take the form of high-pitched ringing or metallic tinkling sounds, called microphony. Some brands of tube are less microphonic than others but generally you should have new preamp tubes checked for microphany before you buy them. In old-fashioned tube hi-fi amps microphany was not an issue, but it certainly is when the tubes are placed in an amplifier head that sits on a violently vibrating speaker cabinet. I have experienced particular problems with the EF86 and ECF82 tubes in my Vox AC10. My prized, original-specification Mullards were notoriously microphonic and were not up to the job. A knowledgeable tube dealer finally helped me out immensely by recommending what I would have thought was a lesser make of tube, but one which certainly turned out to be less microphonic.

If you are running a separate head and cabinet, the most obvious solution is to take the head off the cabinet and place it on a chair next to the cab. With combo amps like Voxes and Fenders this is more difficult (and dangerous) because it involves the partial dismantling of the cabinet and the exposure of electronic circuitry. I usually end up doing it anyway. (*Warning:* remember that even when switched off and unplugged, tube amps can store enough high voltages to give you a lethal shock. Do not attempt to remove or even expose the chassis of your amp unless you are fully experienced in amplifier maintenance, and understand the correct, safe procedures for bleeding high voltages from filter caps and rendering amps safe to work on. Even then, do not touch any internal components with bare fingers – filter caps can re-form their charge even after being drained, and a previously bled cap can still offer a potentially lethal zap. If in doubt, take it to a professional technician.)

Putting The Amp Head In The Control Room

Unfortunately, removing the amp chassis from the cab does not always solve the problem of ringing and microphany because the sound pressure levels from the speakers are still high enough to rattle the tubes. Although I can't claim this as my own, the solution I found – from watching that Metallica video again – is one of the best discoveries I have made in years.

If you are going to separate the head from the speakers, why do they even have to be in the same room? When I'm recording guitars these days, the amp head stays in the control room and the speakers stay in the live room. This has some real advantages. Firstly, microphonic tubes sound better because they are isolated from vibration. Secondly, the sound of the amplifier can be adjusted while you are actually listening to the backing track through the monitors – thus eliminating guesswork and endless trips back and forth to the live room. Thirdly, you don't have to damage your hearing by standing in front of the cabinet while you are trying to get a sound.

It also eliminates the need to run extremely long guitar cables from the control room to the live room. This is good news too, because the capacitance of long guitar cables causes high frequency loss and reduced signal strength. Long cables are also more likely to pick up noise. If you need to run long speaker leads, please make sure that you use good quality multi-stranded copper cable. You don't need to use expensive designer cable; in fact heavy-duty copper electrical cord (mains cable) bought off the roll from your local hardware shop or DIY superstore is fine. Crucially, you should avoid using shielded guitar cable because the large surface area of the shield results in a cable with high internal capacitance. This will react with the impedance of the speaker causing an impedance mismatch between the output stage of the amp and the speaker. If you try to use shielded cable, you will likely discover that new output transformers are very expensive and that your amp will never sound the same again.

Noise And Hum

Electric guitars, especially those with single coil pickups, are liable to pick up noise and hum from any equipment with transformers. If you find yourself in this situation, move slowly around the control room until you find the quietest spot. Computer monitors can cause serious interference problems and should, if possible, be switched off. Sometimes the screens go blank in standby mode but they are still powered up so don't let them fool you. Cell (mobile) phones can also bleed irritating noises through audio systems, even when they are not being used. These always find their way onto tape or hard disc. Remember to switch your phone off!

Studio Attitude

Most inexperienced guitarists (and quite a few experienced ones) make the mistake of being too precious about their sound. I'm not suggesting that you should accept a drop in quality. Some guitarists get so involved in their "own sound" that they fail to see the overall picture. When you are creating a piece of music in a studio you have to adapt your sound to the acoustics of the room, the sound of the drums, the sound of the bass, and so on. Quite often I have worked with guitarists who have failed to grasp that the sound they have carefully honed in the splendid isolation of their bedrooms does not do the job in the studio.

In such cases, alternative suggestions are often treated with sulking and even hostility. This type of behaviour is usually the result of insecurity and immaturity; the more open-minded and enthusiastic you are in the studio, the more you will enjoy yourself and the more people will enjoy working with you. You will also make better music as a result.

There is a difference between being a great instrumentalist and being a great musician. I have met players with stunning technique, theoretical mastery, and not an ounce of musicality. On the other hand, I've worked with technically limited players who can move you to tears with an A minor chord. I believe that a good musician will always try to see the bigger picture and will play to complement the music and the band. Bad musicians are characterized by selfishness, stubbornness and narrowmindedness. Fortunately – unlike raw technical ability – these are characteristics that we all have the power to change for ourselves.

Dealing With Sound Engineers

On the other hand, you also have to know when to stand your ground. Some engineers are insecure and immature too. Generally, these are the ones who want you to record your Jimmy Page-style acoustic number with a DI box because they know more about samplers than they do about microphones – and they're too scared to tell you. Other phrases that betray the rogue engineer are: "It'll be all right with a bit of reverb on it," and the infamous, "I'll sort it out in the mix."

Serious debates and sometimes arguments occur between guitarists, engineers, and producers about whether to record effects. Many studio pros prefer to record dry and leave all signal processing until the mix. They work this way because they know you cannot remove reverb, flange or chorus from a sound once it has been recorded, but you can always add just the right amount during the mix.

There is no way to recreate your amplifier's boingy spring reverb with a Lexicon 224 digital reverb, however. It is the subtle interaction of the effects with the amplifier circuitry that creates the magic. The sound of a certain pedal might be vital to your band's arrangement of a particular song, or a crucial guitar part could depend on your rhythmic interaction with your echo unit as you are playing. There's no right or wrong here, but it's important to remain flexible and open. If I like an effect, I'll print it to tape – but that's just me. You might want to do the same, or you could consider monitoring through the desired effect to get the right feel for your performance, while only recording a dry sound from your amp. You can add the effect back to the dry sound during the mix and find the optimum balance for the song. Ultimately, you will have to decide for yourself, or in discussion with your engineer, the best approach for each song or each session.

Be Prepared

We have all read about bands spending six months or a year recording, and even writing their albums in the studio. Unfortunately this is a luxury most bands do not have. If your budget is small and your studio time limited, you need to be prepared. Your sessions will run more smoothly if your songs are already written and your band is well rehearsed before you even go into the studio. There is nothing worse than losing that excitement because everyone in the band has got their act together except the bass player, and you have to record take after take until the whole band finally gets it right. By the time you have a usable take, you might have lost all the feel and vibe and the recording will not do justice to your band. Be prepared before you go into the studio. Write your songs, learn your parts, and practice like crazy.

RECORDING BASICS

Analog

Analog tape is made from a plastic film backing – usually Mylar or Melinex – that is coated with a magnetic layer consisting of a binding material mixed with magnetic particles. All analog tape has an inherent noise floor; this is the hiss that you can hear when you play a blank cassette in the tape machine of your hi-fi. A consistently high recording signal can mask tape noise. We call this a good "signal to noise ratio," and sound engineers strive for this. Excessive signal levels can also overload the tape, however, resulting in decreased transparency and possibly even distortion. This has always presented a problem for studio engineers attempting to record music with a wide dynamic range. Dynamic range is the difference between the quietest and the loudest sounds in a piece. In the quietest passages, the tape hiss can actually be louder than the music. Typically, classical music and jazz has a wider dynamic range than pop or rock. Various noise reduction systems have been used over the years to minimize tape hiss. You might have seen some of these (e.g. Dolby B, C, S, and DBX) on hi-fi equipment or budget multitrack tape machines. In a recording studio you are more likely to encounter Dolby A or Dolby SR. Engineers quickly developed techniques to use noise reduction creatively. It became common practice in the 1970s to record some instruments with Dolby A and to play the signals back with the noise reduction switched off. This creates an apparent sheen in the high end that sounds quite different from equalization. The British group 10cc treated the breathy vocal pads on their hit single *I'm Not In Love* in this way.

When we are recording to tape, careful attention should be paid to recording level. Tape machines have VU meters, which stands for Volume Unit. Most engineers try to ensure that the level of signal sent to tape keeps the indicator needle on the meter around the 0 VU mark. Some old-school engineers will also suggest that VU stands for "virtually useless." VU meters are notoriously slow and inaccurate and they fail to respond to transient peaks that can push the tape into distortion. A more accurate form of meter is the PPM or Peak Programme Meter. Experienced engineers use meters for guidance but rely heavily on their experience to determine how far they can push the levels onto tape. This will depend largely on the instrument or sound being recorded, in combination with the musical genre itself.

Digital Recording

Digital sounds arrived in our homes on a wave of hype with early CDs. "Perfect sound forever," the marketing deptartments declared, "no noise, indestructible and problem free." As we now know, that didn't prove to be entirely true. Digital recording is in some ways less forgiving than analogue tape. At the upper limit, there is an absolute ceiling. Exceeding this produces a nasty and harsh digital quack. The onset of digital distortion is instantaneous, not gradual. In contrast to analog systems, digital distortion levels can actually increase as record level decreases. Digital recorders are equipped with meters that are designed to respond quickly and register overloads. In my experience, these meters are inconsistent and cannot be trusted (Tascam DAT machine meters are among the culprits). Once again, we need to pay careful attention to recording levels when we are recording digitally.

The debate between supporters of analog and the digital enthusiasts is very intense and can get very heated. Unfortunately it is beyond the scope of this book to get involved. If pushed, I would say that I vastly prefer the sound of analog tape above digital equivalents such as Pro Tools, but I'm not religious about it.

Setting Your Record Level

Mixing desks can be a little complicated, but there are a few guidelines that can help you to minimize distortion and noise from your recording medium and your mixer. Most desks use a fader on the input channel to adjust the level sent to tape or hard disc. The signal is often routed down a group or buss, which can introduce a second, "group" fader.

The best procedure is to set both faders to the zero mark on the channel strip. This is generally around two-thirds of the way up, not flat to the floor as you might think (though marked as a "0" it is actually the "unity gain" level, which means the signal level going through the fader is the same as that entering it from the mike preamp, rather than being boosted or attenuated). Always use the gain on the microphone preamp to control the level sent to tape or hard disc. Aim to maintain an average signal of 0 VU when recording to analog; when recording digitally, set the level just below the point where it starts to peak. If you find that your record level is too hot, even with the mike amp gain turned right down, activate the input pad on the mixing desk and readjust your gain level. If your mixer does not have a pad, you might find that the microphone has one built in, so use that instead.

If your faders are set too low, you will have to turn the mike preamp farther up and this risks noise and distortion from the desk circuitry. Your mike will also be too sensitive, making spillage and background noise more apparent. Some outside broadcasters and film recordists push their faders up to max and run their mike amps at a lower level to reduce microphone sensitivity. Try this trick if spillage is proving to be a problem when you are recording a live band in a studio.

STUDIO LAYOUT

Never worked in a professional studio before, or at least nothing more organised than Joe's demo shack? Don't worry, plenty of good musicians haven't. But a quick look at the basic rooms and facilities such establishment generally offer can help you feel like less of a newbee when you finally get the opportunity.

Control Room

This is the area that houses the mixing desk, the monitor speakers, the outboard effects, and the computers and recorders. It is also where the engineer and the producer sit. Ideally this room will be symmetrical along a central line running between the monitor speakers. Without this, stereo imaging can suffer. The back wall acts as a bass trap and acoustic treatment on the ceiling and side walls minimizes early reflections. To avoid standing waves, the ceiling, and the floor will not be parallel, nor will the sides of the room.

Live Room, Or Studio

This is the area where the instruments are recorded. In days gone by, the reputation of a studio was based on the sound of its live room. Older establishments such as Abbey Road and Capitol were originally designed for orchestral work and consequently had very large live rooms. The advent of affordable reverb devices now enables the engineer to simulate the sound of larger recording spaces digitally. Well, that's the theory anyway. Consequently, large live rooms are less common these days.

The sound of the live room can have an enormous impact on the sound of the recording. In the '70s drums were often recorded "dry" with the minimum possible room ambience. Big drum sounds became fashionable in the '80s with bands like U2 and Simple Minds. To record these, ambient microphones in the live room

RECORDING LEVELS

Rather than indicating minimum or no input, the zero (0) mark on a mixer's faders and VU meters indicates the level at which the incoming signal is neither boosted nor cut. When recording, aim to keep your average signal at or around 0 VU.

were blended with close microphones on the individual drums to create the impression of space and size. For a while there was even a vogue for very bright sounding stone rooms.

Some studios will have several live spaces, often with acoustic separation, but many modern facilities hardly bother with a live room at all. Instead, they have dry booths designed for vocalists that can just about accommodate a drum kit but certainly not a full band. Personally, I find this trend depressing.

Monitoring In Home Studios

One of the biggest difficulties faced by home recordists is inaccurate monitoring. The average box-shaped domestic room is an appalling space in which to listen to music. An acoustic space that is cuboid or rectangular is problematic because standing waves can occur. This happens when two sounds of equal frequency and amplitude are traveling in opposite directions, where the space between the walls contains a large number of different wavelengths. When this happens, standing waves can be built up in many dimensions.

The frequencies where the standing waves occur are called "eigentones," and any sound coming out of the monitor speakers that coincides with one of these eigentones will be emphasized or diminished according to where you are sitting. In practical terms this might mean that your track could have tons of bottom end in your studio room, but the mix will sound bass-light everywhere else. You are faced with two choices: either compensate through guesswork by making all your mixes sound too bassy in the studio, or sort out your room. I suggest that you should disregard the first option, and try some of the simpler means of achieving the second.

Certain everyday materials are capable of very effective sound absorption. Such materials might include wood, carpet, foam or cloth. Large panels of cloth can soak up low frequencies by moving with the sound. Acoustic treatment panels can be bought at studio equipment suppliers but they can be expensive. If you have a restricted budget, try putting some foam panels up on the walls and ceiling. Maybe hang drapes or a duvet across the wall behind your head.

Don't attempt to make your room completely dead – your speakers and amp combination might have problems filling the room with sufficient sound. A certain degree of liveness is natural and even preferable.

Make sure that your speakers are at equal heights, with the tweeters firing at ear level. Sit exactly in the middle of the two speakers and listen to a well-mixed commercial CD. If the vocal sounds thin and unfocussed, try toeing the speakers in slightly towards the center. If the vocal sounds too up-front and the track sounds narrow, move the two speakers outwards slightly in equal amounts. Take your time, listen carefully, and make small adjustments – an inch or so at a time. It's worth optimizing this from the start, because it will affect your perception of every sound you record.

Try to place the speakers away from walls and definitely avoid putting them in corners. Most importantly, do not get conned into buying expensive speakers and amplifiers to cure your monitoring problems. Ordinary speakers, well positioned in a good sounding room are better than expensive speakers incorrectly installed in a bad room!

Many novice recordists squander significant sums of money on expensive "studio" monitors. In the world of professional audio, most engineers continue to mix on hi-fi speakers designed for the domestic market. They do this because they feel comfortable working with monitors that are familiar and representative of the speakers most consumers will be listening to at home.

The diagram opposite shows a suggested layout in a rectangular room. There is no such thing as perfect monitoring, and success will always involve an element of familiarity and guesswork. Try to select speakers that you actually like. Try to arrange a prolonged audition period because you should avoid speakers that make your ears feel tired after a couple of hours. Don't mistake excessive top-end for clarity, or boominess for genuine low-end harmonic integrity – and be suspicious and wary of speakers that are immediately impressive.

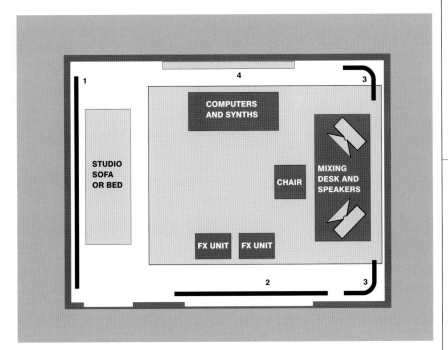

MONITORING ROOM

With only a few changes – and the addition of some carefully placed drapes – most ordinary rooms can be converted into an acoustically sympathetic environment for home monitoring. In the diagram left, drapes or curtains help to deaden the rear wall (1), side window (2), and corners (3), while a bookcase takes sound-absorption duties at a parallel wall (4).

Recording Bass

Tired of just sticking your P-Bass through the desk? Learn how to get a fat, punchy bottom end every time.

CD track 21: DI'd bass

DI BOX

Some engineers reach straight for the DI box when confronted with a bass to record. Units like that pictured above – a basic, passive DI – offer acoustic isolation, while sending more of the instrument's frequency range to tape than most amp's can manage. There are, however, plenty more good ways to record bass guitars.

As with recording electric six-strings, there's far more than one way to capture a good bass sound. The technique you choose to employ will depend on a combination of factors that will include playing style and the sound that proves right for the song, but it's important to know from the outset that you have plenty of options. In some camps, nothing but the DI'd approach is ever considered for the low end; others demand a version of their live, amped-up sound in the studio. In this chapter we'll investigate ways to make the most of each approach, and introduce lots of great methods to blend the two.

Direct Injection

Many engineers feel that bass amplifiers are a necessary evil whose sole function is to provide adequate volume and monitoring levels during live performance. The limitations of amplifier and speaker enclosure design actually degrade the signal from the instrument and should be removed from the equation. Their thinking runs that it is logical, therefore, to plug the bass directly into the mixing desk.

This is the simplest approach to recording bass, and we call it "Direct Injection," or DI for short. It removes all corrupting factors (except the cable) and provides the best chance to capture the instrument's full range of tones, frequencies, and dynamics. The DI box also provides acoustic isolation in situations where amplifier noise and microphone spill could be a problem.

Impedance

As a rule, electric basses (and guitars) are high impedance devices designed to drive the even higher input (load) impedance of amplifiers. Inconveniently, the input stages of microphone amplifiers in mixing desks have low load impedance (as is discussed toward the end of Chapter 3). This mismatch results in a loss of signal (bad), uneven frequency response (bad), and a possible lack of sustain (also bad). This is because the lower the load impedance, the more current the pickup has to provide. Sustain is compromised because the current in the pickups becomes too weak to drive the load as the note decays so the instrument feels lifeless and difficult to play.

DI Boxes

To connect the output of the bass to the input of a mixing desk with minimal level losses and a good signal to noise ratio, we use a DI box. This presents a low source impedance to the preamp. The input impedance of the DI box should be very large – some active models are as high as 10M Ohms. The DI box also converts the signal from unbalanced to balanced. To accomplish this, the signal is split into two inside the DI box and the polarity of one signal is flipped by 180˚. DI boxes have XLR output sockets (also known as "cannon" connectors), with three pins labeled 1, 2 and 3. The screen or earth is connected to pin 1 and the signal is connected to pin 2 (hot) and pin 3 (cold), 180 degrees "out of phase."

When the signal reaches the preamp, the polarity of the signal on pin 3 is flipped back and summed with the signal on pin 1. Any noise or interference picked up by the balanced cable is cancelled in the process, in roughly the same way that a humbucking pickup cancels hum.

In their simplest and cheapest form, DI boxes are passive, non-powered devices containing a transformer to balance the signal and convert impedance. Two parallel jack sockets provide the input and link so that you can place the DI box in line between your bass and your amplifier.

A male cannon or XLR socket provides the low impedance source for the mixer. (When you are gigging, by the way, you should always try to carry two guitar cords. This will help live engineers DI your bass if previous groups have walked off with their spare cables.) Many modern bass amplifiers have DI outputs, and manufacturers who actually live on planet earth will provide an XLR socket too, for convenient connection to a mixing desk. Others use a jack socket, which can make even the most mild-mannered live engineer want to reach for his AK47 on a bad night.

Some, more sophisticated (active) DI boxes need power. This may be phantom power supplied from the mixing desk or mains power, although some work with batteries. Active DI boxes can provide low source impedance without using a transformer, although many still have them. They also provide a volume boost, which is controllable on certain models with a volume pot or an attenuation switch.

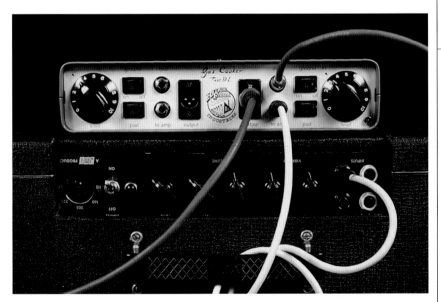

DI BOX CONNECTION

Any quality DI box – such as the active Gas Cooker unit, left – will have a parallel output, or "link," which allows the player to play through an amp while recording from the DI. This is useful either for monitoring the performance through the amp with which the player is accustomed, or for recording techniques which blend a DI'd signal and a miked amp.

This buffering amplifier isolates the pickup from the rest of the system, which is a useful safety precaution. Most DI boxes also provide a ground-lift switch for eliminating noise and earth hum. This may expose the musician to the risk of electric shock if dangerously connected, so some devices use "auto lifting" or "ground compensation diodes." With these, a threshold is set whereby the earth is lifted until voltage rises above a certain point, e.g. 0.5 volt; contact is then re-established.

Transformers vary tremendously in standard and the sound of the DI box – or indeed any audio device – is profoundly influenced by the quality of its transformers. A high-output device such as a synthesizer or an active bass or guitar can be used successfully with a passive DI box. For best results with standard, passive basses and guitars, use an active DI box.

Running Long Cables Without Losses

Many bassists and guitarists prefer to record their parts while playing in the control room. The technical difficulty is that the physical separation between the instrument and the amplifier requires very long cables. High source impedance and instrument cable capacitance can result in high frequency losses and noise pick up. This corrupts the signal and your sound will suffer. Low source impedance allows the signal to survive long cable runs with reduced susceptibility to high frequency losses and noise.

Here is a great trick for running very long instrument cables into amplifiers with minimal losses by using two DI boxes, one active and one passive. Plug the output of the instrument into the input of the active DI box, using as short a cable as is reasonably possible to start with. Take the low impedance XLR output into a microphone line in the wall of the control room or the patch bay of the mixing desk. In the live room, take a cable from the same microphone line and place it into the XLR socket (the output) of a second (this time passive) DI box. Take a guitar cord (jack-to-jack cable) from the "input" socket of the DI box to the amplifier input.

The first DI box provides a low source impedance to help the signal survive a 20 or 30-yard cable run. The second DI box is used backwards to present a high source impedance to the amplifier. You can use this trick with electric guitars as well as electric bass. The balanced operation of the cable also maintains good signal to noise ratio.

DI Recording Vs. Amp Miking

Typically a DI'd bass sound will have a very broad frequency range with transparent highs and clean, extended lows. Les Paul famously advocates the use of low impedance pickups in his Les Paul Recording guitar. He believes that the integrity of the signal – the actual sound of the vibrating string – should be reproduced as accurately as possible. This is High Fidelity!

DI bass can be very effective in certain genres of music, but good results require a competent player and a good instrument. On the other hand, most electric bassists and guitarists do not share this hi-fi sensibility. We prefer to plug our sonically corrupted, lo-fi, high impedance guitars into nasty, distorted, high impedance amps with noisy, unbalanced cables. So there it is: rock'n'roll. DI'd bass can be fine in isolation, but often sounds weak and wimpy in the context of a full-blown mix.

Many bassists prefer to get their sound from their amps – for all the same reasons as guitar players. The bad news is that miking up bass rigs is not always easy or even practical. The first problem is that they always make everything in a 50-foot radius rattle and vibrate like crazy, including doors, windows, light fittings, dentures, the back of the mixing desk, and so on. Engineers sometimes have to listen in the control room at very low volume to determine if the rattle is part of the recorded sound or if it's actually in the room with you. We often find it harder to locate the source of low frequency sound than high frequency sound. After you have applied gaffer (duct) tape to everything, including the studio cat, you should find yourself in a perfect position to start recording the bass. So where do you place the speaker cabinet to make this job easier?

Locating Speaker Cabinets

Speaker positioning is critical for good low-frequency response. If you want a flat frequency response, place the cabinet on a stand or on a chair in the middle of a room – that is, in free space. If the cabinet is near a wall you might experience a 6 dB bass rise. A corner will increase this to 12dB. If you then take the cab off the stand, the floor adds another 6dB. Try your speaker cabinet in several positions in the live room until you identify the best spot.

Microphone Choice

Bass speakers can reproduce low frequencies at volume levels that would give many microphones a hard time. Specially designed dynamic mikes, therefore, are often chosen for the task of recording bass. Common examples are the AKG D12, the AKG D112 and the Electrovoice RE20 (which features a bass roll-off switch). These microphones have frequency response curves that are anything but flat. They are designed for flattery and enhancement, not accuracy. The resonant cavity they use to add depth and power to kick drums can create an uneven response with bass sounds. This means that certain notes will be over-emphasized.

To achieve more accurate results, many engineers like to use condenser microphones such as the Neumann U47 valve or FET models. Quite often I will combine the signals from dynamic and condenser microphones to achieve a blend of their desirable characteristics. Bass guitars produce a lot of low-mid and upper-mid frequency information. It is important to capture these frequencies because most domestic hi-fi speakers are incapable of reproducing the lowest frequencies. If the listener can hear the upper harmonics of a low bass note, the ear can be fooled into believing that it can hear the fundamental. If the upper harmonics are absent, the bass line might disappear on small speakers.

I must urge you, however, not to try out your prized ribbon microphone on electric bass – even though it will sound absolutely superb in the split second before its complete destruction.

Microphone Placement

Engineers commonly put microphones directly in front of the speaker, very close to the dust cap. The sound there is punchy and aggressive, but this technique produces an uneven low-frequency response. This is caused by the microphone

CD tracks 22-24: bass mikes

CD tracks 25-27: mike distance

MIKING UP

As with guitar amps, the most common mike position used on bass amps is directly in front and at the center of the speaker, as with the Neumann U47 FET positioned in front of the Ampeg Portaflex, left. Thanks to our old friend the proximity effect, however, such close miking can result in a boomy, uneven response from some notes. Moving the mike back from the speaker will often give better results.

body, which reduces the area through which sound waves can escape, causing "tip up" in the bottom that adds to the proximity effect I described in the microphone chapters. This can cause some notes to sound significantly louder than others. You will often see engineers diving for their EQs and compressors at this point, but there's no need to panic. Better solutions exist.

Simply move the microphone away from the speaker. The sound from a bass speaker needs space to develop. After all, the audible range of wavelengths extends from approximately 2/3" to 53' (17mm to 17m). It is reasonable to expect that the behaviour of the sound will vary across the frequency range. I usually start by placing the mike about two foot (60cm) in front of the speaker. If the result is boomy I will move the mike further away; if it needs more weight I move it closer.

Most engineers try to avoid allowing too much room ambience into their bass sounds. You can reduce this by placing acoustic screens each side of the bass cabinet. I like to flare them outwards in a "V" shape (with the amp set where the two sides of the "V" join) to avoid phase canceling early reflections bouncing back onto the microphone. This arrangement also helps to throw the sound forward.

FLARED SCREENS

Setting a bass amp within a pair of acoustic screens flared in the shape of a "V" can help to both reduce phase-canceling early reflections, and to throw the sound forward toward the mike.

Boundary Microphones

I often use the boundary miking technique I discussed in *Chapter 3* for recording bass, too. Place your microphone on the floor in front of the cabinet, as in the photo below, and ask an assistant to slowly move the microphone away from the cabinet until you hear a frequency balance that sounds right. Compensate for volume with your microphone amp gain and hit record.

CD track 28 **boundary miking**

CD track 29 **'panel' miking**

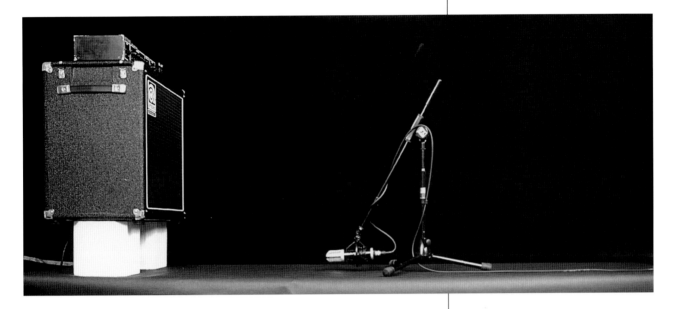

Wood Panel Deflector

Another interesting technique involves a flat panel of wood tilted upwards from the base of the cabinet. The microphone is placed just above the panel, pointing towards the speaker, as below. You can even use a PZM attached to the wood to pick up a little resonance. The wood panel technique is excellent when you are confronted with modern bass cabinets containing a variety of drive units – such as a 15", two 10"s and a tweeter. If you need more-high end then re-position the microphone in a more direct line to the tweeter and adjust the panel. If you have too much top, do the opposite. The panel deflects unwanted sound away from the microphone allowing it to pick up the sound fired directly from the speaker.

BOUNDARY MIKING

A mike mounted just above and parallel to the floor can be an effective way of capturing a good bass sound (top photo). Another variation on the boundary miking technique (bottom photo) involves mounting a PZM on a board angled in front of the bass cab.

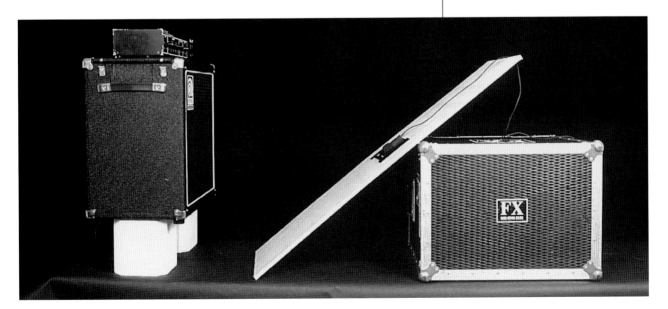

CD track 30: DI plus mike

Combining DI Signals With Microphones

Many engineers prefer to blend a DI signal with a microphone rather than use one or the other on its own. If you like the characteristics of the amp then why not try the DI output from the amp? Alternatively, use a DI box. The microphone signal provides the tone and the character while the DI provides the clear upper-mids and the smooth lows.

Unfortunately this technique can result in partial phase cancellation, which is caused by the slight time delay in the microphone signal. We call this comb filtering. If the microphone is one foot away from the speaker the sound is delayed by 1 millisecond (ms). A two-foot gap results in a 2ms delay. The delay is even worse if the DI box is in the control room with the musician, and the amplifier is in the live room.

If I'm combining the microphone signal with a DI, I always take my DI signal from a box situated next to the amplifier in the live room. The solution is to put the DI'd sound through a delay unit and blend it with the microphone signal. Temporarily flip the DI signal's polarity by 180 degrees to the mike signal, using the phase switch on the desk. Notch up the delay (set to a single repeat) one millisecond at a time and listen to the sound get quieter as the recorded delay is eliminated. Continue past this point and it will start to get louder. Aim for the quietest sound when adjusting the delay time. When you have found it, release the phase switch on the DI channel and the sound should be well phat! Your microphone and DI signals are now time-aligned, and you can balance them any way you like.

This procedure is even easier on a hard-disc recorder. Simply record the mike and DI signals onto two separate tracks and nudge the regions into alignment, one sample at a time. If the bassist was listening to the DI when he was recording then move the microphone region forward in time. If the mike signal was the monitor sound, then move the DI region forward in the arrangement. If you don't, you might end up changing the playing feel as well as the sound.

You might even decide that you like the comb filter effect. You can exploit the partial phase cancellation to fine-tune the bass sound without using EQ.

The modern player demands fine control over bass sounds and the ability to sculpt tone, using equalisation. To this end, bass amps are becoming more and more complex. While this ability to tweak is often crucial due to poor acoustics at concert venues, an amp's punch and power can be sacrificed to parametric EQs and graphics. These features are often unnecessary in the studio. A great way around this when you are stuck with an amp like a modern Ampeg SVT is to plug a simpler, better sounding preamp into the otherwise very good power amp stage. My all-time favorite bass amp is the original flip-top tube Ampeg Portaflex. Turn up this 15W tone monster to the point where it just begins to distort, stick a good microphone in front of it, and enjoy. They're pretty loud, too!

BASS EFFECTS

Fuzz And Distortion

It's also great fun to use effects with bass. I'm talking here about effects of the stomp box variety. Unfortunately there aren't that many great bass effects boxes around – particularly when it comes to distortion and fuzz. Bassists often have to resort to guitar pedals that make the bottom end disappear as soon as they're switched on. I haven't tried the reissues, but the Vox Tone Bender distortion always seems to allow a proportion of the original signal through intact. This gives you fuzz and bottom end.

A little distortion can be mixed in with a boring DI sound to add some sonic interest or even mimic the sound of a real amp. Also check out octave pedals and flangers – especially on fretless. If you can, try the Electro-Harmonix Electric Mistress and the MXR Flanger (Electro-Harmonix are one pedal builder that does offer more bass-friendly effects than many). Experiment with whatever you can get your hands on and use what works. If a guitar pedal gives you the degree of sonic interest or just plain weirdness that you desire but saps your low end, try splitting the signal and blending direct and effected signal to get the best sound.

Filters

I often manufacture a little extra low end during the mix by splitting the bass signal and sending one side through the filter of an analog synth. I like Minimoogs, as well as Korg MS10s and MS20s. Plug into the external input and set the input level to taste. Filter out as much of the high-frequency information as you like and adjust resonance to taste. Compress the hell out of it and ride it underneath the untreated sound. The bass becomes much weightier and it's easier to balance it in the mix.

CD track 31 DI + mike + filter

Compression And Limiting

Compression is a vital weapon in the engineer's armory. We use compressors to help the bass punch consistently through tracks. They also help to compensate for erratic volume levels caused by poor technique. Typically a bass compressor will have a fairly slow release time. A fast attack time will squash the transient peaks that can cause tape saturation and digital overload. This smoothes out the sound, but your bass might lose its musical dynamics and become lifeless. Many bass amps today come with built-in compressors for live use. In the studio, however, the dedicated recording unit is likely to offer much, much better results and significantly greater flexibility.

CD track 32 mike + compressor

Some engineers use a limiter with very fast attack and release times to catch the peaks, followed by a touch of light compression. This can work very well, smoothing the sound and containing the peaks in a transparent and musical way.

I also like to split the signal and blend a little of the uncompressed sound into the compressed signal. If you try this, watch out for phase shift and adjust accordingly.

Equalization

One of the more difficult aspects of mixing is to achieve a bottom end that has a lot of weight but remains punchy and tight as well. One of the best ways of getting a solid and punchy bass guitar sound is to deal correctly with the bass drum sound first.

When you place a microphone inside a bass drum, the sound produced will range from the very highest frequencies – the sound of the beater hitting the skin – to the very lowest – the resonance of the drum and the skin. The bass guitar needs to blend with the bass drum, but both of them are competing for the same frequency space. Without EQ these two sounds will combine to produce a boomy low end, which slows down the track, rather than an exciting, punchy rhythm section.

Mix engineers get around this problem using parametric EQ. First they will accentuate the upper-mid frequencies (around 2kHz to 3kHz) to bring out the click or the attack of the beater hitting the skin. This helps the bass drum to cut through a dense mix. Second, they will remove some of the lower mid frequencies (around 400Hz) to take the boom out of the drum.

Removing the low mids creates a frequency space or hole for the bass guitar and tightens up the drum. The two sounds will then work together more effectively and both can be placed high in the mix without overpowering each other or anything else.

There are no set rules for equalizing bass guitar. Most listeners are familiar with the natural sound of voices, pianos, and acoustic guitars, so they will notice when these instruments have been highly processed. Like electric guitar, the bass can be treated in any way you like, but more often than not you will want to boost the bass, remove any boominess from the low mids, and add a little definition in the upper mids.

MIKING DOUBLE BASS

As with so much recording, the simplest technique for double bass begins with a single mike. For a warmer, bassier sound, position your mike – a Neumann U47 FET in the photo, right – nearer the floor.

CD tracks 33-36: double bass

Double (Upright) Bass

Double ("trouble") bass is an acoustic instrument and I tend to approach recording it in much the same way as I do acoustic guitars. After all, they also boast a large slab of resonating wood.

The most common recording technique is to place a high quality condenser microphone in front of the bridge. Common choices include valve and FET Neumann U47s and U87s, AKG C12s and C414s. If you get in close with your ears, you will hear a concentration of low frequencies around the area of the f-hole and the bridge. Moving the microphone closer to the floor and aiming up towards

ALTERNATE POSITIONING

For a tighter, more focused sound, move the mike nearer to and even above the bridge. A range of positions between these two extremes should enable you to locate the ideal sound, even with just a single mike.

the instrument gives a warmer, bassier sound. Conversely, the sound becomes more focused and less boomy as the microphone is moved above the bridge.

The idea that large capsule microphones have more bottom end is largely a myth. Some jazz recordists use a pair of small capsule Neumann KM84s or B&Ks on a stereo bar aimed either side of the bridge. The mike signals are panned hard left and right.

Wonderful percussive sounds come from the area around the fingerboard, and a second microphone placed close to the fretting hand can add to the sonic interest and sense of realism. As always in multi-mike set-ups, watch out for phase shift.

STEREO BAR

Small capsule condenser mikes are perfectly up to the job of capturing acoustic double bass. Some engineers record jazz bassists by placing two small capsule Neumann KM84s – as in the photo, right – on a stereo bar aimed either side of the bridge.

Ribbon microphones work particularly well with double bass (and cello) and often attract favorable comments from the bassists themselves.

Many players also install high quality piezo pickups, or "bugs," for live use. This can make an interesting blend with the microphone sound and can help in recording situations where separation is not possible. Pickups generally sound a little thin and metallic but can be used to add definition to a lifeless mike sound.

Ultimately, the key to a great sound is a great player. I had the good fortune to record a couple of albums with the notable British bassist Danny Thompson, and he is very easy to record. He taught me that a lot of the older jazz guys learned to

FINGER MIKING

A second mic placed close to the
fretting hand – usually a small
capsule condenser as in the photo,
left – can pick up a variety of
percussive sounds that add to the
sonic interest and realism of the
acoustic double bass.

play the double bass in the days before amplifiers and pickups. Many younger
players tickle the strings because they are used to their amplifiers doing all the
work. The older guys play harder and dig in more. This makes them easier to
record… plus, their anecdotes tend to be funnier.

After reading this chapter, I hope that any bass players who have been
disappointed with their DI'd sound in the past will now have the confidence to say
"bugger off" to the next lazy sound engineer who tries to force them into it. What's
more, you'll be able to tell them how they should do it properly, in their own
language. Good luck.

Effects and Production Tricks

Processing doesn't have to be a dirty word. Do it right, and you'll make the most of your tracks.

EFFECTS: AN OVERVIEW

If you have already tried some of the techniques detailed in previous chapters you might have noticed that your guitar recordings still don't sound quite like those on many of your favorite records. The reason is that producers and engineers use effects such as compression, reverberation, delay, and equalization to further process guitar sounds. Signal processing has often been a mystery to guitarists and musicians in general – until now.

Among guitarists, the word "processing" is somewhat loaded. It conjures up ghastly memories of Tom Sholtz Rockmans, Roland GP8s and P16s, and other so-called "processors." In short, all those ultra-modern types of sounds we used back in the '80s when it "seemed like a good idea at the time." Times have changed, and the way producers and engineers process sound can often be very subtle and sympathetic, even musical. We use compression and equalization (EQ) to enhance and maximize the potential of the natural sound, not necessarily to transform it. We use delay and reverb to "sit" the guitar into the mix or give it its own acoustic space. The result is often that well-processed guitar tracks sound more "real" and "natural" (that is, more like we expect professionally recorded guitars to sound) than un-processed tracks.

Equalization (EQ)

When the signal from a microphone or DI box reaches a mixing desk, the first option that presents itself is equalization. This is because all mixing desks have built-in EQ. The simplest way of thinking about EQ is to equate it to the tone controls of your hi-fi or guitar amp. These basic tone controls, however, will only provide a boost or cut in a frequency range pre-determined by the manufacturer. As engineers we require more flexibility and precision; this is why most mixing desks are equipped with parametric EQ. You have probably used one of these before in the form of a wah wah pedal. Parametric EQs enable us to select the frequency range we wish to change. This requires two control pots: one knob will sweep through the frequencies and the other will apply boost or cut. On more sophisticated mixers, a third control will adjust the "Q factor" or "bell width" – the breadth of frequencies around our selected point.

Some mixing desks have only treble, bass, and one or two parametric EQs; other, more expensive consoles might have five parametrics. In a sense a parametric EQ is like a graphic EQ because you can select the frequencies you want to change. Of course, it would be impossible to put a graphic EQ on every channel of a mixing desk because there wouldn't be enough space. This is where the parametric variety fits the bill in such applications; plus, each band is user definable rather than fixed as on a graphic EQ.

EQ was originally designed as a corrective tool. Its functions were to even out the frequency responses of colored microphones or to alleviate problems caused by imperfect recording rooms. Purist "old school" engineers approach EQ with caution, preferring if possible to avoid it altogether. They do this by choosing appropriate microphones and concentrating on microphone placement. Steve Albini – producer of the Pixies, Nirvana, The Breeders, Page & Plant, PJ Harvey

PARAMETRIC EQ

Equalizers, like this Pultec, can achieve everything from eliminating low-end "sonic garbage" to giving extra cut to a lead guitar part.

and others – is a well-known advocate of this approach. Some recordists argue that equalization is actually a form of distortion: it adds noise, and the delays inherent in the electronic circuitry result in phase cancellation.

Some equalizer manufacturers, such as Neve, Trident, Pultec and API, have achieved legendary status because the phase response of their products is particularly pleasing. In other words, they sound good!

Other engineers, myself included, take a more pragmatic approach. Circumstances often conspire to deprive us of our preferred microphones, and our positioning might be dictated by a necessity to minimize spill. In these situations, EQ can save your ass.

Additionally, during the mixing stage you might find yourself trying to achieve clarity while balancing a snare drum, a lead vocal, some backing vocals, and five guitar parts. All these elements occupy a similar frequency range. EQ can be used to adjust the timbre of each instrument to help it cut through without dominating the others. As a rule of thumb, a high or upper-mid frequency boost will bring an instrument forward in a mix without having to raise its volume, but doing so can reduce tone, power, and weight. The only way to use EQ is to trust your ears and, unfortunately, that requires experience.

If you decide to use EQ, then make sure that all the boosts and cuts are set to zero before you switch on the EQ section. This will ensure that when the equalizer is activated, the sound will not change. Now turn up the boost about half way to maximum, then turn the frequency select knob, sweeping through the frequencies. As you sweep up and down you will notice that it sounds like a wah wah pedal. If a frequency jumps out that sounds good, boost it; if a bad one pops out then cut it. If a sound is well recorded and only needs a little help, I will rarely boost or cut more than 3dB or 4dB. If you need to get really extreme with EQ it can sound unnatural and even have a "ringing" quality to it. You can reduce this effect by dialing in a wider Q factor or bell width if your mixer has that facility.

You can EQ while listening to the sound in solo, but an experienced engineer will always fine-tune the EQ while listening to the sound in context with the other instruments. There is no point in making an instrument sound good on its own if it doesn't work in the mix. The two can often be very different things. On its own the sound might be poor, but in the context of the song it might sound excellent.

In addition to parametric EQ, many consoles have high pass filters, which shelve off low frequencies, and low pass filters which shelve off high frequencies. These are very useful. When you are recording – especially at home – your mikes are likely to pick up a lot of low frequency noise or rumble. Much of this is caused by traffic noise and aircraft, but it might even be unwanted speaker cab resonance, or something else in the room with you such as air conditioning or the drummer farting.

There is no musical benefit to be gained from keeping this sonic garbage; in fact it can clutter up the low frequencies of your mix to such an extent that you will find it difficult to achieve a punchy and clear low end. Use your filters to take out any unwanted noise from the top end and bottom end. On individual tracks you might not notice too much of a difference, but with 24 tracks running it will help a lot.

The best way to use EQ is to ask yourself if the sound actually needs to be equalized before you change anything. If you decide that it does, then figure out what you want to do before you start. Equalization can also be used as an extreme, creative effect and can be a lot of fun. Please don't regard it as a cure-all, however, or as a substitute for recording the sound well in the first place.

I have one last warning regarding the use of EQ. When your listening volume is low, bass frequencies will drop off and high frequencies will be emphasized. Conversely, high listening volumes will emphasize bass frequencies and create a false sense of excitement. If you generally monitor at high levels, make sure that you check the low frequencies at quiet listening levels. If you don't, your music might end up sounding bass light.

Compression

Another vital weapon in the engineer's armory is the compressor. I'm sure that a lot of you will have used compressors in the form of foot pedals or as a feature in your digital processors. Compressors are used to narrow the dynamic range of the signal. This means that they reduce the difference between the loudest and quietest parts. This is vital when we are recording because we need to avoid peaks, which cause tape distortion and digital distortion. We must also maintain a good signal-to-noise ratio to minimize tape hiss and noise.

Compressors are, in effect, automatic volume controls. Since the loudest parts of the music are attenuated, the quieter parts consequently seem louder. This makes the music appear subjectively louder for given sound pressure levels – it creates the illusion of loudness. Think back to the *Introduction* when I talked about the difference between "being loud and sounding loud." You might have noticed an example of this when watching television. A volume setting that is fine for a movie might become too loud during the commercial break. This is because

COMPRESSORS

A vital weapon in the engineer's arsenal, a compressor is a key ingredient in achieving that vital difference between being loud and sounding loud.

advertisements are heavily compressed to make them sound loud; the idea is to sell you that car, shampoo, or fast food – even if you have already gone out to the kitchen in the break to fetch a beer.

The purist (and theoretically correct) approach to compression is that it should be transparent and inaudible. You shouldn't be able to hear the compressor working, and it is a necessary evil to help us cope with the limitations of our recording technology. While there is a lot to be said for this argument, most audio professionals working in the rock or pop field realise that audible compression can actually enhance music by bringing out details and adding aural excitement. In fact, we are now so accustomed to compression that some things can sound strange without it. In the photo opposite you will see that there are five controls: Threshold, Ratio, Attack, Release and Make Up Gain. Here's what each does:

Threshold sets the level at which the effect is triggered in. Since a compressor is an automatic volume attenuator, something must trigger it. This trigger is signal level, and we can control the point at which the compressor begins to work using the Threshold control. The signal will remain uncompressed as long as it remains below the threshold level.

Ratio defines the strength of the compression, which might range between 2:1 and 20:1. At 2:1 an increase in input signal of 2dB is required to produce a 1dB increase in output level; this is light compression. A 20:1 ratio requires an increase of 20dB in the input signal to produce a 1dB increase in output; this is heavy compression.

Attack determines the speed at which the compressor reacts to the volume peak.

Release controls the speed at which the compressor re-sets itself after the signal drops below the Threshold level.

Make Up Gain is like an output level control. Heavy compression might reduce the overall level of the music, so Make Up Gain can be adjusted to compensate for this (although some "purist" compressors do not provide this function).

All of this sounds pretty simple, but it takes a lot of practice to get the best out of compressors, and as usual a lot of it is down to personal taste. The trickiest part is setting the attack and release times because to an extent they are interdependent. Some compressors make it easy for you by having presets for different instruments. Others have automatic attack and release. The best thing you can do is to have a go. You are likely to discover some favorite settings over time, but the material you are recording or mixing will also dictate your compression levels to some extent, too.

REVERB

After EQ and compression the next thing an engineer might consider is reverberation – or reverb for short. When you are mixing you can probably imagine sound in three dimensions, including width and depth, rather than flat, dry, monophonic sound.

Guitars which have been recorded dry or close miked often need a little help to make them sit naturally within the mix. To achieve this, we use artificial reverb to create the illusion that the guitar was recorded in a tiled bathroom, a church or a concert hall. Reverb is actually the sound of echoes that are so close together they appear to be continuous. We can use a combination of volume, panning, and reverberation to place sounds within their own acoustic space.

Plate Reverb
In the old days, studio reverbs came in the form of metal reverb plates, spring reverbs, and reverb chambers. Plate reverbs use a thin sheet of metal suspended under tension inside a frame. The metal plate is attached to the frame using springs. Signals sent to a plate reverb pass through a transducer, much like a speaker, which transfers audio energy into the plate and causes it to vibrate. One or two contact microphones attached to the plate itself then pick up the vibrations and pass the signal to a couple of onboard preamps. These preamps are usually tube based, though later models are solid state. The most famous manufacturer of plate reverbs was EMT.

CD track 37 plate reverb

Plate reverbs allow you to set the decay time using mechanical damping (a felt pad) but not much else. If you want to change the timbre of its sound you have to use the EQ on the mixing desk. Pre-delay is achieved by sending the signal through a delay line before it gets to the plate reverb unit, usually – in the old days – a reel-to-reel tape machine.

Plate reverbs sound dense, deep, and extremely musical. Many studios still use them and they remain the favorite reverb device of many engineers and producers, myself included. The good news is that you can still buy EMT plates from studio dealers for less than £1,000 ($1,600). The downside is that they are enormous, weigh a ton, and pick up extraneous noises such as traffic rumble very easily. For both these reasons – the great sound vs. potential inconvenience in use – a lot of contemporary digital reverb units offer plate-style settings among their hundreds of options, though these are never quite like the real thing.

Spring Reverb

Spring reverbs were extremely popular during the '50s and '60s. They work in exactly the same way as the spring reverbs in guitar amps and are very similar in operation to plate reverbs. The sound is fed into a coiled metal spring and then bounces back and forth along its length. Spring reverbs can sound a little metallic and they sometimes get a bit twangy and percussive when the input signal gets too high. To counteract this, some of the high-end spring reverb manufacturers incorporated limiters to control the transients.

I'm a huge fan of spring reverbs. They are readily available secondhand and names to watch out for are Grampian, Great British Spring, and AKG. The AKG BX15 and BX20 in particular are recommended and readily available used.

Reverb Chambers

The top studios of yesteryear often had reverb chambers. The reverb chamber was constructed in an irregularly shaped room with non-absorbent masonry or tiled walls, and contained a speaker and a microphone. (An irregular shape is essential to avoid standing waves.) Hard objects were often placed in the chamber to diffuse the sound and add complexity to the reverberation. A carefully designed small chamber can mimic the acoustic properties of a much larger space. You can even create a reverb room of your own. Put a clean sounding guitar cabinet or hi-fi speaker in your bathroom (**diagram A**) and connect its input to an auxiliary output on your mixer. Put a microphone such as a PZM in the room and plug it back into your desk. This can sound very effective, but you should make sure that no direct path exists between the speaker and the microphone – you want reflected, echoed sound only. You can also do this in professional studios if they have a good live room. It can do amazing things for drum samples or DI'd guitar and it's a great way to get the guitars to sit well with the drums – especially if the drums were recorded in the same live room.

Digital Reverb

Digital technology has provided us with convenient reverb devices in compact form that offer enormous flexibility and versatility. A typical digital reverb will contain plates, halls, small rooms, large rooms, tiled rooms, springs, chambers, and so on. You can also edit the programs to alter pre-delay, high frequency cut-off, diffusion, and more.

If you are using a digital reverb processor, put your recorded guitar through it and try out the presets. When you have found one that sounds good in the mix, you might like to edit or fine-tune it. Most of these units will allow you to EQ the reverb, adjust the pre-delay, and change the reverb decay time. Some modern processors offer such deep editing I'm sure before long you'll be able to change the color of the wallpaper or choose between shag pile carpet or floorboards in your virtual room.

CD track 38: spring reverb

CD track 39: digital reverb

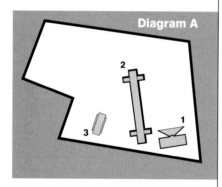

Diagram A

REVERB CHAMBERS

In the "good old days," some of the finest reverb was recorded naturally – in a dedicated room called a reverb chamber. As in the diagram above, you can create a chamber yourself by placing a speaker and a microphone in a bathroom or other reflective room. Here (1) is the speaker, (2) a screen, and (3) your microphone.

Modern digital reverbs are also MIDI controllable. We can use a sequencer or computer to change reverb programs or presets during the mix. This is an invaluable tool for today's mixing engineers because it is sometimes hard to find an effect that works well throughout the course of a song.

DELAY

Digital Delay

We use delay to "sit" instruments into mixes and to create ambient rhythmic effects. Think of the Edge with U2, Andy Summers with The Police, or Dave Gilmour with Pink Floyd. Digital delay units allow us to program the delay times we require with great accuracy.

If a song has been played to a click track we can calculate the delay to match it exactly to the song. If the tempo of the track is 120 beats per minute (BPM), divide 60 by 120 to derive the intervals in seconds between quarter beats. Here, this works out at half a second or 500 milliseconds (ms), so one bar would equal two seconds. MIDI control also allows us to change delay times during mixes.

Many units feature a "tap" control. If your track has not been recorded to a click track, simply punch the "tap" button in time with the track – the delay unit will work out the tempo and adjust the delay time accordingly. If you don't have a tap button, try putting the snare drum or kick drum through the unit and adjust the delay time by ear until the delayed drum falls exactly on the following hit or between the beats without fighting the groove. When it sounds right, take the drum out of the delay unit and stick your guitar back through it.

Tape Delay

In the days before digital delay we used tape delay. A tape delay unit prints the input signal to a spinning tape loop, then plays it back by a separate head before the signal is erased. Different delay times are achieved by varying the gap between the record head and the playback head on the tape machine. More sophisticated units, such as the Roland RE-201 Space Echo, allow you to adjust the speed of the tape loop, though more basic machines often have fixed speeds. Most units incorporate three or four playback heads for selection individually or in combination. I generally select the head that sounds good in the mix, then fine-tune the Varispeed for more precise control of the delay time.

In the old days, to achieve longer times two machines were placed several feet apart on a dedicated Echo Shelf. A single tape loop was then fed between them. You could set the delay time using a tape measure. If the tape was moving at 30 inches per second and the engineer wanted a two second delay, the record head of machine 1 and the playback head of machine 2 needed to be 60" apart.

Although tape echo is a lot more trouble than digital delay, there is something about it that sounds "right." Tape echo units also offer plenty of scope for abuse and sonic mayhem. The early machines were tube-based, and they were always easy to distort. The frequency response of the tape was limited, so the echoes became increasingly dull as they faded away. This created an impression of the sound moving away from you. On old WEM Copicats, the swell and sustain controls allow you to increase the volume of the echo and to send the delayed signal back into the record circuitry. With the sustain turned right up the unit will start to feed back. This echoing feedback is very "playable," and allows you to create interesting, otherworldly, synth-like sounds.

Tape Echo With A Cassette Machine

If you have a three-head cassette deck you can use it as a high quality slap-back tape echo – and you can even use the Dolby to keep the noise down. Feed the machine from an auxiliary send; bring the signal back on a separate channel of your mixer, and press record and play. Most three-head tape machines have a

CD track 40 tape delay

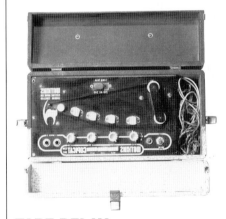

TAPE DELAY

The classic Watkins Copicat tape delay unit, a stalwart of the early British rock scene and probably best known for its use by Hank Marvin of The Shadows. Early Copicats were tube-based, later ones solid-state.

source (input)/monitor selector. Make sure the machine is monitoring from the tape, not the input. This way you can listen to the sound that is recorded on the tape and take advantage of the inherent delay. You can send the echo back to the cassette machine by turning up the auxiliary send on the return channel. This creates a feedback loop, so make sure your volume control is set low because it can get out of control pretty fast if you're not careful. You might also try rolling off a little of the high frequencies on the return channel. The sound you get is an old fashioned slap-back echo, but the delay time is not variable.

Varispeeding Tape Machines

Varispeeding the multitrack tape machine provides some interesting opportunities. A common trick when multitracking power chord parts is to tune the guitar to concert pitch, and then slow the tape machine down very slightly. On the next pass do the opposite – speed the tape up very slightly. Of course, when the multitrack machine is returned to fixed speed, one track will be slightly sharp and the other slightly flat. This produces a natural chorus effect. I have mixed feelings about recording layer upon layer of guitar to produce a wall of sound. Quite often I feel it just turns into sonic wallpaper rather than a wall of sound. If you want to try this technique, record odd numbers of overdubs (that is, three tracks of the same guitar part, or five or seven tracks, rather than two, four or six tracks). Then pan pairs hard left and right, and stick the leftover track in the middle. This is a magic trick which produces big sounds without sacrificing edge and rawness, and the middle track seems to focus the sound and pull the whole guitar part together, making it sound more solid than just left-right pairs.

On another occasion you might find yourself wishing you had a 12-string guitar to play a really cool arpeggio part. The good news is that you can fake it. Record the part once on your six-string, then halve the speed of your multitrack. The pitch of the song will drop by one octave. Record the part again on a separate track; it'll be hard with the track running so slowly, but you can do it. Return the machine to standard speed and the second track will be an octave higher than you actually played it. Mix them together and, abracadabra, you're Roger McGuinn.

Sean Bevan does something similar – though in reverse – when recording guitars for Marilyn Manson. The backing tracks are recorded to multitrack tape at 15 inches per second (ips). The guitars are tracked at 30 ips with the guitarist playing an octave high, twice as fast. The tape is then slowed back down to 15 ips to bring the guitar track back down an octave.

BACKWARDS EFFECTS

Backwards Tape

CD track 41: backwards tape

Another great trick you can use with analog tape machines is backwards recording. You will have heard Jimi Hendrix doing this on *Are You Experienced*. Play the multitrack tape to the end of your guitar solo section and press stop. Very carefully – preferably with a pair of helping hands – remove the tape from the machine and reverse the spools placing the left reel on the right side and vice-versa. When you press play the tape will play backwards through the solo section. If you now record your guitar solo and replace the reels the song will play forwards again but your solo will play backwards.

This produces a weird, sucking effect. When a guitar note is played we hear the percussive attack (or transient), the note sustains, then fades away. With backwards guitar we hear these steps in reverse order. There is an audible fade-in to each note, and an abrupt end. Your tried and trusted licks will also acquire a mysterious, unpredictable quality. Instant psychedelia!

This is a simple effect to set up and achieve; one word of warning, however. Musicians tend to get into backwards stuff late at night when they are "tired and emotional." In this state of mind, it is quite easy to erase something by mistake.

Many engineers have wiped precious drum tracks and lead vocals this way. Just be certain to count your tracks carefully. I sometimes run a length of masking tape along the bottom of the desk and write down all the numbers 1 to 24 under the corresponding faders. I then peel off the tape and replace it upside down. That way you can tell at a glance where your reversed tracks have ended up. Remember that when you reverse the tape reels on a 4-track machine, track 4 becomes track 1, and track 3 becomes track 2. On a 24-track reel-to-reel machine, track 24 becomes track 1 and track 23 becomes track 2.

You might like to record your solo forwards, flip the tape, and then put the solo through a reverb unit and record the effect backwards. This sounds particularly good with wah wah guitar.

Backwards Effects With Hard Disc Recorders

Fortunately you can achieve backwards guitar sounds using modern hard-disc recorders. If anything, it is easier and involves less risk. Simply record your monitor mix as an internal bounce, noting the start and end points. Reverse the sample region in the computer and place it back in the arrangement. Overdub your guitar part with everything other than the backwards track muted. When you have finished recording, reverse the guitar sample region, remove the backwards backing track from the arrangement, and de-mute everything else.

TAPE FLANGING

We're talking *Itchycoo Park* by The Small Faces here – the wacky bit where it all goes "swooosh." Believe it or not, this was achieved using analog tape.

With identical recordings on two separate reel-to-reel machines, start both playing at exactly the same time. Machine A is then slowed down using gentle hand pressure on the tape reel. This induces a comb filtering effect where the delay time induces phase cancellation in some frequencies but not others. Hand pressure is then removed from machine A and applied to machine B. Machine A takes over from machine B as the leader and we hear the famous "swooosh" effect at the point where they swap over. Now apply pressure to machine A once again and release machine B. If you apply too much hand pressure the tape machine will slow down so much that you will hear echo, not flanging.

Although heavily associated with psychedelia and alternative music, legend has it that the men in white coats at the BBC had figured out how to do this back in the early '50s. Modern flangers have never been able to match the intensity or depth of the original method, but some good-sounding units are available. MXR made an extremely good rack-mountable studio flanger, and I still use my Electro-Harmonix Electric Mistress for guitars and other things besides. If you are intent upon trying this, you could buy a couple of mono reel-to-reel machines from a junk shop. You could even buy a Revox or similar machine for around £300 ($500). Not only would you have a device for flanging, you could use it for tape echo and mastering. Properly set up, these machines sound great, run reliably, and will knock the spots off any DAT machine that I can think of.

ROTATING SPEAKERS

If you wanted a "chorus" effect 40 years ago, you needed a Leslie speaker cabinet to get it. These huge devices were originally made for Hammond organs, and feature a two-speaker system with a horn handling the top end and a standard cone driver for the lows. The speakers are driven by an onboard tube amplifier (which distorts nicely) through a crossover system, and are rotated by two separate motors, which are capable of running at two different speeds: fast and slow. The spinning speaker creates two distinct effects. Firstly, as the speakers spin away from the listener, there is a perceived change in volume and also frequency response. Secondly, an induced doppler effect produces pitch modulation. This is similar to the pitch change you experience as a police car drives past you with its siren on. Another classic sonic signature of the genuine Leslie sound is the speeding up and slowing down of the rotors at slightly different paces as the player switches from slow to fast or vice-versa, as the individual motors chase each other to the new setting. Great Hammond organ players, like Jimmy Smith, have used this aspect of the Leslie sound to great effect for years.

If you are lucky you might one day find yourself in a studio that still owns a Leslie, though you will need a preamp to use a Leslie speaker with a guitar. There are several dedicated Leslie simulation effects units. Korg's version is especially good. The rotating speaker effect is notoriously difficult to emulate digitally, however, and nothing yet sounds quite like the real thing.

You can achieve a similar effect with a microphone, a long cable, and a willing volunteer. If you can't get the speaker to spin then why not spin the microphone? Attach a microphone securely to a cable using gaffer (duct) tape, put a foam pop shield over the end to cut down the whistling noise, and with your outstretched arm above your head, start swinging Roger Daltrey style.

Warning! Do not attempt this using precious condenser or ribbon microphones. Anything from a cheap store with the word "professional" written on it should suffice. I once asked an assistant engineer to perform this trick and the poor lad got it hopelessly wrong. The cable wrapped itself around the back of his neck and continued spinning in ever decreasing circles until… well, you can guess the rest. Suffice to say, he was lucky to walk away with his teeth.

Fans of Stevie Ray Vaughan might be aware that Fender used to make a rotating speaker cabinet called the Vibratone. Available in the late-'60s and early-'70s, it was based roughly on the Leslie (the patents for which were owned by Fender at the time), but updated for use specifically by guitarists. Other famous Leslie sound-alike effects include the Dunlop Uni-Vibe and the Hughes & Kettner Rotosphere. In addition to guitars and Hammond organs, Leslie speakers were also used for backing vocals, brass, and strings.

NOISE GATES

A very popular device used to create interesting musical effects is the noise gate. The most common brand found in recording studios is made by Drawmer, but others include Klark Technic and Kepex. Many guitar processors, such as the Line 6 POD, also include a basic noise gate to cut down the hiss and hum on distortion patches. In part of its function a noise gate is somewhat similar to a compressor because it responds to signal level, but instead of acting as an automatic volume control to govern the level it actually opens and closes to let the sound through or block it all together.

GATES

Originally designed primarily to filter out unwanted hiss, hum, and spillage, noise gates are today used to create a range of interesting sonic effects as well.

The usual studio application for noise gates is to eliminate unwanted sound or spillage on drums. A microphone placed close to a snare drum will pick up the snare but also all the other parts of the kit, like the hi-hat right next to it, for example. The snare drum will be the loudest sound in that mike, but you might encounter problems if you decide to add reverb to the snare. The chances are that you will also be adding the reverb to the hat and cymbals at the same time. A noise gate can be set up to allow the loudest sound to pass through, but to silence the quieter sounds.

As you can see in the photo opposite, many of the gate's controls are similar to those on the compressor we examined earlier. In this example they include:

Threshold determines the volume level required to trigger the gate to open. Sounds below the Threshold will be inaudible because the gate remains closed.

Attack adjusts the speed with which the gate opens.

Hold determines the length of time the gate stays open.

Decay adjusts the speed with which it shuts.

Range allows us to mix the original un-gated signal back into the gated sound. Heavily gated drums can sound unnatural or stilted and this feature can help to minimize that effect.

Unfortunately a noise gate can be very difficult to set up using Threshold alone; finer control is needed. To this end, gates often feature these extra controls:

Key Listen allows us to EQ the trigger – the sound that opens and closes the gate – leaving the gated sound unaffected.

Duck reverses the function of the gate so that it closes in response to loud sounds and opens in quiet sections.

High Pass/Low Pass Filter lets certain frequencies through. Open hi-hats are usually louder than closed and can accidentally trigger a snare gate to open. You can use the low pass filter to remove the high frequencies from the trigger. Similarly the occasional loud bass drum beat from an "expressive" drummer can cause the gate to open. Use the high pass filter to EQ out the bass drum. Switch back to Listen and you should find that the gate responds more accurately.

Link synchronizes the two sides of a stereo noise gate. Gate A controls gate B.

For a snare drum – which obviously has an instantaneous attack and not a whole lot of sustain – attack time should be set fast, hold should be long enough to allow the tone of the drum to ring through, and decay should also be fast. If you are using a noise gate to clean up a guitar track by eliminating amp noise, the hold should be set longer and decay should be more gradual. This way you can avoid sudden cut-offs at the end of sustained notes or chords.

Six-String Techno

Noise gates can be used for creative and musical effects as well as for removing unwanted noise or spill. An exciting feature for guitarists is the "external trigger." Key source can be switched to external, which means that the gate can be triggered by a different signal from the one you are gating.

CD track 42: external-trigger gate

Let's take an example. Record your guitar feeding back throughout a track and patch the recorded sound through a noise gate. Put the bass drum, snare drum or even hi-hat from the backing track into the key input of the gate and switch key source to external. With just a little time spent getting the controls set for the right trigger level, you should be able to get the guitar feedback pulsing perfectly in time with the song.

Switching from gate to duck will shift this pulse to the off-beat. A slow attack setting and a short decay can produce some cool backwards effects. Try adding some filtered delays to the pulsing feedback and suddenly you are in techno-land without a sequencer in sight.

Tightening-Up Multitracked Power Chords

Heavily multitracked guitar parts can sometimes lack punch at the front of chords because the timing will be slightly different on each take. Even the best player's timing will vary by fractions of a second between takes, and this can lead to a mushy, soft attack after three or four tracks have been added together. Put the stereo sub mix of the guitars through a linked stereo noise gate but use only one of the takes to trigger the gates from the external key input. Suddenly all the guitars will sound as tight as a gnat's chuff.

Duck'd Delays

Guitar solos can sound excellent with delay. Unfortunately, definition and articulation can be lost during fast passages. Put the delay through a noise gate set to external input and use the dry guitar signal to trigger the gate. Switch the noise gate to duck. The gate will close during the playing passages and the delay will disappear. The gate will then open during the gaps allowing the delay to appear. The result: your runs sound tight and precise, but are followed by an effective, atmospheric delay.

HARMONIZERS

Engineers often apply harmonization to basses and guitars to create a richer, fatter sound. To do this, channel A of a stereo chorus is de-tuned by 3 cents and channel B is tuned up by 3 cents. The bass or guitar signal is sent to the harmonizer and blended to taste. If I'm harmonizing power chords I'll pan the harmonizer returns hard left and right or maybe 8 and 4 o'clock. For bass I'll pan the dry signal in the center and place the effect returns at 10 and 2 o'clock. My favorite harmonizers are made by Eventide and AMS.

Acoustic Guitars

Capture the full richness and body of a great acoustic guitar sound, plus and advanced look at stereo techniques.

The strange thing about recording your own acoustic guitar is that you probably don't even know what it sounds like to start with. It's a little like our speaking voice: we never hear it in quite the same way as others do. With our voice, we hear the sound waves as well as the transferred vibrations through our bones and muscle. I still remember the shock of hearing myself on tape for the first time. When an acoustic guitar is played, the sound heard by the musician is quite different from that heard by the listener. And both are probably different to that which would be heard in the listening position envisaged by the guitar builder. Discerning players often notice that their recorded sound is different and unfamiliar. So how do we record acoustic guitars to get good, predictable results, which aren't a total surprise each time?

How Acoustic Guitars Work

The key to successful recordings is to understand the way an instrument generates sound. When you strike a guitar string you are applying energy to it, but the vibration of the string alone is not enough to produce clearly audible sound. The strings of an acoustic guitar pass over the saddle and through the bridge, and when they are plucked the vibrations excite the thin wooden body; we call this "vibrational coupling." This transfer of energy is most efficient when the string vibrates transversely in a direction perpendicular to the soundboard surface. You can try this out by plucking a string from the side then plucking it by pushing down towards the surface of the soundboard and then releasing it. You will hear the difference.

When the top (or soundboard) vibrates, it generates sound waves, much like a loudspeaker. As the soundboard moves forward, the air that is in front of it is compressed and it moves away from the guitar. As the soundboard moves back, the pressure on the air in front of the guitar is reduced. This is called a "rarefaction," and air rushes in to fill the rarefied region. Through this process, an alternating series of compression and rarefaction pulses travel away from the soundboard, creating sound waves.

The back and sides of the guitar will also vibrate, adding to the timbre of the instrument. Body shape and size is very important because the soundbox determines volume, projection, and tone. The vibrating soundboard also creates sound waves inside the body of the guitar. These internal sound waves in turn facilitate the vibration of the soundboard. The air inside the guitar vibrates more readily at low frequencies than at high frequencies. Therefore, a guitar's low-end response increases with body size because of the greater volume of air behind the soundboard. The soundhole provides a coupling between the internal vibrations and the outside air. If the soundhole is too small or even closed, the quality of the sound is dramatically altered. The Californian guitar company Santa Cruz produces a Tony Rice dreadnought model with an enlarged soundhole modeled after bluegrass picker Tony Rice's vintage 1930s D-28 Martin, which was once owned by Clarence White of The Byrds. This design is intended to increase volume and bass.

Construction, Body Shapes And Woods

CD track 44-47: 4 body styles

The design of the steel string acoustic guitar, as we know it, dates from the mid-nineteenth century when the C.F. Martin company perfected the X brace. Classical guitar makers still primarily use the fan-bracing pattern that Antonio de Torres developed at around the same time. Soundboxes have gradually evolved to become larger – producing higher volumes and emphasizing bass frequencies. The traditional choice of soundboard wood is spruce, which produces a bright, clear tone with good projection. As a spruce-topped guitar gets older, its tone should become fuller and lose its harshness. Cedar is also used – especially for classical guitars – and it has a warm, dark sound that will remain consistent over the years.

Guitar backs and sides also have a strong influence on the instrument's sound. To demonstrate this, try strumming a chord with the back of your guitar pressed tightly to your stomach and chest, and then do the same while holding the soundbox slightly away from your body. Your guitar will sound louder and have better tone when the back is free to vibrate. Mahogany backs and sides produce a warm, bright sound, but for real depth and clarity, top quality instruments are made with Indian rosewood. Brazilian rosewood is even more highly regarded, but it has been very scarce since Brazil imposed a ban on rosewood exports in 1969, and any reserves still available to guitar builders are extremely expensive. Walnut combines the brightness of mahogany with a little extra warmth, while maple produces a full midrange with bright, strong high frequencies, making it a good choice for the back and sides of a guitar intended mainly for acoustic rhythm work, such as the Gibson J-200.

Budget instrument manufacturers will sometimes attach solid wood tops to laminated backs and sides. Results can be good but will never match the responsiveness and tonal complexity of a solid wood guitar. Very cheap guitars will be made entirely from plywood.

These days the most common body shape for steel-string guitars is the dreadnought – named after a British battleship. The curves of the dreadnought are less pronounced than the traditional hourglass shapes of earlier designs such as Martin's 0, 00 and 000. The dreadnought produces a warm sound with good volume and a lot of bass and midrange. The trade-off is less definition, clarity, and high-end sparkle. Many guitarists favor dreadnoughts for strumming, flat-picking, and rhythm guitar work. The various "0" styles are popular for fingerpicking, open tunings, and bottleneck.

Finding The "G" Spot

Before we consider microphones or microphone placement for recording acoustic guitars, we should think about the acoustic space and how it will affect our recording. Guitar players know that the acoustic properties of certain rooms contribute to a musical sound, which can as a result be more inspiring and pleasurable to play with. These spaces might include bathrooms, stairwells or kitchens – places with natural reverb.

If you are recording a solo acoustic guitar piece, my recommendation is to find a space at home or in the studio that inspires you to play. A VU meter on a tape machine will not register feeling – anger, sadness or passion – but people can hear it. If you are enjoying the experience of playing you will make better music, so you should do everything possible to facilitate this.

Take some time to walk around with your guitar, play the piece in a few different parts of the room, and find a place where you feel comfortable and where you enjoy the sound of your guitar – you can call it the "G spot." Remember, it's always best to tell the sound engineer what you are doing before he has set up his microphones.

Microphone Choice

The standard choice of microphone for acoustic guitar recording is the condenser. This is partly because acoustic guitars have a much wider frequency range than an electric guitar and amp combination, and a condenser is generally better able to capture this. Neumann's U87, KM84 or U89 are popular choices. The AKG C414, C451, C28, and C12A are also effective. You might also try a Schoeps 221 or a Sony C37 if you get the chance.

Dynamic moving coil microphones do not have the wide frequency range or the sensitivity to detect the subtleties and nuances of the instrument or the player. I do, however, like to use dynamic ribbon microphones for acoustic guitars, sometimes in combination with a condenser. Although ribbon microphones tend not to pick up the highest frequencies, they are nevertheless capable of producing very lifelike recordings. They are particularly effective with nylon-string or classical guitars. I have achieved some great results with the Coles 4038, although it needs a bit of help in the top end. The Beyer 160 and Royer 121 have quite an extended high frequency response for ribbon microphones and are ideally suited to acoustic guitar recording.

Microphone Placement

CD track 43 2 mikes each/both

If we want a dry, close sound with minimal spillage we need to put the microphone close to the instrument. Novice engineers often make the mistake of pointing the microphone directly into the soundhole of an acoustic guitar. Many people assume that is where the sound comes from but, as we discussed previously, that is only partly true. Remember that the sound of the acoustic guitar comes from the vibration of the entire soundbox. Pointing the microphone at the hole will produce a nasal, slappy tone that will have you diving for the EQ switch *muy pronto*.

The classic "BBC approach" is to fire the microphone across the front of the guitar, positioned at around the 12th fret and aiming towards the end of the fingerboard. The tone captured here is more natural than that from a mike aiming into the soundhole, with good top end – but you might experience a lot of slap from the plectrum contacting the strings, as well as a lack of bass. Since we are trying to record sound waves produced by the vibration of the soundboard, let's try a few other positions for the microphone.

Good results can be obtained by placing the microphone close to the front of the guitar, just below the bridge. This will give you a very warm and full tone with a lot of body. It works well with classical guitars, but the steel-string player might complain about a lack of top end or high frequencies. If the neck microphone is too toppy and the bridge microphone too warm, why not use two microphones and blend them together? We can use each microphone to pick up the timbre of the instrument at various locations along its body. Remember, though, that any time more than one mike comes into play you have to be very careful about phase cancellation.

Many guitarists with arch top or semi acoustic guitars such as Gibson ES-335s or Gretsch models like to blend some of the acoustic sound with the sound from the amp. If the musician is playing in the control room, separation is easy: just turn down the monitors and work on headphones. This trick works particularly well with 12-string semis, like Rickenbackers, when you blend the sparkle and chime from the acoustic sound with the graunch from the amp. Singers who also like to play rhythm guitar "live" while tracking their vocals have been doing this for years without really thinking too much about it – until they tried to patch up the vocal track without patching the guitar along with it. The toppy jangle of a semi or even a solidbody has proved to be the secret ingredient in a rhythm-section mix on plenty of great songs.

Sometimes the recording situation demands that we must use close microphones, but this is not ideal. Acoustic instruments are designed to project.

This means that the overall tone and balance of the instrument can only be heard at a distance. When you play an acoustic guitar your ears are probably 18" or 24" away from the instrument – the listener might be several feet away. When we listen to a grand piano we are unlikely to do so with our heads stuck under the lid. If you have ever experienced a snare drum hit when your head is right next to it, you probably decided pretty quickly not to try it again. My point is that some distance

BBC APPROACH – MONO

Position the mike at about the 12th fret, angled towards the end of the fingerboard and firing across the soundhole.

between the instrument and the microphone will give you a better chance of capturing a natural and realistic sound. You will be able to use one microphone, and you will be able to move that microphone to alter the tone. If you want to create the illusion of a real acoustic guitar when you are recording, this is the way to do it.

BLENDED MONO PAIR

Adding a second mike aimed at the soundboard below the bridge will help you blend a warm, full-bodied tone with the brighter, slappier sound captured at the end of the fretboard.

RECORDING IN STEREO

So far I have been discussing monophonic sound, but most of us are well aware that life ain't in mono, unless you happen to be Brian Wilson. When we close our eyes and listen, we can gauge the direction of a sound source very accurately. We are able to construct an audio image. Our brains decode the information picked up by our two ears by analyzing volume intensity and time differences. The word "stereophonic" comes from the Greek for "solid sound." In the early days of recorded music, systems were monophonic – "single sound." If the ultimate goal of recording is to reproduce sound of such quality that it becomes hard to distinguish the recording from reality, monophonic systems are clearly inadequate. Techniques had to be developed to reproduce sound with the spatial element intact. Obviously this cannot be done with one microphone and one loudspeaker. We have two ears, so we need at least two microphones and two loudspeakers.

Mixing a rock or pop track involves the construction of an artificial stereo image. We do this by positioning numerous mono signals using the individual pan pots on each channel of the mixer. These are a little like the balance controls on domestic hi-fi systems. This is not true stereo, it is merely a range of instruments in a particular recording spread across the stereo field to give the impression of space and dimension. There are, however, various ways that we can use two microphones to create true stereo images. This will be particularly useful if you want to record a soloist or a group of musicians in a natural and realistic way. Steve Earle took this approach when he worked with bluegrass five-piece The Del McCoury Band for the album *The Mountain*, positioning numerous microphones around a live room and recording those which captured the most realistic stereo image of the band playing live. Another fine album recorded this way was *The Trinity Session* by the Cowboy Junkies, which was recorded live using just one stereo microphone.

Spaced Stereo Pair

The spaced stereo pair is not (thank God) a new shoegazing alternative duo. Developed in America in the early '30s by Bell Laboratories, it is probably the most commonly used stereo microphone technique. It simply involves the placement of two microphones, spaced a reasonable distance apart. The signals from the microphones are panned hard right and hard left. This is commonly used over drum kits, in front of orchestras, or simply to pick up room ambience. Human hearing relies on timing differences to determine the location of a particular sound source. Spaced stereo pairs were devised to work in much the same way.

Many sound engineers prefer omnidirectional microphones for spaced stereo applications. Their frequency response is generally smoother and they have extended low frequency capability. The off-axis response also tends to be smoother, allowing the microphone to accurately pick up sound from a broad area, not just a narrow region in front of the microphone.

Cardioid and figure 8 microphones are also used in spaced stereo pairs. Many engineers use them to minimise unwanted spill from other instruments or to reject unwanted room ambience or reverberation. Fans of this technique enjoy the spacious, open quality of the sound and the way that spaced pairs combine very effectively with close microphones. Detractors argue that the stereo image is always vague – not solid – and point out the inevitable comb filtering and lack of mono compatibility.

These drawbacks occur because the distance between the two microphones causes sound waves to reach them at different times. This is compounded by the additional timing differences introduced by the separate hi-fi speakers, and the distance between the speakers and the listener. This problem can be minimized by making sure that the distance between the microphones is three times greater than the distance between each microphone and the sound source. This is called the "Three To One Rule," as illustrated in **diagram A**.

Coincident Pair

If you want to get serious about stereo recording, you will want to explore ways in which you can achieve solid, stereo imaging with minimal problems from phase cancellation. The most obvious solution is to place the capsules of two directional microphones as close together as possible, with the microphones pointed towards the left and right at an angle of about 90 degrees. This is called the "mutual

CD track 48: spaced pair

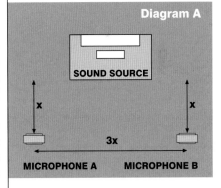

Diagram A

THREE-TO-ONE RULE

To minimize phase cancellation when recording using a spaced stereo pair, remember to keep the microphones three times as far from each other as they are from the sound source.

CD track 49: coincident pair

angle," and it can be varied to adjust the width of the image. The height of the microphones above the sound source can also be adjusted to fine-tune the stereo image; the area of pickup in front of the microphones is called the "acceptance angle." Alan Blumlein invented this technique in England in the '30s, and called it the "coincident pair."

Blumlein discovered that the brain could be tricked into interpreting the differences in volume or intensity between the two microphone signals as timing

SPACED STEREO PAIR

A pair of matched mikes spaced a distance apart provides a fairly straightforward method for recording in stereo.

differences. Of course, the close proximity of the capsules ensures negligible phase shift or comb filtering because the time differences between the sound waves hitting each individual capsule are negligible. Therefore, coincident pair recordings show good mono compatibility.

To make stereo recording easier, many manufacturers build stereo microphones. These are essentially two microphones housed within the same chassis, with individual capsules, which rotate independently to allow for different angles. The two channels into which the stereo mike is plugged should be panned hard left and hard right, and the width of the stereo image varied by changing the angle of the capsules. An acute angle produces a broad image and a wide angle narrows it. AKG built a classic example, the C24 (which was effectively two of their C12s housed together), and Royer now even offer a stereo ribbon microphone.

Microphones used as coincident pairs should be matched as closely as

possible. They can be set to cardioid or figure 8. Most engineers choose small-capsule condenser microphones for this application, aiming the microphones inwards towards the center of the stereo picture. Large capsule microphones tend to have large bodies that can cast an acoustic shadow across the pickup areas of other microphones. Therefore, when used in coincident pairs, such mikes should be aimed outwards.

COINCIDENT PAIR

To record with a coincident pair, place the mikes' capsules close together, aimed left and right at an angle of approximately 90 degrees.

CD track 50: mid-and-side

Mid-And-Side

The "mid-and-side" (also known as "sum-and-difference") pair was also invented by Alan Blumlein, and is a variation on the coincident pair. This is a somewhat "magical" technique that produces a stereo image from a single mono figure 8 mike, while filling in the center of the sonic image with a second mono mike. The key to it all is splitting the signal picked up by a sideways-mounted figure 8 mike and reversing the phase of one side of it. Read on to find out how to do it.

MID-AND-SIDE PAIR

This is a relatively simple technique to achieve. The mid-and-side pair captures a full stereo image, and is also mono compatible.

Microphone A (Mid) directly faces the sound source while microphone B (Side) is placed "sideways" right above or below mike A, firing side to side in a figure 8 pattern. The pickup pattern of microphone A can be cardioid, omni or figure 8. The single mono output from microphone B is split into two and brought up on two separate channels of the mixing desk. These channels are panned hard left and hard right and the polarity of the right channel is reversed using the phase switch on the desk. Set the output of the mixing desk to mono (or pan each track to center if you don't have a mono switch on your master channel strip), and then bring the faders of the two side channels level and adjust their microphone gains to achieve maximum phase cancellation. You'll know when it's right because the sound will disappear when the signal levels are matched. Switch the output bus of the mixing desk back to stereo, pan the two channels for mike B's split output to hard left and hard right respectively, then bring up the signal from microphone A on a third channel of the mixer panned to the center. A wide stereo image should appear that is full and solid due to the "mid" mike aimed at the center of the source. A good tip is to stick the two side faders together using a bulldog clip.

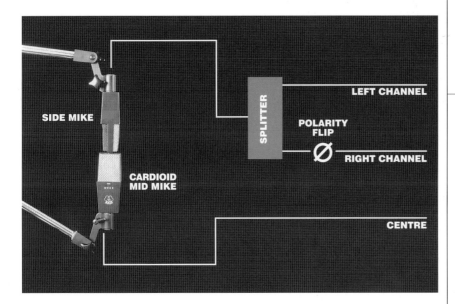

MID-AND-SIDE PAIR

A pair of AKG C414 mikes used in "mid-and-side" configuration. The diagram shows how the signals from the mikes are used to create a stereo image.

By altering the balance between mid and side signals, the stereo width can be adjusted from mono to such wide stereo that the image appears outside the speakers. This technique offers all the other benefits of angled coincident pairs plus total mono compatibility. In mono the side signals will cancel out but the signal from the mid microphone remains intact. This is also a great technique to use when you need a stereo recording but you don't have a matched pair of microphones. The mid and side microphones can be completely different.

Dummy Heads And Jecklin Discs

Another specialist technique is "dummy head" recording. Two omni-directional microphones are placed at about the same spacing as a pair of ears either side of a plastic disc with sound absorbent material on each side or a dummy head These devices are designed to mimic the acoustic "shadow" of a human head. You can make your own Jecklin disc from a circle of plexiglas (perspex) about 8" to 10" in diameter, and some acoustic foam. This technique can produce extremely realistic recordings, especially when replayed on headphones. Over speakers the stereo image is not that accurate, but it works as well as that from a spaced stereo pair.

You could try a dummy head arrangement because the beauty is that you have your own real head (or real dummy) to use. Place an omni-directional microphone next to each ear, pointing down towards the guitar. Pan the signals left and right and voilà – a true stereo acoustic guitar sound. Players who have tried it comment on the accuracy of the result. Be careful about phase cancellation and also avoid spillage from monitoring headphones by using closed-back designs. For mono you could place an omni or cardioid microphone above the player's head. Try an omni somewhere in front of the guitar. What about blending this front mike with the binaural pair either side of the player's head? The possibilities are endless.

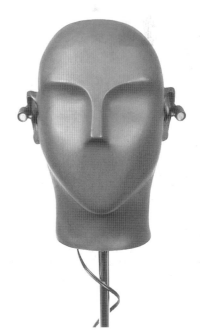

A REAL DUMMY... HEAD

If your guitarist objects to the implications, purpose-made dummy's heads are available.

| *Acoustic Guitars*

An old interview with Ry Cooder got me thinking. He was talking about the way Robert Johnson preferred to record facing into a corner. The recording engineer who recorded Johnson suggested that he might have been shy or nervous. Cooder said: "Does that man sound nervous to you?" Of course he wasn't, he was "corner loading." Try it! Playing into a corner with nice reflective walls will

DUMMY HEAD – STEREO

Using the guitarist himself to record with the dummy head technique can yield results that sound extremely realistic to the player, capturing much of what the ears hear in the playing position.

dramatically increase low frequencies and produce a natural type of compression. You can record using this "corner loading" facility particularly well using the dummy head technique described just now.

Simply set up as you would otherwise, but with the guitarist playing into a good reflective corner, and place the mikes at each ear as usual. They will pick up not only all of the guitar sound that a dummy head setup in the middle of a room would pick up, but they will capture the full-bodied sound with increased lows from the corner loading, too.

CORNER LOADING

Take a tip from Robert Johnson: playing into a corner can boost low end and offer a rich, full bodied acoustic guitar sound. This can easily be recorded using the dummy head technique, too.

DUMMY HEAD – MONO

To use the dummy head technique in mono, simply subtract one of the stereo mikes. The remaining mike can also be blended with a mike placed at the front of the guitar – but beware of phase cancellation problems.

CD track 51: 'real' dummy head

The Aperture Effect And Smear

If the sound source lies directly in front of a microphone – on a plane precisely parallel to that on which the mike's diaphragm lies – the sound waves hit all points on the surface of the capsule simultaneously. In such a case all points on the

Acoustic Guitars

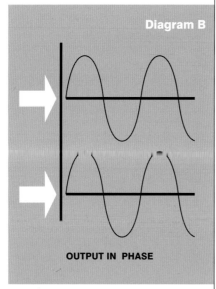

Diagram B

OUTPUT IN PHASE

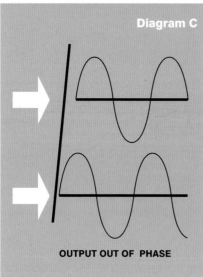

Diagram C

OUTPUT OUT OF PHASE

APERTURE EFFECT

As shown in the diagrams above, a sound source hitting different parts of the microphone's diaphragm at different times can cause phase cancellation, even within the same mike. The resulting "smear" can lead to indistinct stereo imaging.

CD track 52: plectrums & tone

diaphragm move in phase, as shown in **diagram B** here. If the sound source is located at an angle to the microphone, the sound waves will hit different parts of the diaphragm at different times, as shown in **diagram C**. When this happens, various parts of the capsule will be moving out of phase. The signal produced is therefore an average of the signal taken over a time "window." The duration of the window is a function of the speed of sound and the size of the diaphragm. This phenomenon is called the "aperture effect," and the effect it produces acts as a low pass filter.

As the sound source moves away from the center – off axis – the response curve of the microphone drops off as frequency goes up. Eventually this will fall to zero when the aperture of the capsule spans one wavelength.

The aperture effect is not much of a concern for mono recording, but accurate stereo demands greater levels of precision. Coincident recording relies on intensity or volume levels; therefore image stability has to be independent of frequency. A coincident pair above a drum kit should produce a solid image of a snare drum slightly to the left of center. If the high frequency content of the snare sound is attenuated by the aperture effect but the mid and low frequency content is not, the image of the snare drum will be indistinct. We call this phenomenon "smear." In this area, the central imaging produced by the mid-and-side technique outperforms standard coincident pairs, but it deteriorates towards the sides.

Sound Choices

All these stereo techniques have their strengths and weaknesses. Which one you choose will depend on circumstances, your microphone selection, personal preference, and a little experience. Try them all and see what works for you.

If you have made it this far, you will have acquired a good grounding in acoustic guitar recording techniques. The problem is that knowing how to record an acoustic guitar does not mean that you will get a great acoustic guitar sound. A piece of Korean plywood will never sound like a Gibson J-45 or a Martin 000-28. As an engineer, you cannot be expected to work miracles and, unfortunately, a great recording of a really bad guitar is unlikely to win you many friends. Such is the lot of the engineer.

The elements that make a great acoustic guitar sound are spruce, cedar, rosewood, and mahogany. Add to this some phosphor bronze, a sympathetic recording space, decent microphones, and a committed musician, and there are no excuses.

STUDIO TRICKS

Strings

Many experienced acoustic guitarists avoid fitting new strings to their instruments on the day of a session. Brand new strings can be bright and may cause tuning problems if they have not been properly stretched or allowed to settle down. Studio time is money! When a string is attacked with a thin plectrum it is bent to a sharp angle before it is released. This creates more high frequencies than fingering, which bends the string to a radius, so the condition of your strings and your playing technique work together to some extent to determine the high-frequency content of your acoustic sound.

Tone is also influenced by plectrum thickness: thin plectrums sound brighter because they bend with the string, thus sharpening the angle. Thick ones are more rigid and sound fatter because they produce less high frequency. A friend of mine recently gave me a very old genuine tortoiseshell pick. It is three sided, very rigid, and shaped to a point. It has all the tonal solidity and power of a thick plectrum with all the high frequencies and clarity of a thin pick. I love the sound and I would be distraught if I lost it! A session guitarist should be comfortable with various gauges of pick, and that goes for strings too.

Tracking Up

CD tracks 53-55 tracking up

Producers often record acoustic rhythm parts twice, panning one take left and the other right. This can be very useful, because variations in the rhythmic emphasis in each take can result in some interesting stereo effects. Instead of recording the same thing twice, try putting a capo on the third fret or fifth fret and re-learning the chords in the new position. Record an open A major part, for example, then double track it with a capo on the fifth fret using an E major shape. This will give your second guitar part a different tone and will make the whole thing both bigger and more defined.

Nashville Tuning

CD tracks 56-60 Nashville tuning

Another great production trick for acoustic guitar is "Nashville tuning." Sometimes a song cries out for an acoustic guitar, but if it has lots of guitars already an extra acoustic can make everything too boomy and unclear. Take off the wound E, A, D and G strings, then replace them with the high octave strings from a 12-string set (or, if those aren't available, simply the D, G, B and E strings from a second standard set). Tune these strings up to E, A, D and G and play as normal. Your acoustic guitar will now produce the crisp, octave-up jangle of the high strings from a 12-string but without the boom of the low strings, and will sit into any track without taking up too much space. You could use variations such as changing just the E, A, and D. Also try tuning up individual strings such as the D or maybe the G.

Flanged Reverb

Sometimes it's hard to make an acoustic guitar "sit" in a mix. When we add reverb it either sounds too wet or too dry, with no point in between. Try plugging an auxiliary send from your mixing desk into a flanger and then into a reverb unit. It seems crazy, I know, but it sounds great.

RESONATOR GUITARS

CD track 61 National resonator

Resonator guitars have experienced a major resurgence in popularity in recent years, and with good reason. Played well and recorded right, a reso can produce one of the most powerful and evocative sounds in the guitar world. In order to think logically about how we can best record resonator guitars and to see how we might apply mono and stereo techniques already discussed, it makes sense to first take a brief look at a few significant aspects of their construction.

Back in the inter-war years of the 1920s and '30s, guitarists were the poor relations of the music world, struggling to be heard above the drums, piano, and horns. The electrified acoustics of Charlie Christian and his contemporaries were a thing of the future. In an effort to achieve more volume, big-band guitarists such as Eddie Lang resorted to mammoth archtops with frighteningly thick strings. There was another option, however: the resonator guitar.

These instruments had cones of spun aluminum that worked much like built-in speakers. The most famous of these guitars are the metal-bodied Nationals, which we associate with early blues players like Son House, Bukka White, and Blind Boy Fuller. The earliest models had three 6" cones and were known as Tri-Plates. The cones were arranged in a triangle with two on the bass side, one on the treble, and a T-shaped bridge joining all three. They were available in Hawaiian (square neck) or Spanish (round neck) styles, with four levels of sand-blasted body decoration. The bodies were made from an alloy of copper, zinc, and nickel commonly known as nickel silver or German silver.

The Tri-Plates proved very expensive to manufacture and maintain. Soon after their introduction, National brought out a model with a large, single resonator with a circular wooden bridge-support mounted in the center. This is known as the biscuit bridge. The first models were called the Style O, the Duolian, and the Triolian. These models evolved over the years from slotted to solid headstocks, while also changing from a 12-fret to a 14-fret neck joint, echoing the evolution of standard steel-string acoustic guitars. New models are built in all of these formats and more are available today.

Wooden bodied resonators were also available from about the same time. These are generally known as Dobros after the most common brand offering this style, and are more associated with country music. Dobros also use a single resonator, but there are differences in the construction. The Dobro resonator is dish-shaped with a center portion that protrudes upwards. The bridge is also different – known as a "spider bridge," it has eight legs that span the dish-shaped cone and conduct the vibrations to the sides of the resonator.

Resonator guitars behave very differently from flat-top acoustic guitars, so we take an entirely different approach to recording them. The key to successful reso recording generally involves capturing the desired blend of cutting, mid-heavy frequencies coming from the cone itself and the mellower, warmer sound coming from the soundholes in the upper bouts. While many of our mono and stereo techniques already discussed can be applied to resonator guitars in the fundamentals at least, in doing so we need to take account of the different ways they produce and project sound compared to traditional acoustic guitars. For in-depth tips on reso sound and recording, see the interview with world famous National player Bob Brozman in *Chapter 10*.

Amplifiers

Without a great sounding and well recorded amp, you'll never get a satisfying electric guitar sound. Learn to make the best of your amplification.

We may love them, we may hate them, but as guitarists – unless we are exclusively acoustic players – we've all got to play through them sometimes. All of which means we really ought to learn as much as we can about the running and operation of guitar amplifiers in order to be able to get the most out of them, and to get them sounding their absolute best in the recording environment. The first half of this chapter, therefore, introduces a lot of technical information; but stick with it, and you'll be better equipped to make the right amp choices in the studio, and to keep those amps sounding their best.

What They Do

In essence the purpose of an amplifier is to make a quiet signal loud. It takes its electrical power from a battery or converts AC electricity into Direct Current (DC), and uses the input signal voltage to control the delivery of that power to the speaker as audio. The output signal is an alternating current that is analogous to the input signal. Wavelength and frequency remain constant, but amplitude is increased (see **diagram A** below).

AMPLIFICATION

In theory, an amp's job is to take the signal at its input and boost it to a louder signal at its output, with the fewest possible tonal changes along the way. (The diagram shows an input signal, A, and the amplified signal, B.) However, where guitar amps are concerned things are never that simple.

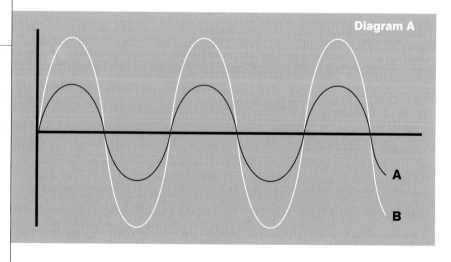

Diagram A

A

B

The theoretical ideal in amplifier design demands zero deviation between the input signal and the output signal except a current boost. Frequency content must remain the same. This is what we mean by "high fidelity" or hi-fi. Differences between the input and output signals which are induced by the amplification process are called "distortion."

All tube guitar amplifiers have a similar layout to that shown in **diagram B**, right, which includes the following components.

Power Supply   Converts alternating current (AC) into direct current (DC) using a transformer, a rectifier, and a network of resistors and capacitors. The transformer steps up the voltage and isolates the amplifier from full power current. The rectifier can be a diode tube (e.g. GZ34 or 5Y3GT) or two or four solid-state diodes, and it converts the AC voltage to pulsating DC (see **diagram C**, following page).

The pulsating DC passes through several capacitors known as filter capacitors. These capacitors allow AC voltage to flow but block DC. The residual ripple in the rectified voltage drains through the capacitors to earth, leaving "clean" DC. The filter caps in the power supply of a guitar amplifier need to be quite large in order to store enough electrons to meet power supply demands at high volumes. Values between 10 to 40 microfarads (generally written as mF or μ) are typical in guitar amps, with larger values called for in more powerful amps that deliver higher voltages to the power tubes.

If the demand on the power supply is too great, the amplifier's response sags. This is a particular characteristic of tube rectifiers, and many players prefer it to solid-state rectification because of the softer, compression-like feel it gives their pick attack while playing. The value of the resistors in the power supply is chosen to match the current drawn by the circuit. If the value is too small, the high tension (HT) voltage will be too high for the tubes to handle.

First Stage Preamp – This will employ one half of a twin-triode tube or a transistor plus associated components. The function of this stage is to provide a fixed voltage gain – that is, it amplifies the signal voltage to a level where it can be further processed.

Tone Circuit – In most guitar amps this involves a passive network of capacitors and potentiometers (variable resistors) that act as high and low pass filters. (Some amps, most notably Vox's Top Boost AC30 models and some Matchless models based on this design, use active, interactive tone circuits that use a further tube or half of a twin-triode tube in their tone-shaping circuitry – but these are far less common.)

Volume – A variable resistor, typically 500k to 1M ohm (logarithmic)

Second Preamp Stage – Signal level drops as it passes through the passive tone circuit so the second stage of the preamp is used to compensate for any losses. In high gain amps, this stage is also used to provide additional gain for overdrive and distortion.

Amps employing "cascading gain" preamps, such as those pioneered by Mesa/Boogie, will commonly link a number of preamp stages purely to generate high gain levels for preamp-generated overdrive.

Power/Output Stage – This is where the large signal voltage is converted into a large current flow. The phase inverter/driver (a role performed by another preamp-style twin-triode tube in tube amps) divides the signal into two and places one side 180 degrees out of phase with the other before delivering it to the output tubes. It also further amplifies the signal.

Most tube and transistor amplifiers employ a push-pull design, where one side "pushes" the signal while the other "pulls." In response to a signal, one will pass more current while the other passes less. In a tube amp, the twin-triode tube feeds this split signal to each half of a pair or quartet of pentode output tubes – unless

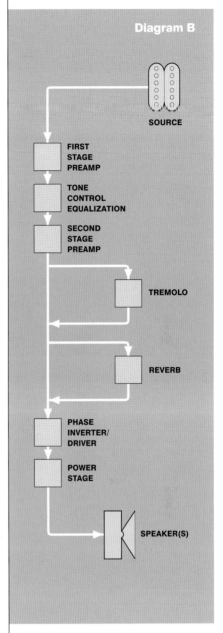

Diagram B

SOURCE

FIRST STAGE PREAMP

TONE CONTROL EQUALIZATION

SECOND STAGE PREAMP

TREMOLO

REVERB

PHASE INVERTER/ DRIVER

POWER STAGE

SPEAKER(S)

AMP STAGES

All tube guitar amps employ a signal chain that passes through similar amplification and tone-shaping stages, even if the circuits and tubes in these individual stages differ. Some, as in the above diagram, also include effects such as tremolo and reverb (as do many '60s and '70s Fenders), but such extras aren't part of the basic amplification process.

| *Amplifiers*

the amp is a low-wattage, single-ended design, powered by only one output tube. Because there is no partner to share the output load in such a design, such amps are always class A, with the single output tube running flat-out for the entire signal cycle (more of which later).

POWER SUPPLY

While its primary job is to deliver the voltages which the tubes feed on, the design of the power supply – whether it is solid-state or tube rectified, what type of filter caps it employs, and so on – plays an important role in any amp's feel and response.

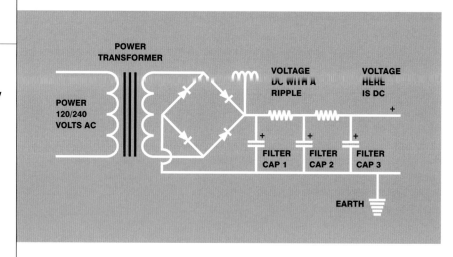

TUBES

The Triode

The simplest type of tube used in audio circuits is the triode, so called because it relies on three internal elements plus a "heater." After pioneering work by Thomas Edison and John Fleming, the triode tube (or thermionic valve in the U.K. – valve for short) was invented by Lee de Forest, who called the invention the Audion. This tube contains a heater (filament), a cathode, an anode (plate), and a control grid, all vacuum-sealed inside a glass container much like a light bulb (though early versions were also constructed within metal tubes). The lack of oxygen inside the vacuum ensures that the internal components cannot burn.

The power supply section of the amplifier converts the AC power voltage into a DC voltage, which is connected across the cathode and the anode. A small voltage – typically 6.3 volts AC or 12.6 volts DC – is fed to the filament, causing it to glow orange and heat up the cathode. The heated cathode emits negatively charged electrons that flow towards the positively charged anode. This is called thermionic emission. Charge then flows between the cathode and the anode inside the tube.

The input signal is sent to the control grid, where it regulates the flow of charge between the cathode and the anode. As the AC input signal voltage rises and falls, the flow inside the tube does the same. By placing a resistor (R1) between the anode and the positive power supply, the varying current will be converted to a varying voltage on the anode. The voltage fluctuation between the anode and cathode is much larger than the fluctuation on the control grid. The signal has been amplified.

Twin triodes are commonly found in the preamp and phase inverter/driver stages of audio amplifiers. Common examples include the 12AX7, 12AT7 and 12AU7 (ECC83, ECC81 and ECC82 in British circuits). These triodes are used in Marshalls, Fenders, Voxes, Boogies and just about everything else – and in fact it is rare indeed these days to find a tube guitar amp that doesn't contain at least one 12AX7.

The Tetrode

Tetrode tubes were developed to overcome the problem of capacitance between the control grid and the anode. A second grid called the screen grid – which is

TUBES – TRIODE

Using only three elements – called the cathode, anode (plate), and grid – in addition to its heater filament, a basic triode is capable of amplifying a signal.

connected to earth at signal frequencies – was added between the anode and the control grid. Tetrode tubes give greater gain than triodes and operate at higher frequencies, but they also introduce more distortion so they are seldom used in audio applications.

Pentode

The next development was the pentode – named after its five elements plus heater which used a third grid called a suppressor grid. This is connected to the cathode, either internally or externally. The pentode retains the high-gain/high-frequency advantages of the tetrode without the high distortion levels. Small-bottle EF86 pentodes are commonly found in hi-fi preamps, and are used in some Vox and Matchless guitar amp preamps as well. Famous power stage tubes include the EL34 (Marshall, Hiwatt), EL84 (Vox, Matchless, Overbuilt, Bad Cat and others, and even smaller contemporary Fenders, Boogies, Peaveys and more), 6V6 (vintage Fender and Gibson), and 6L6 (Fender, Ampeg, Mesa/Boogie).

Occasionally, designers will use hybrid tubes within a circuit. The Vox AC10 used an ECF82, in which a triode and a pentode are combined within a single glass housing.

TRANSISTORS

Contrary to what most people believe, the transistor was not invented by Bell Labs in 1945, but by the physicist Dr. J. Edgar Lilienfeld in 1923. Bipolar transistors are made from a sandwich of semi-conducting materials called n-type and p-type. This is why we have PNP and NPN transistors. They have three elements: the emitter that releases electrons (like a heated cathode); the collector which collects them (like an anode); and the base which controls electron flow (like a grid).

Transistors do not need heaters to make them work. If a positive voltage is applied to the base (making it forward biased) and a higher positive voltage is supplied to the collector, then current will flow: electrons leave the emitter and flow to the base. Most of the electrons travel on towards the collector. When the signal from a guitar pickup or microphone is applied to the base, this affects the flow of electrons through the transistor by controlling the charge concentration at the junctions.

Early bipolar transistors were made from a material called Germanium, and many audio enthusiasts claim that Germanium transistors sound warmer and more musical than the silicon transistors that later became the industry standard. This is a word you will hear most these days when vintage fuzz pedals are discussed, as some units with Germanium transistors are highly prized by many players.

A transistor can be configured as a common collector (emitter follower), common emitter, or common base circuit, but the latter is rarely found in audio applications. The voltage gain of a common emitter circuit (right) is determined by the ratio of the collector resistor (R1) and the emitter resistor (R2). Output is taken from point A. In an emitter follower or common collector circuit, the output is taken from point B. The voltage gain is less than one, but current gain is quite high.

Field effect transistors, or FETs as they are generally known, work differently to bipolar transistors. Such transistors also have three connections: the source, the drain, and the gate. In FETs, however, the current flows through a single piece of semiconductor material. Current flow is controlled by voltage on the gate, which has an opposite polarity. Base current controls the current flow in bipolar transistors, but voltage is used in FETs just like in tubes.

MOSFETs (metal oxide semiconductor field effect transistors) are a variation on the FET. The drain and the source are separated by a substrate of opposite polarity. A layer of metal oxide separates the gate and the substrate.

FETs have higher input impedance than bipolar transistors and are commonly found in the input stages of amplifiers. MOSFETs offer high speed and extended

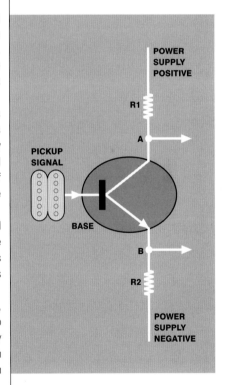

TRANSISTORS

Like a triode tube, a transistor contains three elements – called the emitter, collector, and base. But a transistor can amplify a signal without help from any form of heating element (filament).

frequency response and are used in high-power applications, so you will frequently find them powering the output stages of solid-state guitar amplifiers.

TUBES OR TRANSISTORS?

Power-Up

The most obvious operational difference between tube and transistor amplifiers is their power-up characteristics, although in many ways this is the least significant difference between them. Tubes take time to warm up because the heaters have to bring the cathodes to operating temperature before they will function. Transistor amplifiers respond instantly when they are switched on, and this can create a nasty thump as the power surges through the circuit charging the capacitors. Most modern amplifiers feature protection circuitry to prevent this potentially speaker-blowing characteristic from doing any damage. Nevertheless, it is a wise precaution to ensure that volume levels are set to zero before switching on a transistor amp.

Sound

The old cliché holds that tube amps sound warm and transistor amps sound harsh. This perception can be traced back to the introduction of transistor amplifiers in the mid-'60s. By that time tube amps were highly developed, and they were sounding very good. The early trannies did not match up.

Most tube hi-fi amps of the day operated in class A, only becoming distorted at very high power. In such amps the signal's transition from linear to distorted is gradual, and even the second-harmonic distortion characteristics are generally pleasing – adding a perception of warmth. In contrast, most of the early transistor amps would saturate suddenly, and the resulting distortion was very harsh and unpleasant. The usual target distortion measurement of the time was 0.1 per cent. This figure was fine for tube amps – which eased gradually into distortion and sounded pretty good along the way – but transistor models with this level of distortion sounded dire. Manufacturers were forced to make much higher powered transistor amplifiers to provide sufficient headroom.

Theoretically, all properly engineered hi-fi amplifiers should sound the same. If the goal is zero distortion then this requires the amplifier to effectively "disappear." Real life, however, is more complicated. Legend has it that one Japanese manufacturer produced an amplifier in the '70s with distortion levels so low that they were un-measurable. It was a total flop; everybody who heard it hated it. People get used to their equipment and come to regard the familiar as correct. When presented with a more accurate amplifier or set of speakers, we often still cling to the belief that the original is better.

Personally, I like to use tube amps in my studio monitoring setup – Leak TL50 Plus mono blocks, to be specific. If you measured their distortion figures they would probably look bad, but I can listen to them all day without experiencing ear fatigue … and they do help to keep the place warm.

Distortion characteristics are of vital importance to guitar players because the failings of a hi-fi amp are the joys of a guitar amp. Guitarists have by and large stuck with tube amplifiers because they like their distortion to be controllable and musical. Bassists have demonstrated more willingness to embrace solid-state technology in an effort to achieve clean sounds at high volume. Personally, I really like transistor amps in certain guitar applications. Before you start screaming "heretic" and call the tone police, I want to make it clear that I'm not talking about Gallien-Kruegers or other such '80s rubbish. I mean late-'60s trannie amps with reverb, tremolo, and fuzz. It's the only way I know to get that spitty, reverbed "boom chugga" sound achieved by Luther Perkins on my favorite Johnny Cash records, or that elusive Italian "tone" on the Ennio Morricone soundtracks. After years of frustration with Fender amps I have seen the light. Of course, many designers of such mid-'60s transistor amps were trying to build the very best guitar amps they could, but using the "new" solid-state technology. The majority of modern trannie amps, sadly, are produced solely because they are much less expensive to build than tube amps.

But back to hi-fi and monitoring amps for a moment. When evaluating a monitor amplifier, take your time. Firstly you need to allow yourself to get used to it, and secondly, the true character of the equipment only reveals itself over prolonged periods of listening. If you are choosing a monitor amp, don't go for the model that immediately impresses. Try to assess how your ears will feel after you have been listening to it for 12 hours straight. Good equipment can also be demoralizing because it may reveal weaknesses in other parts of your system, such as harsh speakers or a badly engineered crossover.

Tube microphone preamps are extremely popular in the pro audio world. Vintage units from the '50s and '60s such as the Telefunken/Siemens V72 and V76, RCAs, Altecs, and Pultecs are becoming highly sought after. Modern manufacturers such as TLA, Aphex, Drawmer, Manley, and Avalon are also producing tube equipment. Predictably there is also a following for vintage solid-state. Collectors are paying big money for Neve, API, and Trident preamps. Of course some are celebrated for their technical shortcomings as much as for their strengths.

With all of the above – as with your guitar amps – look for good all-around sound and pleasing tone first when making your buying decisions, and try to put the tubes vs. transistors argument out of mind when auditioning the gear. Some current makers in particular are going to great lengths to imply the superiority of tubes and hinting at the presence of such in their own designs with names that include the words tube and valve when the "real" tubes in many of these products (especially in the lower price ranges) do little more than glow. If the tube onboard isn't powered to full voltage and performing its full function, you might as well be paying less for good sounding solid-state equipment; in any case, plenty of vintage – and modern – trannie audio equipment is great sounding gear.

TUBE TYPES & CHARACTERISTICS

A working knowledge of audio tubes is helpful for musicians and recordists alike. It is often necessary to carry out running repairs, substituting one tube for another at a pinch. A guitarist or engineer can also shape the tonal spectrum of an amplifier by interchanging compatible tubes. All tubes produce distinctive sounds, and their personalities are particularly in evidence when overdriven. Many factors influence the performance of a tube in an amplifier, including circuit design, bias setting, plate voltage, as well as the effects of ageing. The following should be treated as a guideline to the general characteristics of each tube rather than as a definitive description.

Preamp Tubes
12AX7/7025/ECC83 – This double triode is the most widely used audio preamp tube in the world. You will find this one in Marshalls, Fenders, Boogies, Voxes, and pretty much everything else. The U.S. 12AX7 and European ECC83 is characterized by a warm, round, and musical sound. The 7025 is a direct replacement that offers more gain and extended high frequencies, but is getting harder to find too. All of these tube types – if of quality manufacture – overdrive smoothly in appropriate circuits, and offer amplification factors of 100 per side with reasonably low noise. They also seem a lot less susceptible to microphony than other preamp tubes.

12AT7/6201/ECC81 – Very similar to the ECC83/12AX7, this tube can actually be substituted in an emergency in some circuits, although the cathode bias resistor

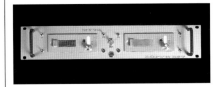

TUBE MIKE AMPS

Two Siemens/Telefunken V72 tube mike/line amps, in a rack. This was the type of mike preamp fitted in the EMI mixers at Abbey Road studios in the 1960s, as used by The Beatles.

will probably need to be changed in the long run. It is rarely used in the first gain stage of an amplifier because of its lower amplification factor (60), and instead shows up most often acting as a phase inverter/driver, or in a reverb circuit. Some players like 12AT7s if they are looking for a cleaner sound with more headroom. They are commonly seen in tube hi-fi amps such as Leaks, as well as some microphone preamp circuits, because of their low noise and characteristic brightness in the upper mids. They are found in Fenders, early Mesa/Boogies, and low-power Vox amps such as the AC15.

12AU7/6189/ECC82 – Another double triode; in fact 12AX7s, AT7s and AU7s (ECC83s, 812s and 82s) are all basically the same tube with varying electrode spacing and grid pitch to achieve their different qualities. Some people feel that the 12AU7 is bland and lacking in character. This might make them a poor choice for guitar amps, but their lack of coloration makes them popular with hi-fi manufacturers such as McIntosh and Audio Innovations. Both Ampeg and Leslie amplifiers use them, and they also crop up in some positions in vintage Vox AC30 and Gibson amps. With an amplification factor of only 20, they are typically employed as phase inverters/drivers.

12AY7/6027 – This tube is extremely close to a 12AX7/ECC83 and is your best bet for a swap in an emergency. Its amplification factor, at around 44, is somewhat lower but it has low microphony and noise, and can be substituted for a 12AX7 (and vice-versa) without biasing problems. Sonically it is rich, smooth, and open. The 6072 is the military version, and some aficionados consider it superior, offering a clearer and more forceful sound. This tube is commonly found in the first preamp position in '50s Fender and Gibson amps, and many players looking for hotter sounds from their original tweed amps substitute a 12AX7 for the vintage-correct 12AY7 to drive the preamp a little harder (though often this was first done almost "accidentally" by many guitarists as the AY7s became harder to find). Nevertheless, stock levels for these remain fairly high, but they can be quite expensive, and might need to be sourced from a specialist supplier.

5751 – This is an interesting substitute for the 12AX7. It has lower gain and it is very difficult to drive into distortion, but it sounds clear and open. If you are looking for a super clean twang from your amp, then this tube is worth trying. U.S.-made examples are readily available and comparatively cheap.

EF86/6267 – Unlike the other preamp tubes mentioned above, this one is a pentode, not a dual triode. This means that it has three grids and produces significant gain, with an amplification factor even higher than that of the 12AX7, and with extended high frequencies. This tube has very low noise for a pentode and is used in hi-fi applications as well as some guitar amps such as the Vox AC4 and AC10, and the Matchless DC/30. They are also used in tube microphones such as the Neumann U67, where the wiring is altered to turn them into mock triodes. EF86s can sound quite forceful and edgy but many players like that, especially contemporary rock players. Their performance in guitar amps is somewhat compromised, however, by their high microphony. Beware that the connection layout of an EF86 is different from the tubes mentioned above, even though it is built in a similar-sized nine-pin glass bottle. You cannot interchange EF86s with dual triodes without revising the circuit.

6SL7 – Very early Fender, Ampeg and Gibson amps used these large eight-pin double triode tubes instead of the smaller nine-pin 12AX7s and 12AY7s. They have an amplification factor of 70 – slightly less than a 12AX7 – but microphony and noise are low. Sound quality is warm but very clear, and they are popular among hi-fi manufacturers.

6SN7 – Used in old tweed Fenders and Gibson amps, this dual triode is also a large eight-pin tube. It was popular in preamps as well as the driver stages of power amps. They were very popular with the military and were used for missiles and space applications, so they should be good for a few years of Sunday afternoon jam sessions down the Dog And Duck. Sound quality is regarded as excellent, though they are known to mellow with age. Stocks of the 6SN7 and the 6SL7 are drying up, which can create problems for the owner of an early Fender or Gibson. Should you need to convert to 12AX7s, conversion adaptors are available to help you avoid punching holes in a vintage amp chassis in order to fit the smaller nine-pin tubes sockets required.

Power Tubes

6L6/5881 – This is the tube we associate with the high-powered offerings of Fender, Mesa /Boogie, Ampeg, Soldano, and other builders of big American amps. It sounds crunchy, crisp, and sweet with a metallic and bell-like chime. They have great midrange and distort nicely in a controllable and natural way. Fair stocks of Western-made brands are still available (though the highly desirable examples like RCA and Tung-Sol are getting extremely expensive), and some good newly manufactured varieties are finally beginning to appear, too. Although broadly interchangeable, there were originally slight differences between the 6L6 and 5881, and certain older amps specified one or the other, though in recent years the two names have generally been used to denote exactly the same tube.

EL34/6CA7/KT77 – When Jim Marshall started making guitar amplifiers in the early '60s it is widely acknowledged that he took his inspiration from the original Fender Bassman. Nothing wrong with that; the Fender company probably took their circuits straight out of Leo's late '40s radio engineer's handbook. The 6L6s used by Fender were more readily available in the U.S. than in Europe. Jim Marshall looked around for a suitable alternative and, after a brief flirtation with the KT66, settled on the much-revered EL34. We associate this tube with the sound of the classic Marshalls and Hiwatts – in short, the "British sound." They distort easily with a recognizable compression, bite, and crunch.

6550 – Throughout the late-'70s and much of the '80s Japanese and American distributors sold Marshall amps with 6550 tubes instead of the EL34s found in the European spec'd models. Since 6550s were manufactured in the U.S., it made economic sense for the American distributors, who had to cover the warranty and spares situation. 6550s were commonly used in amplifiers intended to provide clean, high-powered sound, such as Dynaco and McIntosh hi-fi amps and Ampeg SVT bass amps. They can also be found in Sunns, Peaveys and Dumbles. If you are a rock or metal player looking for a cleaner, punchier, and more muscular sound, you might prefer the performance of 6550s in your Marshall to the softer and crunchier stock EL34s. Blues-rockers and classic Brit-rockers, however, are likely to prefer EL34s. 6550 and EL34 tubes are not interchangeable without re-biasing your amp, changing a few resistors, and modifying the feedback connection. If in doubt, take your amp to a qualified professional.

6V6 – These were used in lower-powered amps by Fender, Gibson, Silvertone, and Supro, among others, and have a reputation for great tone, pure and simple. They are smoother than their big brother the 6L6, are pushed into distortion more easily, and will put out only about half the 6L6's maximum wattage. Their tone is sweet and smooth, while retaining a certain bite and clarity. Some players attempt to squeeze more power or headroom out of their small amps by swapping their 6V6s for 6L6s. The 6L6 will certainly work in the circuit, but the amp should be re-biased by a technician. Also, the higher heater current required by 6L6s can put a strain on (and even burn out) some smaller power transformers. My recommendation would be to take the money you would have spent on a new set of quality tubes and the bench charge for re-biasing and put it towards a second 6V6 amp – so many of them sound great, and are excellent for recording. Generally collectors and players view low-powered amps as the poor relations, and you can sometimes pick up great bargains. That way you can play in stereo and you'll always have a spare!

EL84/6BQ5 – In some ways EL84s are the European answer to the 6V6. They provide the complex, harmonic saturation we associate with Vox and Matchless amps and were also used in many Gibsons and low-powered Marshalls. They distort readily, especially in class A guitar amp circuits, but they were also very popular in the old days with hi-fi manufacturers such as Leak for their lower-powered designs. Vox used no fewer than four of these tubes to coax 30 watts from their classic AC30, and many other amps have been designed around this same output section, including models from Mesa/Boogie, Peavey, Orange, Laney, and many other boutique makes as well. Perhaps a touch more brittle and "high-frequency-saturated" sounding than the 6V6, the EL84 is nevertheless responsible for countless classic rock guitar sounds, and is certainly the "little brother" of the Brit-sound family.

KT66 – This was the tube used in the early Marshall JTM-45 amplifiers, because it was more available in the U.K. than the 6L6s or 5881s around which the Fender Bassman – from which Jim Marshall drew his inspiration – was designed. The original GEC unit was built in a glass bottle that flared out at the top and looked as beefy as it sounded. The KT66 offers more headroom than the EL34. It also has more clarity and an extended frequency response. KT66s were famously used in the Quad II hi-fi amps, and are a big part of that amp's great sound. Good examples are expensive but worth considering if you are playing contemporary rock with dropped tunings and you need more power and focus in the bottom end. They will go straight into your old JTM-45 if it has been carrying something else in more recent years, and will also substitute for 5881s or 6L6s in old Fender Bassmans and the like – and sound huge too! Most amps build around EL34s will require some changes to fit KT66s, however, so consult a good tech.

KT88 – Basically a KT66 on steroids. Marshall used this tube in their awesome 200W Major amplifiers. They also show up in McIntosh, Dynaco, and Leak TL50 hi-fi amps as well as Sunn bass amps. A great clear, punchy, and muscular tube with great tone; Billy Corgan of the Smashing Pumpkins uses them in his Marshall JCM800 and some bass players like to put them in their Ampeg SVTs.

Many players fret endlessly about their tone, trying different effects, replacement pickups, and exotic cables, while completely ignoring their tubes. Significant sonic differences are apparent between the tubes produced by various manufactures, and even changing between makes of the same type of tube can fine-tune your tone. Original Mullards and new old stock (NOS) American RCAs are now very sought after by originality obsessed vintage amp collectors and tone hounds alike. Sadly, this has pushed prices up dramatically. But are the old classics that much better? Unfortunately, the answer is often yes. For too long, many manufacturers of expensive amplifiers have been content to use poor quality tubes of dubious origin. At best, the inferior tubes will compromise your tone; at worst, they can cause unreliability. A tube upgrade can substantially improve many amps that arrived stock with inferior tubes.

Don't worry; good quality, great sounding, affordable alternatives to the NOS originals are widely available. Your best bet is to find a reputable tube supplier (easily located over the internet these days), call them up, and talk over your requirements. If your amp has output tubes running in push-pull you will need to ask your supplier to match up a pair or a quartet. This usually involves a small "matching fee," but it is essential if you want your amp to work at peak efficiency. Take the time to shop around for the best price and avoid bogpoko, specialist guitar tube companies that match, grade, and re badge Chinese and East European tubes. Their products are often fine, but some people might say that they exploit your tone paranoia to extract obscene amounts of money from you. You can decide!

Some amps have auto-biasing circuitry and others, like the modern Ampeg SVTs, make it easy to set the bias yourself. Most amps – unless cathode biased like Vox AC30s (and their derivatives) or tweed Fender Deluxes – will require a bias check to be carried out by a qualified professional every time power tubes are replaced. This will ensure long tube life and optimum performance.

(Here's a tip to halve your rebiasing requirements. If you are planning to buy a matched pair of output tubes that have characteristics you know you will be happy with, and are going to get your amp rebiased along with it, buy a matched quad instead. Then, when the first pair wears out, you can pop in the second pair from the matched quad without having to rebias.)

Preamp tubes are self-biasing and you can swap them yourself without checking the circuit afterwards. In this instance you can let your ears guide you, swapping in different makes and types until you achieve the tone that pleases you most. Make sure you let the little guys cool down first, though, or you'll burn your fingers.

If you play hard, often, and loud, you should probably change your tubes every six to 18 months. If you play only occasionally and at low levels, there's no reason why they shouldn't last for years.

Class A Amps: The Myth And Mystique

The hot phrase in tube amps in recent years is "class A." Many players feel they need an amp that fits this description, and manufacturers are ever eager to offer products that do so ... or purport to, anyway. The difficulty is – in terms of strict definition – that what guitarists have come to associate as the "class A sound" and what actually determines a class A power amp design are often not necessarily one and the same. (In short, an amp doesn't have to genuinely be class A to produce what guitarists have come to consider the class A sound.) The result: many recent makes of amps marketed as class A are in fact class AB designs.

Aside from being aware of any potential deception, it's even more important to understand right from the top that this isn't necessarily a good or a bad thing – and an amp that sounds the way you want it to sound should always be your ultimate goal, whatever it's supposed operating "class." But it's worth taking a look at a little of the science behind this white lie told by marketing people so that you can better understand what your amp is really doing, and why it sounds the way it does ... or doesn't.

Operating class distinctions such as "class A" or "class AB" are not designations of different quality such as, for example, food quality labels that say "grade A beef." They merely distinguish different types of amplifier function, as defined by very clear, fixed parameters in their design. The class A designation was never intended to indicate that such an amp is better than a class AB amp, even if pasting the label all over advertising literature quickly begins to imply this.

A class A amp is one in which the output tubes (two or more of them, in the case of a push-pull amp) are biased so that all are on for the full 360 degrees of the signal (waveform). In a push-pull class AB amp, the tubes "share the load" of the waveform, as it were, with each shutting down for a portion of the signal wave while the other continues to drive the transformer. The class A is a less-efficient power producer, but can be one of a number of ingredients which result in what players describe as a "hot," "juicy," "tactile," or "tubey" feeling amp, with a smoother onset of distortion and more even-order harmonics. The class AB is capable of higher output levels, with a tighter response and more headroom, but a very slightly harsher onset of distortion when pushed into clipping. Keep in mind, of course, that this is how a tweed Fender Bassman or a Marshall Plexi functions – and these are not "second class" amps in the distortion stakes!

The confusion (and ease of deception) arises from the fact that the class A designation is just a small part of what makes – to name a classic of the breed – a Vox AC30 sound the way it does. Equally, if not *more* influential are its cathode biasing, lack of a negative feedback loop in the output stage, and sweet, glassy, easily distorted EL84 tubes. Design a class AB amp with cathode biasing and no negative feedback loop and, voilà, you've got a more saturated, softer responding,

---

TECHNICAL TIPS: BIASING AND FEEDBACK LOOPS

BIASING

"Cathode biasing" is the simplest, least efficient method for biasing output tubes in guitar amps, and is most often seen in lower-powered vintage combos. With the more efficient fixed bias approach taken with most larger and many modern amps (which, confusingly, is often achieved using a variable circuit and must be re-set when tubes are changed), the tubes' cathodes are connected to ground and a negative voltage applied to the grids. Cathode biasing lifts the cathode from ground with a large but relatively low-value resistor, plus a bypass cap. In the right design, this less-efficient technique can result in a slightly more distorted, more textured sound, which is appealing to some guitarists. Also, to replace output tubes in most cathode-biased amps, you merely need to pop in a new, matched set. In the majority of fixed-bias amps, rebiasing is required when output tubes are replaced.

FEEDBACK LOOPS

"Negative feedback" is the term used for a technique of tapping some of an amp's reverse-phase signal where it occurs before the phase inverter and feeding it back into the final post-output tubes and post-OT signal at the amp's output (speaker jack). To generalize somewhat, this has the effect of damping the output and keeping distortion and signal peaks under control – which is a positive thing if improved headroom and maximum loud-clean capabilities are among the designer's goals. Removing this negative feedback (or simply building an amp without it) produces a higher-gain amp relative to the same volume settings, with a more open, raw, and sometimes "wild" feel, particularly at lower volumes. This sounds like it would always be desirable in amps that will be played with some distortion content, but that's not necessarily so. Another benefit of a negative feedback loop is that it helps an amp to achieve a better, more accurate frequency response at higher volumes, where an amp without the loop might really begin to freak out, to use the technical term. A big amp run hard will often yield a rather more controllable distortion thanks to the presence of a negative feedback loop.

Many amps which feature negative feedback loops can easily be fitted with a bypass switch to eliminate this loop from the output, giving the player the option of both sounds. A simple mod, it should nevertheless be carried out by a qualified tech because of the potentially lethal voltages in proximity to the necessary wiring changes it requires.

somewhat looser, and more "tactile" amp. In short, one which sounds, most guitarists would agree, a lot like a great class A amp should. (Note that single-ended amps like the Fender Champ, Vox AC4, Gibson GA 5, Orange AD5, Cornford Harlequin, and Cornell Romany are always class A, because of course that lone output tube can't shut down through any of the waveform.)

Biasing an amp for true class A severely limits its efficiency – in other words, its volume capabilities. (A lot of energy is wasted by not letting that tube shut off, even when it isn't doing much.) So this isn't practical for a lot of builders, who need to squeeze maximum wattage out of the components and designs their proposed retail selling price will allow. Cathode biasing and a lack of a negative feedback loop are quick ways to approach that sound. If Leo Fender had thought it would sell more amps (and had been a little less scrupulous, even if anybody cared one way or the other at the time) he would have marketed his late-'50s tweed Deluxe as class A, as it shares these design elements and is an excellent example of that characterful sound – though it is undeniably a class AB amp. Give it a pair of EL84s in place of its 6V6GTs, and a Celestion Alnico Blue speaker in place of its Jensen, and you can bet it would start sounding more and more like a Vox AC15.

Too many builders today are willing to slap on the erroneous label because it's not an easy thing to disprove; not many players, techs or product reviewers are likely to open up an amp, hoist it onto the bench, attach the oscilloscope and other measuring gear, and graph out its operating class.

What should you do about it? Well, not much. The reason it's worth knowing all this is that, on the upside, if you're looking for that sound that everyone always referred to as "class A," you don't necessarily have to get it from a class A amp. Make your search not among amps that say "class A" under the logo, but which are built with cathode biased output stages and no negative feedback – using EL84 output tubes if you like that sound in particular – and you'll be casting your hook in the right pond at least.

So does all this mean we should cast aside class AB amps? Not a chance! As I said at the start, it's not a better or worse thing, but a matter of more accurately defining the sound you are looking for. Remember, tweed Fender Deluxes and Bassmans, blackface Twin Reverbs, Marshall Bluesbreakers and Plexis, Mesa/Boogie Mk Series and Rectifier amps, and Soldano TLOs are all examples of class AB amps, and none of them are sounding too shabby. Get the amp you want for the sound you need – but know what you're buying.

BIG AMPS, SMALL AMPS

I want to explode a few myths that have built up surrounding amplifiers. The most common of these is that you need a big amp to achieve a big sound in the studio; often the opposite is true. Legend has it that Jimmy Page – commonly associated with Marshall stacks and Les Pauls – was actually more inclined towards Telecasters and Supro amps in the studio. Billy Gibbons is also known to regard his 15W tweed Fender Deluxe as his all-time favorite amp.

There is a major difference between a guitarist's requirement for live performance and for his studio work. This was particularly true in the late-'60s and early-'70s, when the PA systems were woefully inadequate. Musicians had to provide the volume if they wanted to be heard, and to hear themselves. This is why Vox AC15s, AC30s, Fender Bandmasters and even Marshall 50-watters no longer do the business. I believe that a culture of machismo built up over high-powered amps, and it lingers to this day.

A wonderful story that was passed on to me involved an American who was famous not for being the best guitarist in the world, but for being the loudest. On one occasion in the studio, he insisted that the only way to get "his sound" was to use all ten of his 100W Marshalls at full volume and that he also had to stand in the room with his amps. The absurdity of this should be apparent – because it's likely that the engineer was only using one or two microphones in the first place. An additional problem was that regular studio monitor headphones and amplifiers cannot compete with a thousand watts of Marshall power, and he couldn't hear the backing track. To get around this, our guitar hero had commissioned special headphones with high-power driver amplifiers. Something went wrong; the volume of his first chord was so intense that he lost consciousness. As he lay twitching on his back, his big semi-acoustic Gibson was feeding back so violently that it was actually bouncing on his stomach. Obviously he stayed like this for some time. The studio staff couldn't switch off the amps due to the noise … and also because they were so convulsed with laughter. You'll be relieved to know, though, that our hero recovered, and is still playing to this day.

A high powered Marshall or Hiwatt can sound amazing when it's turned up to Patent Applied For in a big room. The problem is that nowadays, most studios are small and the volume can be too much for the room. It's also very difficult to achieve good results with big, cranked amps when they have to share the room with the drums, bass, and vocals. This is when you hear the dreaded "you'll have to turn down" from the engineer. Personally, I hate saying that to guitarists because we all know that the amp will not sound as good when you wind it back below the "sweet spot."

Anyone with experience of traditional tube guitar amps – ones with one or two volume knobs – knows that the amp has to be turned up to a certain level before it comes to life. Anything below this sounds flat and dull; what's more, it is harder to play. The real magic in tube guitar amps comes not only from overdriving the preamp tubes but also from distorting the power tubes. The distortion characteristics of power tubes are different to preamp tubes. The little fellas tend to have a fizzy, more compressed sound whereas the big ones have a more rounded and musical tone. Overdriven power tubes are also more responsive to the player's touch. When you play light or turn your guitar volume pot down, they sound clean. Turn up or play hard and they distort. In other words, you can play the amp as well as the guitar. Your amp is not there simply to make your guitar louder or to act as a high volume buzz box; it can be an instrument in itself.

OK, let's think how to avoid the dreaded "turn it down." It's no use refusing point blank – the engineer will not be asking you because he doesn't like your sound, it's probably because he has problems with spillage or rattling snares. It is more than likely that everyone else in the group would prefer you to turn down, too. So how do you get that great cranked-up tone without getting thrown out of the studio (or your group)? One simple answer springs to mind: use a smaller amp.

This is not a joke; many top guitarists have known for years that 4W or 10W amps can sound huge on record. Quite often they keep quiet about it in interviews, thinking their image might be blown if they admit that their monster tone was made with a Fender Champ. A lot of the great guitar sounds of the '50s and '60s were made with little Fender amps, Gibson amps, and also budget stuff like Supros and Silvertones and Danelectros.

Many people feel that those small-amp sounds are exciting because the amp is operating way beyond its design parameters. When this happens, random and unpredictable things start to occur – many of which can result in some fantastic guitar sounds on record. When you turn up a Marshall JCM800 or Mesa/Boogie Dual Rectifier it produces a different sound – preamp distortion. These amps are designed to do this and the circuits are operating quite comfortably. This isn't necessarily worse, but it isn't perhaps as ragged or exciting either.

Don't just take my word for it. Here's how Stones guitarist Keith Richards put it to *Guitar Player* magazine way back in November 1977:

"I never use an amp in the studio that I use on stage. I mean, stage amps are far too big. Probably the biggest mistake inexperienced players make is thinking that to have a lot of volume in a studio you need a huge amp. It's probably the opposite. The smaller the amp, the bigger it's going to sound, because it's already going to sound like it's pushed to the limit. Whereas you can never push a Marshall stack to its limit in the studio because it will always sound clean."

The point I'm making (with a little help from Keef) is this: why bother having a really cool 100W Marshall, Hiwatt, Soldano, Mesa/Boogie or Fender amp if you can never turn the volume past three and a half? I've seen guitarists spend hundreds on distortion pedals, compressors, graphic equalizers, power soaks, etc. etc., all in an attempt to emulate the sound their amp produces naturally when it's cranked up. If you still can't get the "big amp = big sound" thing out of your head, look at it like this. In the studio, whatever amp you play through will be captured by a microphone diaphragm that may be less than an inch in diameter, transmitted down a hair-thin wire, recorded as imperceptible magnetic particles on a tape ... and eventually reproduced through speakers that might be anything from the half-inch diameter of your headphone drivers to the 4" to 8" diameter of the average home hi-fi units. In this environment, physical size no longer matters; sonic size is everything.

Tube Rectification

Another wonderful thing about cranking up amps with tube rectifiers – as so many smaller amps do – is that the amp will compress naturally. This is often referred to as "sag." At high volumes the demand on the power supply can be too much and volume doesn't rise in proportion to the physical effort put into the playing. Consequently the guitar is easier to record because it has no transient peaks. Power tubes themselves will also induce some compression-like characteristics when pushed hard, but the effect is more noticeable in tube-rectified amps. The Fender Bassman reissue comes with a tube rectifier for recording and a solid-state rectifier for gigging. On the other hand, if you want a tight, firm, immediate response in all circumstances, an amp with solid state rectification might be more suited to your requirements.

Tube rectifiers also allow for a gentler start when you power up, which is healthier for the tubes if there is no standby switch. Smaller amps also allow engineers to use their high quality condenser microphones very close to the speaker without worrying too much about damaging capsules. The microphones will sound happier, with far less tendency to distort. Ribbon mikes can also be used with reduced risk of damage. I also advocate the use of low-powered amps for clean sounds. I achieved a monster sound with a Neumann U67 placed right against the speaker of a Fender Champ on a recent project; the amplifier was turned to 1.

None of the above is intended to imply that a big amp can't sound great, too. But you will stand the best chance of doing a large amp justice if you record it in a large, properly designed live room in a professional studio – and fewer of us have access to those these days for any kind of affordable money. Even so, a big amp is still going to be more of a challenge to mike up and record. For me, small amps have the magic in the studio. They consistently prove a lot easier to work with, and a lot better sounding when put to the task of recording.

In concluding this section on small amplifiers, let me ask you to remember that a 100W amplifier is not twice as loud as a 50W amplifier – it is only 3dB louder. Or as Nigel Tufnel might say: "That's three louder." The relationship between power and volume is not linear. Each doubling of power produces only a 3dB increase in volume. Speaker efficiency is often neglected in this equation, too. Typical values for guitar speakers are around 85dB, which represents an efficiency of less than 10%. To assess speaker efficiency, a speaker is fed with 1W of amplifier power and an SPL measurement is taken at a point one metre (three feet) away. A speaker efficiency of 10% means that 90% of the amplifier's power is wasted – usually turning to heat. If you like the tone of your little amp but feel the need for more volume, try buying a more efficient guitar speaker. A unit with an efficiency rating of 91dB produces a 6 dB increase in volume versus an 85dB-rated speaker.

Amplifiers

The perceived volume increase is the same as bumping up the power of your amplifier from 25W to 100W. Check the ratings of a few speakers, and you might be surprised. For more on this subject, see the next chapter, *Speakers And Cabs*.

Unnecessary Features

As an engineer I have noticed, with dismay, the trend towards complex circuitry and so-called "features" on modern guitar and bass amplifiers. I have lost count of the number of times I've seen guitarists referring to the manual simply in order to dial up a funk tone. You know the types of amp I mean: the ones with the pull switch mid boost, three stages of gain, four channels, a graphic EQ and a MIDI socket. I assure you, I'm no Luddite – I couldn't survive in my profession if I was – but in the studio many of these amps can disappoint. I feel that they are best employed by the gigging musician with a small car who needs to access a wide range of sounds at the click of a footswitch, and in that environment they function very well. (The chances are that many of the pros you see using such amps on stage are recording with something else, by the way.)

Seriously: the more electronic circuitry your guitar signal passes through, the more it loses. Complex equalization, high-gain preamps, even tremolo and reverb circuits will rob your music of tone, punch, and power. Many of the amplifier hot rodders achieve their results by taking circuitry out rather than putting stuff in. A great example is the tone-stack bypass (or "tweed") switch modification for silverface Fenders. This mod skips around the two or three-pot treble, mid, and bass tone section of one channel of the amp and leaves it with just a single volume and tone control – and a much hotter sound besides.

I have often noticed that "techo" guitarists, who use equipment of this do-it-all sort, seem to be perpetually dissatisfied with their sound. Attempts to cure the problems often involve the purchase of rack-mounted compressors, parametric equalizers, and other such nonsense. It is expensive and naive to throw money at a problem rather than address its root cause.

An engineer friend told me a wonderful story about a bass player he worked with. In his quest for "punch," this hombre had assembled a rig which consisted of a Yamaha 6-string bass running into an Alembic preamp. From this it went into a dbx parametric EQ, a dbx compressor, an ART multi-effects unit and, penultimately, through an Aphex Big Bottom aural exciter (not what you think) and finally into a 500W Crown power amp and Trace Elliot cab consisting of one 18" speaker, four 10s, and a tweeter.

All afternoon this guy protested that he had "no punch" and blamed the engineer. Six hours of studio time were lost stripping down the rig and rebuilding it one piece at a time to finally discover that the battery in his bass was flat. These are the moments when an appreciation of the absurd comes is useful for the long-suffering studio engineer.

If you want great rock, blues, country or R&B tone then plug a well set-up guitar into a cool sounding amp. Add a couple of choice stomp boxes if you need them, and get on with it. You'll be much happier.

My general experience has been that multi-channel amplifiers (and I mean the channel-switching variety) try to be all things to all players. While some of them do this very well, my usual advice would be that if you want a great Fender sound, use a Fender; if you want a great Vox sound, use a Vox; and if you want a great Marshall sound, use a Hiwatt (OK, or a Marshall if you have to).

COMBINING AMPLIFIERS

CD tracks 62-63: combining amps

In the same way that multi-channel amps are compromised, so are all the classic guitar amps. I mean by this that you might find, after testing a broad range of possibilities, that no single amp is "perfect" for a particular song, or contains quite all of the frequency range and sonic elements you want to capture. Some Fenders, bigger ones especially, sound brittle and nasty when they are distorted (if you can make them distort in the first place); Vox amps have an incredible midrange but not much crunch and very few super highs and lows; Marshalls have everything that Vox amps lack, except that beautiful musical midrange. In fact, I always get the best results from separate head and cab Marshalls when I dial the midrange out, Metallica style.

The solution to this is to use combinations of amplifiers. For the perfect British sound, try combining a Vox AC30 with a Marshall. This will give you an incredible spread of frequencies with more musical clarity – especially if you are running the Marshall distorted and the Vox cleanish.

For high-gain rock with tone, I love to combine a Marshall with a Mesa/Boogie – preferably a Dual Rectifier. The Boogie will give a smoother, saturated midrange to the weight and crunch of the Marshall. It will also yield a sound that feels easier to play because of the texture and ease of distortion.

Another startling combination I tried recently was a Vox AC10 with a Matchless

MULTI-AMPING

Sometimes combining two or more amps will yield that perfect sound that one alone just can't achieve. Above, a Vox AC10 and Fender Tremolux are linked using an ordinary stereo effect pedal.

Lightning '15. The Matchless had more punch and clarity and a broader spread of frequencies. I felt that the midrange of the Vox had more sweetness of tone and it distorted better. Together, they sounded amazing. Swapping the AC10 for a hot-running vintage tweed Fender Tremolux offered another great guitar sound: classic tweed power-tube distortion, grit and texture, but married to a classy, rich harmonic spectrum from the Matchless.

You can have great fun combining amps in the same way that you can microphones. Stevie Ray Vaughan was famous for it, and went to some real extremes to get his legendary "tone" at times. Think about it: your tone would be pretty fat, too, if – aside from those .013-gauge strings and strong fingers – you linked up a Vibroverb, a Super Reverb, a Marshall Major, and a Dumble 150 Steel String Singer. (Though miking them up and getting it all to tape could be a challenge, as we have already discussed.)

You can link amps via a stereo stomp box or a dedicated pedal (a number of manufacturers offer them). You can run a guitar cable from a parallel input on amp 1 to the input of amp 2, but tone is likely to suffer as a result of the drop in input impedance. Another problem you might encounter is a loud 50Hz hum as soon as you connect amp 2. The solution to this is to disconnect the ground (earth) from amp 2 so that it can ground through amp 1. If you do this, please note that it is potentially fatal to play an amplifier with no ground connection. You must remember to reconnect it as soon as you have finished using the amplifier in this way (that is, grounded through amp 1). If you do lift the ground, write "no ground" on a piece of masking tape and stick it across the controls to remind you.

OK, I accept that combining tweed Fenders with vintage Hiwatts might seem like fantasy stuff for some readers, but don't dismiss the concept too soon. Combining amps can still be an effective recording technique even if you don't have anything nearly as high-end and exclusive on hand as this, and you can get great results from the weirdest, cheapest stuff. Have a go with whatever you can rustle up – a Marshall "Valvegrate," perhaps, blended with a Peavey Classic 20. Whatever. And good luck.

Speaker

The sound comes out here, and the right speaker and cab can make a world of difference to your amp's tone.

It can be far too easy to get wrapped up in all the potential ingredients that contribute to your electric guitar tone – pickups, strings, wood types, preamps, tubes, power amps, and so forth – without pausing to consider where the sound comes from. Simple: your speakers.

Whatever components play a part in the signal chain that shapes every note you play, the humble speaker is still what takes the sound to the listener, or indeed to the microphone. Admittedly, an amount of DI recording has always occurred, and better-sounding direct-to-board units are available all the time – digital amp emulators, tube preamps with speaker simulators, and so forth – but the majority of recordings are still made by miking up amps. (In fact, in a miked amp the speaker's effect as a low pass filter and the resulting attenuation of high frequencies plays a big part in what we have come to consider a "great guitar sound" – which is why straight DI'd guitar often sounds strange and "unnatural" to us, even if it is a more realistic rendering of the electric guitar's natural sound.)

Amp techs who know their stuff have long declared that your speakers (and speaker cabinet design) are responsible for 50 per cent of your tone, but the speaker is often the last thing a player considers in an effort to overhaul an unsatisfactory sound. Replacing a stock speaker with a different type, even of the same size, can instantly alter your amp's sound more than any other single change – and be the quickest, simplest, and potentially cheapest way to convert a mediocre combo into a tone machine that sounds great and is easier to play.

It's not always just a matter of installing a "better" speaker, however, so knowing a little about the general tonal characters of a number of speaker types can prove valuable to any guitarist. That said, cabinet type and design can themselves play a major part in shaping your sound. Therefore, let's take a brief look at both of these major ingredients: driver type and cabinet design.

DRIVER TYPES

Vintage, Or Low Powered Speakers

You can split guitar drivers very broadly into two categories: "vintage," or lower-powered types; and "modern," or higher-powered types. These can also generally be divided into "British" and "American" sounding units, though most larger manufacturers today cross the border between the two.

In the '40s, '50s and early-'60s, guitar amps rarely carried speakers rated higher than 15W to 30W power handling, and indeed guitar amps in the early days rarely put out more than the upper figure. These were fine used singly in the recording studio, or in multi-driver cabs at dance hall volumes. But push them hard and they started to "break up" in sonic terms, adding a degree of speaker distortion to the amp's own distortion when played near the peak of operating capacity (or well below it in some cases … gotta love those tweed Deluxes).

As guitarists found themselves in bigger and bigger venues, requiring higher clean volume levels, amp builders sought out more robust speaker designs – but these cost more than the cheaply built, lower-rated drivers, so weren't in fact universally employed. For their own part, a lot of players who weren't seeking absolute "clean clean" enjoyed the edge, bite, and apparent compression that a little speaker distortion added to their sound. Lower-powered drivers – with all their gorgeous, inherent "flaws" – quickly became a big part of the foundation of the rock'n'roll sound.

In the U.S., Jensen were far and away the most respected – and for a time, most used – manufacturer of lower-powered speakers, and their 12" P12R (15W), P12Q (20W), and P12N (30W), and 10" P10R (15W), played a huge part in the signature sounds of classic amps from Fender, Gibson, Ampeg, Silvertone and others. Each of these models has its distinctive characteristics, but together they are broadly characterized by bell-like highs, somewhat boxy but rather open and transparent mids, and juicy, saturated lows (to the point of flapping, farting-out, and all-round low-frequency freakout in the lesser-rated models). All of which combines to produce great, sweet, tactile, clean sounds when driven a little, and gorgeous, rich overdrive when driven a lot.

All were built using alnico magnets, paper cones, and paper voice coil formers, which proved to be essential ingredients in the vintage driver formula. Depending on costs and availability, most of the same manufacturers also fitted units from Utah, Oxford, CTS, and others, which more often than not shared some of the Jensens' characteristics (provided they were alnico-magnet designs), but were rarely as revered by players.

Many of the more popular Jensen models are available again from this revitalized maker's Vintage Reissue line. These capture at least some of the originals' tonal characteristics, though materials are not 100 per cent exact matches between the new and old units (though the alnico magnets remain on the

TECHNICAL TIPS: SPEAKER DISTORTION

Distinct from amplifier distortion, speaker distortion occurs when a driver is pushed near to its operating limits. The voice coil and paper cone begin to fail to translate the electrical signal cleanly, and as a result produce a somewhat (or sometimes severely) distorted performance. Put simply, the paper cone begins to flap and vibrate beyond its capacity, and introduces a degree of fuzz into the brew. Like most distortion, this form of speaker "clipping" happens for broadly similar reasons to those which make tubes distort, though the mechanical function is different.

To keep the concept clear in your head, imagine two different amps. Amp A is a 60W Mesa/Boogie MkII with a 100W EV driver, running with the cascading gain preamp cranked, but the master volume down to about 2/10; the sound you hear is definitely distorted, but that is coming entirely from the amp; the speaker is operating well within its limits. Amp B is a 15W Vox AC15 running flat-out into a 15W Celestion Alnico Blue speaker; the sound you hear is part distortion from the floored amp, and part distortion from a speaker hit with very nearly more power than it can handle … and the result is a wilder, more uncontrollable sound – but a great one, by many standards.

"P" models). Eminence builds a number of vintage-styled drivers (and is in fact the manufacturer behind many own-label speakers from Kendrick, Fender, and others). The smaller builder WeberVST also offers some highly respected vintage-repro units.

British Or American?
On the other side of the Atlantic, Elac, Goodmans, and Celestion were building 10" and 12" speakers that weren't a world away in design from the Jensens of the U.S. Using pulp-paper cones and alnico ring magnets to achieve power handling conservatively rated at from 12W to about 20W in the early units, these appeared most famously as the Goodmans Audiom 60 and (Celestion-built) Vox "Blue Bulldog" G12 in the Vox AC15s and AC30s of the late-'50s and early '60s.

By far the more famous and highly sought-after of the pair, the Celestion unit has sweet, rich, musical mids and appealing (if not over-wrought) highs, with not tremendous low-end reproduction but an extremely flattering tonality overall, and great dynamic range. In short, they're one of the most beloved guitar speakers of all time. It was (and, in Celestion's very impressive reissue form, is) a highly efficient speaker, too, offering 100dB (measured @ 1W/1M), as opposed to figures ranging from less than 90dB to around 96dB for similar Jensen units. This means that a pair in a 2x12" cab topped with a 30W Vox AC30 chassis makes for a pretty gutsy combo indeed, despite the apparently low numbers on paper.

Celestion evolved the British driver du jour into the ceramic-magnet G12M "Greenback" (rated 20W to 25W) in the mid-'60s, when they were generally found in multiples of four inside the classic Marshall 4x12 cabs that helped broadcast the rock message to the masses in ever larger arenas and at ever greater volumes. The Greenback is warm, gritty, and edgy, with a not particularly firm bottom end but plenty of oomph when tackling the output in numbers, especially in a closed-back cab. (And remember, four of them together can take 100W, and better share the low-frequency load without flapping out.) This speaker, as much as any amp, typifies the "British sound" sought by so many blues-rock guitarists.

In the '70s the slightly higher-rated G12H took on a heavier magnet to give a tighter low-end response, but otherwise continued with the Brit sound tradition. Fane, too, deserve an honorable mention for some good sounding lower-powered speakers that they've produced over the years, as well as the sturdy drivers that helped give many Hiwatts, for example, their legendary big, bold sound.

Modern, Or High-Powered Speakers
As many higher-powered guitar amps evolved to cope with the larger concert halls, builders sought speakers that could take the full punch and transmit it relatively uncolored, as undistorted as possible. All contemporary manufacturers offer a few models of this type, but early classics came from the American makers JBL and EV. The former helped to make early 100W Fender Twin Reverbs into some of the loudest combos in the States, while EVs were Randall Smith's preferred choice of speaker to take the brunt of the cascading-gain blast in his compact (1x12") but powerful early Mesa/Boogie combos.

JBLs present a rounded midrange with an edge of bark and nasal honk, and ringing, occasionally piercing highs. Various popular EV models down the years have tended to be muscular, balanced, and aggressive, while still musical and fairly "hi-fi" in a guitar context, and remain the top choice for some rock soloists.

Today, Celestion's Classic Lead 80 and G12H-100, a number of Eminence models, and others offer the similar power-handling capabilities and firm-yet-musical response in bigger amps. While an ability to handle massive power levels sounds like a desirable characteristic for any speaker, you'll already have perceived the trade-off: firm, robust drivers barely flinch when hit with the full whack from lower-powered amps like, say, a Fender Deluxe Reverb, a Vox AC15, or a Matchless Lightning '15 – all of them great recording amps, as it happens –

and the tone resulting from this partnership can therefore be somewhat tight, dry, and constipated. Getting back to that old speaker distortion ... hey, in many circumstances we like it, and when it comes to achieving a characterful, semi-clean crunch or distortion sound at lower volume levels it can be a real boon. For mega-watt rockers, however, who need a firm sound on the big stage, for either bold clean playing, high-gain distortion, or gut-rumbling low-string riffs, the advent of high-powered drives was – and remains – a godsend.

The alnico camp includes such all-time classics as the Jensen P10R, P12R, P12Q, and P12N; JBL D120 and D130; and the Celestion Alnico Blue (aka Vox "Blue Bulldog"). Other than the P12N and the JBLs these are all sub-30W drivers. It's not impossible to built a high-powered alnico unit, however, and in addition to the robust, big-magnet JBL drivers, Britain's Fane still offers a 12" alnico-magnet speaker rated at 100W.

As for the ceramics, the classic models are probably loved by as many players as are the alnicos above. Among them are the Celestion Greenback, "H," Classic Lead 80, and Vintage 30 models; Jensen "C" series drivers; and all of the much-loved EV models.

EFFICIENCY AND SENSITIVITY

Guitarists may have put some thought into the general "sound" of their speakers but the majority fail to consider the effect that speaker sensitivity will have on the volume of their amp. Speaker sensitivity is the speaker's efficiency in translating watts into sound. As discussed earlier in this chapter, the speaker plays a big part in determining the decibels (dB) that an amplifier is capable of producing, and is as important as an amp's watts rating in generating that thing we call volume.

Sensitivity is not related in any way to power-handling ability. There are 15W speakers rated at 100dB (measured @ 1W/1m), and 100W speakers rated at 97dB. Remember what we learned before: every doubling of an amp's power creates only a 3dB increase in output. Hit our illustrative 15W and 100W speakers in turn with the signal from, say, a good 15W tube amp, and the lower-powered speaker will give you twice the audible volume – and probably sound better in the process if you're a rock'n'roll fan, with more speaker distortion and coloration

TECHNICAL TIPS: ALNICO MAGNETS

Players have raved for years about the great mojo of alnico-magnet speakers versus ceramic-magnet units. The science behind all this is difficult to quantify here, but there is certainly something to it.

Alnico is an alloy of aluminum, nickel, and cobalt. It's used in speakers (and vintage-style or high-end pickup magnet assemblies) and is generally regarded as the "musical magnet." Thanks to the relative scarcity of cobalt – and high prices from the early '60s onward – it's also an expensive alternative, especially when you need to gather together enough of it to manufacture a big magnet for a high-powered driver.

As a rough rule of thumb, alnico speakers tend to be musical, sweet, and harmonically rich without harshness. Ceramic speakers are characterized by muscular, aggressive, punchy performance (though both of these are generalizations, and either type – if well designed – can also possess elements of the other's characteristics). In the early days of ceramics, the material was chosen because it was relatively affordable. This also translated into ceramics being the magnet of choice for heavy, firm, high-powered modern units.

added to the mix). Hit the pair of them with a 60W Mesa/Boogie MkII cranked to full, and the sensitive 15W speaker will blow; it's important to remember that high efficiency does not equate to high power-handling capabilities. Stick in one of the new Celestion Centuries, however, rated at an astonishing 102dB and capable of handling the Boogie's full 60W, and you've got a loud little combo.

What all this means is that you can make your amp of choice far more muscular by fitting a speaker or speakers with a higher sensitivity rating. For example, you might convert a 20W combo fitted with a Celestion G12M-25 "Greenback" (97dB) that just won't cut it at gigs into a club player's dream by putting in a 100dB Celestion G12H-30. As much as this would seem to be generally a "good thing," a more sensitive speaker might make your much-loved recording combo too loud for optimum studio use. Alternatively, you just might prefer the sound of its original, less efficient driver – or find equal reason to swap down from a loud, sensitive speaker to a juicy, softer, insensitive one.

Referring back to our beloved tweed Fender Deluxe, Tremolux and the like, these originally came with Jensen P12Rs and P12Qs, which weren't highly efficient volume producers ... but sounded delightful.

SPEAKER SIZE

Size matters, but bigger isn't always better. Far and away the majority of guitarists pump their air with 12" speakers, but plenty of great amps carry 10" drivers as well: the tweed Fender Bassman, Vibrolux and Super Amp; the blackface Fender Tremolux and Super Reverb; the Vox AC10 and the Matchless Lightning '15 210. A few great combos carry 15s, namely Fender's tweed Pro, brownface Vibrosonic, and blackface Vibrosonic Reverb. All of the above – including countless combos and stacks carrying 12s – are stunning guitar amps.

It's a common misconception that 10s are inherently "bright and trebly," while 15s are "bassy and woofy." It ain't necessarily so. A decent 15" speaker designed for guitar amp use will be capable of producing as much audible treble as any 10" driver – or at least more than you probably want to hear anyway, at full whack on the treble control. On the other hand, a pair of 10s offers more speaker-cone surface area than a single 12", and are capable of reproducing a more solid, forceful fundamental, provided their frequency response dips to the lowest-produced notes on the six-string guitar (as most do).

The size of the cone has more effect on attack and response times – that is, the delay between plucking a string on the guitar and the speaker coaxing audible airwaves into motion. At one end of the scale, 10s have a faster response due to the shorter distance the cone has to travel, which results in crisp, articulate notes and a speedy attack. This can also translate to more lively-seeming highs, though not necessarily more high frequency content as such.

At the other end of the scale, 15s – with their much larger, deeper cones – are slower to get moving and pumping the air, the result being a slightly less articulate attack. As you would expect, 12s fall between the two, offering a good compromise, hence their broad popularity. (We're talking tiny fractions of a second here, but it all contributes to the resultant tone.) Singly, 10s do have trouble giving enough oomph to your lows, while 15s can get too "flappy" for some playing styles. This was the very reason that Mr. Fender changed his Bassman from a 1x15" to a 4x10" in the mid-'50s. Yeah, it's a classic *guitar* amp – but the change to a 4x10" succeeded in making it a better bass amp in its day, too.

CABINETS

In addition to the sound of the drivers themselves, the cabinet you bolt them into plays an important part in shaping your sound. Cabinet design and resulting tonality could make a book in itself, but there are a few major factors and formats worth understanding to begin to pin down your requirements. These include the choice of open or closed-back designs, single or multiple drivers, cabinet wiring, baffle construction, and wood types.

Open Or Closed Backs?

Simply bolting a piece of wood across the back of a box or leaving it open can be one of the single greatest tone-influencing aspects of a cabinet's design. Open-backed cabs accentuate the higher frequencies, with a wider, more "surround-sound" dispersion. They generally offer a broad, well-rounded, transparent, and relatively "realistic" sounding frequency response. Their low-end response, however, tends to be somewhat attenuated. This is due to the partial phase cancellation that results from sound waves that come from both the front (driver pumping forward) and back (driver pumping backward) of the cab and reach the listener – or the microphone – at the same time. This isn't usually enough to cause the alarming phase cancellation problems discussed earlier in Advanced Microphone Techniques (Chapter 3), but it does influence the overall sound signature of open-backed cabs … sometimes for the better, sometimes for the worse, depending on what is required for the type of music you play.

The same phenomenon means that if you stand anywhere but straight in front of an open-backed combo, it's likely to sound louder than a similar but closed-back amp, with a more "omni-directional" sound projection. Again, depending on your requirements, this can make it either more of a challenge to mike up, or more appropriate to achieving your desired sound.

Closed-back cabs offer a tighter, fuller, low-end response, with more directional sound projection that comes straight out from the front of the speakers. Sometimes this comes with slightly spongy, compressed-sounding mids (though often this element is accentuated by the drivers popularly included in such cabs), and slightly attenuated highs. A closed-back cab will also be relatively quieter than a similarly loaded and powered open-back cab if you stand to the side or, obviously, behind it.

In a nutshell, you can think of the "open-back" sound as the gritty, edgy, full-throated wail of a Fender tweed Deluxe; the bright, bold twang of a Twin Reverb; or the juicy, sweet mids of a Vox AC30. Think of the "closed-back" sound as the bowel-rumbling blast from a Marshall Plexi, or the foundation-rattling roar of a Mesa/Boogie Triple Rectifier stack.

Single Or Multiple Drivers?

The number of speakers in your cab obviously plays a big part in determining how much air you're going to move. But there are some less obvious tonal differences if you run through a 1x12", a 2x10" or a 4x12". To understand this concept thoroughly, cast your mind back again to the discussion of phase cancellation in Chapter 3. The major principles are covered there, so I won't retread all of that ground. In short, the more speakers you bolt into a cab, the more potential you create for phase cancellation between drivers. Even speakers of the same make and model react a little differently to the signal presented to them, and of course they are in slightly different positions relative to the ear of the listener, or the microphone. So the variations in sound waves they produce inevitably result in some phase cancellation.

This slight "blurring" of the sound from phase cancellation in multi-speaker cabs can indeed be a good thing in some circumstances. It contributes to many classic sounds and might be exactly what you want to achieve. It can also sometimes make life harder in the studio … or easier, if miking up each of two speakers in, say, a Bluesbreaker combo and blending them correctly creates the sound you're looking for. Yet again, it's all about the right sound for the right track – but it's worth knowing in advance which formats might be more difficult to record than others.

Some makers take advantage of the complementary interaction of two or more speakers in a cab by mixing entirely different types of drivers. Matchless use one juicy, soft Celestion Greenback and one tighter, brighter Celestion G12H in their D/C-30 cab, with excellent results. The designers at Trace Elliot selected a Celestion Vintage 30 12" and a 10" Vintage 10 for the Gibson Super Goldtone combo, and it helped to create a great-sounding amp.

This is something you can try yourself. If you are tempted to replace both speakers in a twin-style cab, try replacing just one first. That might be enough to change the sound for the better, and the mix of speaker types might make for a richer, more complex sound. (Of course, always mix speakers of the same impedance. That is something you do not want to mix'n'match.)

Related to this, and with any multiple-driver cab, is yet another factor that will have its say in your sound: how the speakers are wired together.

Cabinet Wiring

We're talking series versus parallel wiring here, or indeed a combination of the two. This can be a very complex issue (hey, like so much we have covered up until now!). But it's not hard to comprehend at least enough of the subject to know roughly how it affects your tone. Roughly speaking, all speakers interact with the amp's output transformer and, through that, its output tubes, to create different degrees of damping and resonance according to impedence and how hard you're driving them. For this reason, the way you wire together two or more speakers will affect your tone.

Speakers wired in parallel tend to damp and restrain each other a little more, offering a slightly tighter response and smoother breakup – all of which is highly desirable in some circumstances. Speakers wired in series tend to run looser, with less damping, resulting in a more raw, open sound – which is, yep, highly desirable in other circumstances. If you have a 2x12" or 2x10" cab with two 8 ohm speakers and an amp with 4 ohm, 8 ohm and 16 ohm outputs, you can test it both ways and decide which you prefer.

Two 8 ohm speakers in parallel will create a 4 ohm load, while in series they'll create a 16 ohm load, so set you amp accordingly. Be aware, however, that if one speaker in a parallel set-up blows, the other will keep functioning and the amp (namely the output transformer) will remain safe for a time, though you should still shut it down pronto and replace the blown speaker. When one speaker of a series-wired pair blows, your output will die instantly because each speaker relies on the other to complete the signal flow, so dive for that power switch before your OT starts to fry! This is most likely why Fender wired all of their earlier multi-speaker cabs in parallel, rather than anything to do with tonal differences between the two.

Baffle Construction

The speaker baffle is the board at the front of the cab to which the speaker is bolted. The way it is fixed to the cabinet, as well as its thickness and wood type, will affect the overall sound. Thinner, more loosely fixed baffles will vibrate more, and pass more vibrations into the rest of the cabinet too, creating cab resonance and standing waves that add to the sound of the speaker itself.

Vintage cabs, as a rule, tend to be built this way more than modern cabs. The classics of the breed include Fender's tweed amps from the late '50s, like the 5E3 Deluxe, the 5F6A Bassman, and their brethren. These are built with "floating baffles," attached to the cab's front panels by a pair of screws at each of two sides of the baffle only. When cranked, the whole cab begins to sing – and the amp reacts that much more like an instrument in itself. For the right style of music, this can sound great, but otherwise the tone can be perceived as woolly or blurry.

Fixing the baffle tightly to all sides of a sturdy, thick-wood cab tends to restrain cab vibration and baffle resonance, and translates a greater proportion of the pure speaker tone into the resulting sound. In general, this can mean a somewhat more controlled response and tighter lows.

Wood Types

Important too are the types of wood from which the cab and baffle are built. Broadly speaking, plywood and chipboard offer less cabinet resonance than do solid woods (well, less and lesser respectively, if you will). This can be desirable for some designs, where the amp builder has factored in precisely what he wants from his amp and drivers, and doesn't want too much unpredictable cab sound to get in the way. On the other hand, the resonance that does occur in a chipboard or MDF cab – and there will always be some of this – can sometimes sound dead and "unmusical."

Solid wood cabs, usually built from pine or similar soft woods, as used in the early Fender, Gibson and Vox cabs and others, offer a more uniform, musical resonance and, unsurprisingly, a woodier tone. To some ears this can be slightly indistinct and unfocused; to others, it is sonic beauty incarnate. Either way, it's a contributory factor to some of the greatest sounds of rock'n'roll history.

GOOD, BETTER, BEST?

So which of all of the above is best for you, especially as a studio recordist? Sorry, but only you can decide. Little of what we have covered here – vintage or modern and American or British speakers, fixed or floating baffle, series or parallel wiring – is a strictly "better/worse" choice. It's all a matter of choosing the right tool for the job, and the one which best suits your sonic tastes and playing style.

The importance of all this lies, as ever, in understanding the vast range of tonal choices available to you. Never ignore the major role that speaker selection and cab design play in the tonal recipe, and you'll be better able to achieve the results you want from your amp. Experiment, mix'n'match, and see what you can come up with.

Where previously you were convinced you needed to lay down another wad of cash for a vintage Marshall half-stack to get the sound your band requires on a couple of tracks, you might discover that injecting your 12W Fender Princeton Reverb through the studio's in-house closed-back 4x12" pulls off an impressive JTM-45 impersonation. And it will be distorting a lot quicker and sweeter, and is a hell of a lot easier to record. Cool, huh?

Pros Talk

A series of revealing interviews with the industry's key producers, musicians, and technicians.

STEVE ALBINI

Steve Albini first came to prominence in the 1980s as the guitarist and leader of hardcore punk band Big Black. Since then he has carved a distinguished career as a sound engineer and producer working with artists like Nirvana, PJ Harvey, The Breeders, The Pixies, Page & Plant, and countless others. At the same time, he has pursued his own musical interests as guitarist in the bands Rapeman and Shellac.

Albini shuns the title "Producer," preferring instead to be called a "Recordist." His approach to recording is purist, exclusively analog, and rooted in traditional engineering techniques more commonly associated with classical music and jazz. For some bands, an Albini album seems to be a rite of passage. His purist and non-interventionist approach captures the essence and true sound of the groups he works with, rather than some air-brushed, candy-coated, radio-friendly interpretation designed to please record company accountants and corporate executives.

I spoke to Steve Albini at his studio in Chicago, Electrical Audio. He has a reputation among some musicians for being formidable and intimidating; previous Albini interviews I had read seemed to confirm this. Others consider him easy going and a pleasure to work with. In person he is measured and articulate, and speaks with authority and real feeling about his subject. He can also be very funny, with a cutting, dry wit. In this world of computer recording, plug-ins, digital effects, and amp modeling, Albini's views might sound quixotic, strange, and isolated. So, is this a man tilting at windmills on the lunatic fringe of professional audio or is he a voice of reason, independence and integrity? Read on, and you can decide for yourself.

What are your preferences when it comes to electric guitars?

I have none, really. I'll go with whatever the artist is using. I don't like to make editorial decisions when working; it's my job to get the sound onto tape in the most flattering way possible.

I will say that I prefer simple guitars, and the fewer controls and switching combinations they have the better. Otherwise too much time can be wasted with too many options.

Do you feel the same way about amplifiers?

Absolutely. In my experience, if it has more than five knobs you have a problem. That applies to guitar amps and especially bass amps.

You are a guitarist yourself, so what are your personal preferences?

Old Fender Bassmans.

Tweed or blackface?

Blackface. I like transistor amplifiers too, in certain applications, for a gritty, edgy type of sound.

Which microphones do you prefer?

Generally I'll go with a BBC/STC 4038 ribbon mike. I like that a lot. The Royer is a very good microphone and it sound very close to the 4038. They did a great job with that microphone. If anything it's a little brighter than the 4038 and has a slightly higher output level.

The RCA microphones are good too – the 77s, the 44s. They also made a cheaper microphone called the RCA Junior that was probably intended as an

> **"I'll very occasionally use a DI if something is going to be very low in the mix, but my opinion is usually that if it's going to be that quiet, then it probably shouldn't be there anyway."**

announcer's microphone in schools and shopping malls. It has a slight presence lift that works very well for guitar. I like Beyer ribbon mikes too. I have 160s, 130s and the 500. I'll very occasionally use a DI if something is going to be very low in the mix, but my opinion is usually that if it's going to be that quiet it probably shouldn't be there anyway.

Do you ever tilt ribbon microphones forward to get a little more top end?

You know, I don't – and I'm not sure that the extra little bit of tension that gravity puts into the ribbon is actually adding top end. I think it's more like a slight bass attenuation. I sometimes use a condenser microphone in combination with the ribbon. I quite like Neumann U67s and sometimes I'll use an AKG C414 in a figure 8 pattern. In cardioid I find them a little harsh and edgy.

Did you ever go down the Shure SM57, SM58, Sennheiser 421 route?

I did do that early in my career, but I realised very quickly that it wasn't a realistic option for me.

When you use more than one mike, is there anything you do to minimize phase shift?

Some degree of phase shift is inevitable, especially in the high end. I will try to maintain an equal distance between the speaker and each microphone.

Generally the microphone is aimed directly into the center of the speaker cone, but if I'm using two microphones I might have one slightly off center, especially if I'm going for a stereo effect. Generally I place the microphones about six to eight inches away from the speaker; I am more likely to adjust the angle of the microphone to adjust the tone than get into using equalisation.

Do you sometimes mix ambient microphones with close mikes?

I do, sometimes with the microphone near the floor and sometimes up in the air. If it's just meant to provide a bit of distance from the cabinet, like its supposed to be providing some sort of slight ambient clue without being a very reverberant sound, then I'll generally try to put it in a place where it's hearing a lot of close reflections, and that's generally a few feet off the ground.

Do you ever mike the back of cabinets?

Yeah, I have occasionally, but it's been out of curiosity, not because it's actually functional. You can try any random thing and it will do something, occasionally. In terms of day-to-day functionality you tend to find those things that do the meat and potatoes version of the job and stick to those techniques. If you have time to kill or someone really wants you to, then you'll do something wacky.

Do you have any preferences for mike preamps?

Well, my experience has been that microphones that have electronic outputs, that is transformerless outputs – unless they have an output impedance that mimics a transformer, like 150 ohms to 300 ohms – those can sound strange feeding an input transformer on a mike preamp. I've been told that what happens is that the source behaves like a virtual short because a lot of transformerless microphones have a vanishingly low output impedance in the order of a few ohms, and that behaves as a short to the input transformer, then the feedback is improperly applied from the output of the circuit back into the input transformer. That causes distortion and loss of headroom. Before you hear distortion and loss of headroom I've actually heard a hardening of the sound where the low frequencies don't speak quite as you would expect them to.

So I tend to match transformerless microphones with transformerless electronics. I quite like the George Massenburg preamps. I'm also very happy with the preamps in our recording consoles here, which are Neotek consoles; I like them a lot. We also have a bunch of microphone preamps that are made out of old Ampex tape recorder amplifiers, 351 mike amps, and we have customized those rather heavily, that is made quite a few modifications to make them more suitable for use with modern microphones in a modern studio. We put phantom power and pads on them.

We also have some Ampex MX 35 mixers which are quite nice, I use those a lot. We have mike preamps by John Hardy, by Sytek, by Neve. Greg Norman, a guy who works here, has also made a few preamps and we have used those as well; they sound good.

Do you go for the old tube stuff at all, like Telefunken V72s and V76s?

You know, I've used V72s and V76s and I didn't like them. Every time I've been in a studio that has them I've felt obliged to plug them in and turn them on and listen to them, just because I keep thinking that there must be something that I'm missing. But I think they don't have much headroom and sound kind of muddy. I'm not a fan, I have to say, of that circuit. The Neve mike preamps that are equally revered by generally the same people are great. They've got really ballsy low end and really clear high end.

> **"It's once in a blue moon, once in a brilliant blue moon, that I will ever put a compressor on an electric guitar."**

Do you use much compression when you are recording?

I have to say for guitar, it's once in a blue moon, once in a brilliant blue moon, that I will ever put a compressor on an electric guitar. Generally speaking, if the dynamic range is too wide in a coarse sense, like the verse is too loud, that's the type of thing you can contend with very easily just by moving a fader. I'd rather do that than run the signal through more electronics.

Do you feel the need to compress acoustic guitars or electric bass?

Electric bass, yeah. I'll take a couple of dB off an electric bass. Anything more than that and I feel you are starting to overwhelm the natural sound of the instrument. It's rare for me to knock more than 2dB or 3dB off.

For electric bass I'll generally have two channels. I'll have a mike that's got a very heavy low frequency presence, then another one that's a little flatter and cleaner. For example, a Beyer 380 for the low frequency microphone and a condenser for the high end. I might knock a few dB off the low frequency microphone with a compressor like the Urei 1176 or a Massenburg compressor or a dbx 160. I'll send the clean microphone straight to tape. The sound ends up being a blend of the two of them, so the effect of the compressor is even less.

I'm not a fan of the sound of compression as an effect. I feel that it can overwhelm almost any sound, so I'm careful about how much compression I use. It's rare that I will plug in a compressor, and when I do I might have to try three or four before I find one that isn't irritating.

Do you tend to use tape compression?

No. And to be honest there are many, many references in the literature to tape compression, and I think most of them are fictitious. We have done pretty extensive experimentation here at the studio trying to find the onset of tape compression, and you really have to run the machines like a baboon to get tape compression. You have to be overloading it by 18dB to 24dB, running so much hotter than would be feasible.

People who talk about tape compression are talking generally about something else, like a nice even sound balance or a good frequency spectrum. If the effect that they were relying on was tape compression they would have to be driving the machine and the electronics of the desk so hard. It is possible to set up a machine so that it is recording in compression but that is such an abuse of the format, I have trouble believing that people would actually like that sound or would do it intentionally. If you hear actual tape compression it sounds lousy, it sounds awful. People who attribute some magical greatness to analog recording and use tape compression as their descriptive term for that, I think are talking out their ass.

Do you use hard disc recording or are you exclusively analog?

I've never done a session on a computer. I've done one or two sessions where I had to work on digital multitracks, and as far as I'm concerned there's still no reason to go down that route. Analog recording is still in my view the best way to make records.

Even though the recording is going to end up in digital form, on a CD?

Well, my thinking about it has always been that your master tapes are going to be there forever and you should make them sound as good as you can. If someone chooses to listen to it on a CD or a cassette or an MP3 file or whatever, that's the listener's choice. That's the distribution medium at the moment. The historical record that is the future is the master tapes, so I want to make sure that those are as good as they can be.

That means analog tape?

Yeah.

Are you going to half-inch or one-inch tape?

For stereo masters I always use half-inch. I think one-inch is a bit of a red herring; there are technical problems with azimuth stability and tape travel on one-inch machines that I don't think have been properly addressed. It's a bit of a fashion now, but I don't see it as an improvement over half-inch.

Which are your favorite tape machines?

I'm quite happy with a lot of different ones. For multitracks, I think Studers can't be beat. Ampex multitracks sound fantastic but they are a little hard on the tapes physically. The Studer A80, 800, and 820 are all fantastic sounding machines.

   The 820 is so easy to work on, a really beautiful tape transport, an incredibly gentle tape transport, with absolutely seamless punches. Functionally, the microprocessor control in it is absolutely brilliant, you can store different tape alignments and you can store the session data direct to tape as a little data burst. It's such a perfectly engineered machine; I don't think tape machines could have gotten better after that.

Do you use MCIs at all?

I have, they're OK. Only about 70 per cent of them is working at any given time, but it's always enough to make a record. They have really bad contacts; MCIs used an automotive connector called the Molex for all their audio connections. Molex connectors are not designed to go through the number of cycles that they have to endure in a tape machine. The pins also tend to tarnish and the contacts lose tension. There are a lot of problems with them, but they are good sounding machines when they are working.

Do you tend to run at 15ips or 30ips?

For rock music I'd say that 90 per cent of the time it would be 15ips using the CCIR or IEC EQ curve. For stuff that's got more detail, more high frequency detail, especially stuff that's not meant to sound heavy in any respect, that I'll generally do at 30ips. If it's a questionable case, I'll record a little piece of music at each speed and then listen to compare the two.

> ## "I cannot stand the sound of electronic pickups in acoustic guitars! It's the most irritating, piercing, shrill, phoney sound."

Let's talk a little about acoustic guitars; do you have any preferences?

I like to record acoustic guitars very simply; a couple of microphones at most. I cannot stand the sound of the electronic pickups in acoustic guitars! I cannot stand it; it's the most irritating, piercing, shrill, phoney sound. That's up there with the POD and Amp Farm and the Rockman in terms of its irritation level on me. I really cannot stand it, it's undeniably cheap.

Interviews: Steve Albini

The hallmark of the amateur?

I don't even think of it in terms of professionalism; if that sound is supposed to represent an acoustic guitar then they have failed. I do like small diaphragm, especially metal diaphragm condensers like the Neumann KM56, Neumann SM2. I quite like the Sony C37, and I've had good luck with the small Altec tube mikes, the 165, the 175. And some of the Pearl microphones – PML or Pearl, whatever they call themselves.

Have you tried the Schoeps 221?

Yeah, that's an outstanding acoustic guitar microphone. It's especially good for classical guitar because the clarity of that microphone is really special. It doesn't sound "bright" necessarily, but it sounds really clean and you can really hear the details of fingers moving across strings. I quite like that microphone. There's a Russian microphone called the Lomo 1918 and I've used that quite a bit on acoustic instruments. I've used it on fiddle, acoustic guitar, mandolin, ukulele. I think that's a great, general-purpose acoustic guitar microphone.

There are two new cheap microphones that really rate highly. For general-purpose acoustic guitar use I really like the Audio Technica 4051. It's a cardioid, condenser single membrane microphone, and for the money it's the best microphone ever. I use it on a lot of different things, great bass response, really clean high end. Maybe there are occasions where it's a little too hollow in the midrange but generally speaking it sounds good.

There's another Audio Technica microphone that I quite like called the Pro 37R. It's a very bright microphone but it's not brittle. It's clear rather than scratchy. I use that microphone quite a bit on instruments that have a lot of high frequency content where I need to preserve it, but I don't want it to become irritating. I think those are about $100 – an unbelievable bargain.

> **"It's a cardioid, condenser single membrane microphone, and for the money it's the best microphone ever."**

What do you think of the rush of cheap Chinese capsule condensers that have come on the market such as the Rode mikes?

They are of almost random build quality; you basically have to try every one in the shop to see if you can find one that's good. I have to say that I haven't found myself using them on any occasion. I have listened to them in other studios but I haven't found myself wanting to use one.

Do you tend to use more than one mike on acoustics?

Generally I'll have a microphone on the bass side and a microphone on the treble side. Sort of angled up and pointed at the player's hand. If it's a strumming rhythm guitar then I'll generally simplify it and only use one microphone. If it's more melodic, like more single-note lead line stuff, then the player's usually seated and that makes mike placement a lot easier. I know that there are a lot of rules of thumb that a lot of people use when miking acoustic guitars, like you should point the mike at the neck joint or at the 12th fret. I've tried all that stuff and I've never been able to get anywhere with it. I've had to experiment and find techniques that work for each circumstance.

Do you get in there with your ears and try to find a sweet spot?

Well, if you're listening and it sounds bad, you don't want to put the microphone there. One thing I've found is that if the instrument is quite boomy then you want to keep the microphone away from the soundhole. A lot of low frequency energy comes out of the hole. If the instrument is thin and weedy, then you want to get the mikes in closer to get a little bit of a proximity boost. I like to have the mikes a couple of feet away if I can; if I'm doing a stereo location recording rather than a stereo effect recording, I like to hear a little bit of a reflected sound on the instrument to make it more realistic. It's not always possible to get any space around it if you've got a group playing.

Which mike patterns do you prefer – cardioid, omni, figure 8?

It kind of depends. I've found that figure 8 mikes are very useful at attenuating spillage because they have such good nulls at the sides.

I've found that when I switch condensers to figure 8, I get a response more like a ribbon mike. I've often wondered if the side rejection helps to eliminate all the sonic garbage bouncing off the side walls.

It has better rejections to the side and you do get a bit of proximity boost, so I think that's a realistic assessment. I do use all types of pickup pattern. Occasionally – if there's an acoustic guitar playing un-amplified as part of a rock band and you've got a lot of bleed – one thing I've done that's worked out well is to use a very small microphone made by Crown, called the GLM. It's about the size of a paper match. I've had reasonable results by taking 2 of those and physically mounting them to the guitar on either side of the bridge. The microphone itself is not actually touching the soundboard of the guitar, but it's maybe a millimetre off it. That gives you enough of a signal that you can keep the spillage under control even if there is a fairly loud ambient sound.

To digress, when you are recording in stereo, for example over a drum kit or an acoustic guitar, do you use spaced stereo or coincident techniques?

If I'm using just two microphones to record the instrument, then it will be coincident stereo – an MS (mid-and-side) pair, a Blumlein pair, or crossed cardioids. If I'm using a stereo ambient recording to supplement a close recording I'll have those spaced pretty wide and at a distance.

Moving on to bass, you mentioned earlier that you tend to use a dynamic mike and a condenser. Which condensers do you prefer on the bass?

Generally large diameter condensers. There's an Audio Technica mike called the 4033; it's a budget condenser mike but I've found that it works well in that application. I like FET Neumann U47s. I haven't had too much luck with the tube equivalent or the East German Neumann CMV 563. I honestly don't know why, but they somehow don't sound quite as clear. I have actually used small diaphragm condenser mikes in rock situations where you have an aggressive sound that you want to record. I have used AKG 451s, Altec microphones, quite a few different things. I would say that the low end is the meat and potatoes; for that I'll generally use a Beyer 380 or an Electrovoice RE20. Generally speaking, I want something that's got a good bass response that goes quite low.

Do you ever use AKG D12s or D112s?

D112s on occasion, but they have a hollow midrange, they're not a full-spectrum sound. For people who have a very aggressive sound it can be flattering. I'm not crazy about D12s in any application; I've never really liked them for anything.

For placement do you like to get close into the cabinet or do you prefer a little distance on the microphones?

For bass guitar generally it's quite close to the speaker, just because at a distance you tend to get such a build-up of midrange frequencies. I have used ambient recording on bass for some stuff. If it's a very busy arrangement that's sometimes counter-productive. If it's really simple you can make it more realistic by having an ambient recording as well.

We haven't talked much about equalization. Do you tend to EQ much when you are recording and mixing?

When you are mixing you are generally fine-tuning things, so you do need to EQ things occasionally there. In recording it's more rare that I will EQ something, but I'm not religious about it. I'm willing to if I need to, but I try to get it right before it goes to tape.

Do you EQ or compress mixes at all?

I don't use buss compression on mixes. Again, I don't like the sound of it, I don't often see that there's a use for it. It's being done defensively now by a lot of people to make their mixes sound "louder." I think that's a poor compromise. I would much rather have it sound better than louder.

Some people equate the two!

Yeah. So I'm not a fan of buss compression. There have been times when I have been putting a mix together where I think that everything sounds good, like the balance sounds good but there's not quite enough clarity or high-end energy to the mix as a whole. And in that situation I will take the whole mix through a mastering equalizer and try to open it up a little bit without having to go into the individual sounds and carve them up. That has been quite useful.

Which makes of EQ do you favor?

There's a Massenburg equalizer that I quite like, and a Sontek equalizer that's very similar that I've used. There's an equalizer made by a company called NTI. It's a fairly crude equalizer in its capabilities, but I think it sounds great. It provides unnoticeable EQ, like if you want some high end you can click in some high end and it sounds a bit brighter, but you don't have any of the piercing quality that regular equalizers can sometimes give you. I have used some passive equalizers that I have quite liked. There's one made by Universal Audio and I ended up with a number of channels of them. Here, in-house, we made up an amplifier to go behind it. I use that equalizer as a buss equalizer occasionally.

> **"I think mastering should be a subtle art; you should be doing very little, because things should be pretty much done by the time they get to the mastering engineer. When the mastering engineer is effecting an enormous change in the recording then that implies that somebody dropped the ball along the way."**

I'd like to ask your views on the "square wave" mastering that everybody seems to be into these days, where everything has to sound louder that everything else.

Well, for a lot of the music it's being done to, it doesn't matter to me because I hate that music. There are occasionally records that would have been better left alone that are still being subjected to this. I think anyone who listens critically to anything can tell that it sounds bad. Everyone is making this trade-off between having something sound good and something be loud. It's a defensive position and one I don't support.

I think mastering should be a subtle art; you should be doing very little. I'm not saying that because it's a philosophical concern, but because things should be pretty much done by the time they get to the mastering engineer. When the mastering engineer is effecting an enormous change in the recording then that implies that somebody dropped the ball along the way.

I don't think that it's true in every case that every record that has ever been made has needed the degree of compression and brightening that's been used on it. There are a lot of things that enter into it; one of them is that a number of non-professionals are mastering records now and they are enthralled by the power of the process. They are amateurishly excited by what they are capable of, and I think that's the sort of thing that will be resolved in time when people realise that good mastering is worth paying for. Even if what you are paying for is for them to do virtually nothing.

To conclude, what are your preferences for monitor speakers?

I can get used to anything, although I do have some slight preferences. I'm not crazy about Yamaha NS10 speakers, I think they're kind of painful to work on for long periods. In that regard, I really like the B&Ws that I have been using for years. The B&W 805 Matrix speakers are what I use for near fields. They are fantastic speakers and they are not fatiguing at all; I can work on them all day and that's a really important consideration. Having said that, I have liked some Genelec speakers. There's one particular model called the SE30, I believe, that has a ribbon tweeter and I think that's an outstanding monitor. I like the small Westlake speakers. I've used small Tannoy speakers. For me it's not critical what they sound like, but it is critical that I get to spend a little time with them before I have to start making critical decisions. Basically, I can get used to anything.

CHRIS TSANGARIDES

From his humble beginnings as a tape op and general gopher hussling at the center of the early-'70s British rock scene, Chris Tsangarides has risen to produce many of the greatest names in rock and metal. He has developed a justly deserved reputation for his ability to take some of the biggest, loudest live acts in the business into the studio and capture every drop of that stadium-level energy and excitement on record.

In the 25-plus years since he graduated to the producer's chair, Tsangarides has pushed the faders for Judas Priest, Black Sabbath, Ozzy Osbourne, Thin Lizzy, Yngwie Malmsteen, Japan, Ian Gillan, Killing Joke, Depeche Mode, Exodus, Anvil, and many, many more major rock acts. In addition to his technical skills he is known as a great "manager" of artists in the recording environment. He is credited for having the necessary attitude to coax the best performance out of a group of musicians, in addition to knowing how best to get it on tape.

What are your favorite guitars for recording?

I think that there are two guitars that will cover most things. That's a Strat and a Les Paul, those two are the workhorses. You either go for the single-coil twang sound from the Strat or the heavier, mellower tone from the Les Paul. I'm not averse to anything really; whatever the guy wants to use.

Some of the guys you work with must have some tasty vintage pieces?

Absolutely, good grief, real Stradivarius guitars, things you wouldn't want to touch because they are so valuable and priceless. Other times, any old piece of crap, a plank of wood with some stuff on it that the more modern bands use, I suppose.

What about amps?

To be honest, nowadays I've got my own. A company from Poland have built me a model called a Sound Man and it's based on a Hiwatt/Marshall traditional English old style amp with EL34s and proper old transformers, resistors, and capacitors. When you open them up you can see that they are handmade. A proper amp!

   I'm not much of a fan of the digital modeling stuff, although I will admit to using them. They are good for effects, but all they are doing is trying to emulate what we used to do with the old amps. Because I happen to play guitar, over the years I have managed to collect most of the classic amps. And the people I work with will either end up using their own stuff if they are absolutely adamant or they will see what I have and say, "Let's have a go," and end up using my amp or some of my vintage Hiwatts, Ampegs, Marshalls. Generally, I prefer a 4x12 and a head over combos, because combos in studios tend to sound like combos. The studio is the one place where you can turn it up and people won't shout at you.

> **"I'm not much of a fan of the digital modeling stuff, although I will admit to using them. They are good for effects, but all they are doing is trying to emulate what we used to do with the old amps."**

Do you think the volume you can get up to depends on the size of the room you are playing in?

Definitely, I think so. Because in a small dead room if you crank up a 100W amp it will just die, but in a big old open place it will just ring and ring.

And drive the room properly?

Absolutely. And it's important to suss out what sound we are after and make sure that the room I am going to use has got enough room for it to breathe.

What microphones do you generally choose for guitar?

Now I've gone back to my old Neumann U47 FET, about eight inches away, and either Schoeps or Neumann U87s for distance.

Do you go for Shure SM57s?

Sometimes if it's a problem guitar then I will. The 57 will color it so it doesn't sound like it does coming out of the cabinet.

| *Interviews: Chris Tsangarides*

Do you place your mikes in the center of the cone or off-center?

Mainly center, to get more punch – and it seems more direct to me. Having said that, I will move mikes around to find the sweet spot.

Do you use any exotic techniques for getting mike positions?

Yes, my handspan! My handspan away from the center of the cone (*laughs*).

Have you ever measured your handspan?

Yes, it's about nine inches. I've got small fingers but a bloody wide palm!

Do you ever use ribbon mikes?

Yes, I've got an old Coles 4038 mike and I like that sometimes if I want a grungey old racket.

So you tend to use ambient mikes?

Always. The distance depends on the size of the room and the sound I'm trying to get. If I want a huge, great reverb, they will tend to be a long way away and maybe not pointing directly at the amp. Normally I would put a mike 12 to 15 feet away, sometimes closer if I'm going for a fuller, "air" type of sound rather than ambience.
   I don't record them on the same track; the close mike gets panned on one side and the ambience on another, and if I double-track the guitar I reverse the panning for the second guitar to give it a bit of a wall effect.

Do your ambient mikes get placed up in the air or do you use boundary techniques?

Boundary sometimes, but I will start off with a pair that are a distance away. I'll walk back from the amplifier to find the spot that I like. Because of the distance the sound will cancel itself out at certain frequencies, so when they're playing solos you get some interesting panning effects going on. That depends on what key they are in ... well, it's normally E anyway (*laughs*).

A as well, surely, or G if you are Ritchie Blackmore?

Exactly! It helps and just sounds good. You can get some really good effects and it's not necessarily noticeable immediately, but when you really start listening you think, "Wait a minute…" The best thing is when you start pulling the ambiences out of the mix, you think, "Good God, what's happened there?" It sounds so "by itself" and direct. At the same time I'm not averse to doing that sometimes. At least if the ambience is recorded separately, I'll have the option to mess with it later because people don't always record live, and you never know what you are doing really so you have to busk it.

Do you use much compression?

Yes, I do. In the '80s I always compressed sounds before they got to tape, but these days I tend to leave it pretty much flat and compress afterwards, in the mix. I've got a Chiswick Reach valve stereo compressor, and some EARs from Esoteric Audio Research that I tend to use on guitars. And sometimes those TLA valve jobbies that are sort of valve. Well… they have a valve in them.

A placebo valve?

Exactly. If I'm working away from my studio I'll see what they have. I like Manleys, Ureis, and I really like Teletronix levelling amps.

Do you compress heavily?

Sometimes, but it's usually 4:1 with a quick attack and slow release to begin with, then I tweak it about a bit depending on what type of guitaring they are doing.

What about EQ?

Yeah, but it depends what desk I recorded it with first. I use Focusrite sometimes if I want it to sound tougher – the Blue mike amp with the EQ. I like Focusrite EQ on guitars, they are really quite good. Neve and Pultecs too, but it's only ever a bit of top and a bit of bottom. But modern bands like to take all the middle out.

> **"I knobbled another reverb trick from Zoot Horn Rollo of Captain Beefheart's Magic Band. They used a little Fender Champ, opened up a grand piano, put a weight on the sustain pedal, put the amplifier inside the piano, and mic'd up the soundboard."**

Do you use digital reverbs?

There is one digital reverb that I just love, it's cheap and nasty and wonderful because I guess it sounds like a spring reverb, maybe. It's the Yamaha Rev 500, and the settings for guitar in that tend to be quite good. If I can get an EMT echo plate I'll go for that and maybe delay it with some tape, because once you have heard one of them, when you go back to the others you start hearing all the fizz.

Do you ever feed the guitar signal through some speakers out into the live room to get an ambience effect?

Yes, oh yes, absolutely. I knobbled another reveb trick from Zoot Horn Rollo of

| *Interviews: Chris Tsangarides*

Captain Beefheart's Magic Band. They used a little Fender Champ, opened up a grand piano, put a weight on the sustain pedal of the thing, put the amplifier inside the piano, and miked up the soundboard. It was a unique, unusual sound. Those were the old days when at best we had an echo plate, an ADT delay machine, and the studio toilet.

Do you have any favorite acoustic guitars?

Actually I like the British maker Tom Mates. He builds them with a hell of a lot of love and they sound wonderful. I'm not a fan of electro acoustics for an acoustic sound, that fizzy twang is just not right. You need to mike them and do it properly. Martins I like very much, they have always recorded well, and old Guilds as I recall.

Do you prefer to record acoustics in mono or stereo?

Stereo. I like putting microphones above the player's head, a couple of inches forward, firing straight down, one somewhere near the hole, one up on the neck. If you fire a microphone directly at the soundhole you tend to get all the boom, so you need to angle it.

   The thing I always find with strummed acoustics is that you either get that ridiculous all-top-end-and-no-beef sound, or a boom that's good for nothing. You have to find the spot where the guitar sounds present and he can strum along as loud as he likes. It's all down to the mike and where it is. The minute you get a compressor on it because you really want to hear it suck, you get Boom Central and it's like, "Oh my God!" The hardest part is always finding the sweet spot, but you do eventually, and it's wonderful when it happens.

Do you prefer coincident or spaced stereo techniques?

Spaced, just because I like to put different reverbs on each microphone to make it different. I'm always trying to make things different. That works best on picking styles. On the strummy stuff you're wasting effort, really, putting all the reverb stuff on there. I don't tend to use a lot of reverb on acoustic if it has been done properly.

Did you ever get into dummy head recordings?

Now, funny you should say that. There's a lovely one that Schoeps make and that's phenomenal. I use it for overheads on drums. It's more spatial, more extreme, and more out-of-phase I expect. Whatever: it's wide and transparent.

Do you compress acoustics much?

Sometimes, with a nice old valve compressor, but I try to keep it as natural as possible really without too much fret noise. I don't mind a bit of fret noise, that's what happens, but if you start getting into too much treble it starts sounding horrible and louder than the instrument.

Any bass and bass amp combinations you like?

You can't go wrong with the old Ampeg SVT. For the rock stuff it's pretty much that. With rock and metal stuff I tend to use two sound sources: a big old clean, thumping bass and another one that's filthy as hell. I also take a direct signal from the DI output on the back of the clean amp. I don't tend to DI straight from the instrument unless it's an active bass. With that mixture, between the three you tend to get what you are after.

> **"You can't go wrong with the old Ampeg SVT amp. With the rock and metal stuff I tend to use two sound sources: a big old clean, thumping bass and another one that's filthy as hell."**

So you are overdriving one of the bass amps?

One of them is overdriven, normally with the preamp turned up so it distorts a bit. If you get a bit of growl in it, once everything else is in the mix it blends its way into the guitar territory, because bass in rock shit is normally what the guitar riff is doing. I will always compress a bass going to tape – again the EAR or the Chiswick Reach, depending what's going on.

And EQ?

Not really. If it's a Fender Precision or Jazz through an Ampeg you know exactly what it's going to sound like; if he's using his fingers or a pick, it's got that sound. Having said that, I like the sound of the old Wal basses.

What mikes do you go for on bass?

On bass it used to be an old AKG C12A, the one that looked like a 414 with a nuvistor. But I use a small-capsule Schoepps now or a Neumann KM84. There's a hell of a lot of bass end on those KM84s.

I think some people make the mistake of equating bottom end with large capsules.

Exactly. And with the Ampeg cabinet it uses 10" speakers, and it has that sound and the transient response.

How close do you get with the microphone?

A good foot away because my theory – in my warped mind – is the lower the frequency, the longer the wavelength, and I find that if the bass is in a room where you can move the microphone away from it you can put a few mikes up and try some room on it and see what happens. I always loved the bass sound on the old James Brown records, and it semed to me that it came out of the speaker, rolled around the stage, and fell off the end.

All the other mikes were probably picking it up.

It's got to be, hasn't it? And the guys were using Marshall stacks in those days.

I read something once where an engineer said that "spillage is the glue that holds everything together".

Absolutely right. Brilliant! I wish I'd said that.

Do you prefer to work with the amp head in the control room and the cabinet in the live room?

Yes, always. With long speaker cables.

It's great, isn't it?

Yes. Quite frankly, yes.

ALAN MOULDER

Alan Moulder started out as a guitarist, playing in local bands in his hometown of Boston in Lincolnshire, England. After a brief stint as a tea boy at Trident studios in London, he took a job at the Ministry of Agriculture. Four years later – having had enough of agricultural administration – he returned to Trident, where he graduated from tea boy to engineer. His early work with The Smiths and Antenna soon gave way to dance music and remixing.

In the late '80s and early '90s he furthered his reputation working with the "shoegazing" bands My Bloody Valentine, Ride, and Slowdive, and enjoyed chart success with Shakespeare's Sister. He worked with The Smashing Pumpkins on Siamese Dreams and Mellon Collie And The Infinite Sadness and, more recently, with Trent Reznor of Nine Inch Nails on The Fragile. Moulder is known for his adventurous, "anything goes" approach to recording. He is inspired by the latest technology, but still uses traditional formats where appropriate.

Other than plastic Maccaferris, of course, what are your preferences when it comes to guitars?

I don't have any, really, they all have their individual sounds. I suppose you just pick what guitar you want for the sound. The ideal thing is that you have enough there to do what you need rather than get all the sounds out of one guitar.

Do you find that the people you are working with favor certain types of guitar?

It does go in cycles a bit. It seems to be Paul Reed Smiths with the metal guys. The indie guys are still Jazzmastering and Stratting it, and Les Pauls fit somewhere in the middle.

Are people using vintage guitars much?

Yes, especially the Jazzmasters and Strats; I've worked with a few people who have used old Strats.

What kinds of amps are you running across at the moment?

A lot of people have been using separate preamps with power amps, like a Boogie power amp or something and various Marshall preamps. I quite like the Digitech stereo preamp, either the 2112 or 2120. I've found those pretty good because they have two preamp stages, one tube and one FET, so you can basically drive out of that to your stereo power amps to a couple of cabs and you have a massive sound. It's actually in stereo but it sounds like it's double-tracked because you've got quite a different stage on each side. I've used those a few times and I've thought those sound pretty good.

> ## "You can basically drive out of that to your stereo power amps to a couple of cabs and you have a massive sound."

Are you still using traditional amps like Voxes and Marshalls?

Yeah, I've been using those too. I've been wanting to try out those new Diesel amps but I haven't had the chance to have a look yet. And there's the new Line 6 amps; they're good.

What do you think of the POD and Amp Farm?

I think they are incredible, really, for what they do and how they do it. I've found with PODs that they are great for getting a sound up quickly that's pretty playable, but I don't think you can track them up. I find that if you have one on its own it can be good but if you start getting a lot of them together it doesn't seem to gel together well and it starts sounding a bit funny, you know? A bit "grey" sounding, or something like that.

A useful tool for a one-off sound here and there?

Exactly, and if you are not doing a lot of guitars they're kind of fine. They don't necessarily sound exactly like the amp they say they sound like, but they still sound pretty good. I've certainly used the Amp Farm plug-in a lot on things; not necessarily on guitars. I think they're good… but I would also say don't throw all your amps away yet.

Moving on to microphones, which ones do you use for electric guitars?

I've got stuck using Shure SM57s and Sennheiser 421s. I do find that they are a great combo; put one on each speaker and blend them in about fifty-fifty and it seems to work well for me. The 421s have a lot of bottom and top, not a lot in the middle – and the SM57s take care of all the middle. It tends to sound the way the amp sounds out in the room to me – actually pretty faithful. Other times if I'm going for a more characterful sound I like the Coles microphone. I think those are really good too.

> **"I've got stuck using Shure SM57s and Sennheiser 421s on electric guitars. Put one on each speaker and blend them in about fifty-fifty and it seems to work well for me."**

Steve Albini uses those Coles mikes, I understand.

He does, I've just been in his studio. I was there for a couple of weeks. It was fantastic. His microphone collection is absolutely amazing; I hadn't even heard of half of them.

Do you use condenser mikes much on guitars?

I might use one for ambience, a Neumann U87 or another valve mike.

It's not something you often do?

Unless it's a pretty raucous sounding guitar I'm going for, I don't generally use a lot of ambience mikes. Not if it's a big rhythm sound I'm going for. I really do like it as dry as possible.

Does that mean you place the dynamic mikes quite close to the speaker cone?

I have it nearly touching the cloth, and also I generally put them right in the center pointing directly at the dust cap.

Is that to get more edge and bite?

I guess that's it, yeah.

Do you ever mike the back of cabinets?

I have done sometimes on AC30s or other combos – I sometimes throw one around the back. I generally do that if I'm looking for a little extra character. It's not something I'd normally do. If something's not working, I'll generally try something in that direction.

Are you into any exotic techniques for finding mike placement?

Again, I can do that; it depends on the part. A lot of the time I'm recording guitars that are in your face. It's the nature of the beast for what I do. Sometimes for odd sounds I'll go for the sum-and-difference (mid-and-side) stereo miking. Get a couple of amps side by side and put a baffle down the middle; I think that's great and a lot of fun if you have the room to fit it in the track.

> ## "A lot of the time I'm recording guitars that are in your face."

Are there any guitar sounds from records that you have made that you feel most proud of, sounds that maybe even define your work?

Well, let me think, that's a tricky one. I really like the sounds we got on the last Nine Inch Nails album because a lot of them were such untraditional guitar sounds. Sometimes we just chained a whole lot of pedals together and DI'd straight into the board, and again some of the sum and difference we did in ambient rooms. That was when I got to play around a lot with the sounds. And working with My Bloody Valentine, I would point to the rhythm guitar sounds that Kevin did – though I can't claim that defines what I do. I wouldn't say there's one thing that does.

Do you tend to record with compression and EQ much?

I tend not to, I tend to try and avoid both unless it's for a specific effect. With DI'd sound I'll generally EQ and compress to give it a bit of life.

Is that because you prefer to leave that for the mix or does that philosophy apply to the mix as well?

At the mix stage I may compress it, though generally not a lot if it's a rhythm sound. I may even use the channel compressors on the mixer. I put them in sometimes just to warm it up a bit. Maybe EQ if that's what's needed. I find that getting it at the start without compression or EQ gives you a bit more flexibility.

If you are going for really big sounds, do you tend to "track up," recording the same guitar part over and over again to build up to that wall of sound?

Generally not, I usually only go for two guitar tracks – and for a chorus or something I'll kick in a super-distorted guitar. I have stacked them up just to see what happens, and it's not a lot more, really.

> **"I usually go for two guitar tracks – and for a chorus or something I'll kick in a super-distorted guitar. I have stacked them up just to see what happens, and it's not a lot more, really."**

If you're recording two mono signals, do you tend to pan them hard left and hard right?

Pretty much. I play around with that to taste. On certain boards if you pan them in just a fraction it can make it sound more powerful, but quite often it's hard left and hard right, as long as the guy can play tight enough.

Let's talk a little about acoustic guitars now. Do you get to do much of that any more?

Occasionally, yeah. Acoustics, I think, are quite difficult, and I think it's really guitar dependent. Certain guitars record really well and it doesn't seem to go according to price. The Jesus And Mary Chain used to hire a Yamaha that was worth around £120 [$200] but it recorded great. I've had great sounding Martins, but there's nothing I can say always works.

Do you have a starting point for mike placement on acoustics, or do you suck it and see?

I'll aim for below the soundhole and the bridge, somewhere around there. I'll generally aim it towards the hole but I like to stand in front of the guitar to see if I can identify a sweet spot where all the sound seems to be. Just listen and wherever the sound seems to be, put the mike there.

Do you close-mike acoustics, or do you prefer a bit of distance from the guitar body itself?

Again it varies, but not too close. Generally at least six to eight inches away is as close as I get.

Do you ever blend in the signal from a piezo pickup if the guitar has one?

Yes, I do that sometimes, but I generally record them separate. That can work really well to add a sheen to cut through the track.

Do you have mike preferences for acoustics?

I've been using the B&Ks quite a lot; I think they're pretty good.

The omnis or the cardioids?

Either. The B&Ks sound pretty good on acoustics – kind of open. I used to use Neumann KM84s a fair bit. Failing that, any great valve mike that happens to be around; they generally sound good.

I always find that if you can start from the point of capturing it as you hear it in the room then you can decide what else it needs to fit in with the track. I guess that's why I like B&Ks – they do that.

What's your approach to compression and EQ? Do you use more with acoustic guitars?

With acoustics I tend to use a little more compression. I might even use desk EQ, but that's the last thing I'd reach for. I'd use the compressor for picking or less strummy parts.

To bring out detail as much as contain the sound?

Yeah, and maybe to add a little sustain.

What are your favorite compressors?

I've used some of the old Neve compressors, the blue ones where the VU meter goes up and down. They can sound pretty good. Some old Pye ones that they have at Konk, they're really good on acoustics. You know Konk don't you?

Yes, the old Kinks studio in London. Any other compressors?

Beyond those there's always the old faithfuls, like the Urei 1176.

Do you have any particular settings for acoustics?

Slow attack, fairly fast release. On the 1176 I always like to push all the buttons in because it always sounds really good, brings it right up in your face. It will vary, but generally around an 8:1 ratio.

Any favorite bass and amp combinations?

Bass is also difficult for me and it depends on the instrument a lot. I've found that if you have a classic old Fender P-bass it will work pretty well. In the early '90s for all those shoegazer bands we used to use those headless Steinberger basses. They didn't sound very good on their own but they used to sit in the track really well. It was weird, we used to A/B basses, and other basses would sound much nicer on their own, but in the track the Steinbergers used to just sit in there and didn't seem to have any dead spots.

That might have been because of the graphite construction.

Yes, I think that was it, because with old P-basses everything sounds great, but there's one note that sounds 20 times louder than every other note. Then there's always the note that's 20 times quieter than all the others. Again I will use a variety of basses; they all have their own sound. When I was working with The Smashing Pumpkins they got this really old Epiphone bass that seemed to have a whole octave lower than any other bass I've used.

Was that a semi-acoustic?

No, it wasn't a semi-acoustic. It was kind of short-scale and quite thick wood and it had real super-low-end.

I've often wondered with the short-scale thing whether the decreased tension on the string produces a rounder, warmer tone. You get less cut and zing in the top end but you get a lot of lowness.

That's interesting; that's the sound this one had, yeah.

What about amps for bass?

Well, I've had great use out of Ampeg SVTs, both the old and the new, as everyone probably will have. I've liked the Hartke.

With the aluminum speaker cones?

Yeah, I like their cabs. I've had good results from Ampegs with Hartke cabs. I worked with a bass player in a band called Emotional Fish once and he had a great sound, and he had one of the old Ampegs and one of the new both together and that sounded fantastic.

How do the new and old Ampegs differ?

The old ones seem to have a bit more rasp, they kind of distort a bit easier without that obvious fuzz pedal distortion. You seem to be able to get that edge out of them a bit better. The new ones are pretty good, they're still fairly robust.

Do you ever do that trick with Ampegs where you use an external preamp and just use the Ampeg as a power amp?

I think that's what this guy did, he used the old one as the preamp and drove the power amp of the new one. I haven't done that with anyone else.

What's your microphone choice for bass?

Neumann U47 FET. If I need a bit more bite I'll put a Shure SM57 or a Sennheiser 421 on the speaker as well.

Do you mike close or distant?

Fairly close, probably about 6" to 8" away.

Into the center of the cone?

Pretty much. With the U47 I'll probably angle it slightly pointing downwards towards the cone so it's firing across the capsule.

Do you tend to take the DI off the bass as well?

Yeah, I've got an ADL valve DI that I generally use. I'll record it separate, check the phase and – again – it works well just for adding presence.

Compression and EQ?

It varies. As standard, I'll compress it a little bit, but if it's in a room that's not that big and it's driving the room pretty hard you don't really need to. The room's doing that for you. My compressor settings are slow attack, and again the release varies with the speed of the song and what they are playing. Generally slow attack so you get all the attack of the sound.

Do you ever get into re-amping at all: recording a DI signal and putting it through an amp later?

Occasionally. A company called Little Labs do a box that's really good for that because it drops the level. There's another box called Re-amp, I was trying to get one when I was in America. I think that will make re-amping so much more feasible. Otherwise you're always pissed off trying to get the level right. So I do sometimes do it, but not always.

> **"The old Ampegs distort a bit easier, but without that fuzz-pedal distortion. The new ones are still fairly robust."**

Are you a fan of keeping the amp head in the control room and leaving the cab in the live room?

If I can do it and it doesn't degrade the sound I will. Some studios have great tie lines for that and it works great, just because of the ability to fiddle with the amp controls easily.

Do you ever end up putting effects on bass?

Sometimes a distortion or flanger, but I always make sure that the DI is pure.

A lot of bass players suffer because it seems that most distortion boxes are designed for guitar.

Yeah, and you lose the low end. Big Muffs are pretty good and there's a pedal I've been using called a Swollen Pickle, which was made by Way Huge. That has got the most bottom end of any pedal I have come across. It's kind of like a Big Muff with more low end, and if you can find them they're worth having. The guy who built them now works for Line 6, so Way Huge have gone down and they stopped about four years ago. They had some pretty good pedals.

> "There's a pedal I've been using for bass called a Swollen Pickle, made by Way Huge. That has got the most bottom end of any pedal I have come across."

What's your favourite bass flanger?

MXR probably.

The rack mount, or the stompbox?

The stompbox. Also the Phase 90. Do you know any good ones?

I like the rackmount MXR.

Is that the blue one?

Yeah, do you remember those? They had them down at Blackwing studio.

Oh yeah, they are great.

I like my Electro-Harmonix Electric Mistress pedal, too, especially the filter matrix switch. I also use harmonizers sometimes.

I do that, a bit of Eventide.

Do you have any preferences among large capsule microphones?

Not really, because I've had to work in so many different studios, and back in the early days there was no budget and you had to make do with what was there. I tend to do use what's there rather than hiring in the same stuff all the time.

Do you have any preferences between digital and analog for recording?

I still try to use both. Digital is great for what you can do with it, and I think that sometimes things can sound better on digital. A lot of the time I'll go straight to Pro Tools, that'll be the way things are going at the moment. I'll sometimes dump certain things to tape to help the sound and then dump it back in. Tape can really help you out because of its compression, especially for bass. Sometimes even for guitars where you can keep bouncing them down to get tape degradation as an effect as well. So both, I can't really say I've got a preference.

BOB BROZMAN

Bob Brozman was born in New York in 1954, and has been playing guitar since he was six. He was captivated by the sound of resonator guitars when he discovered them at age 13 and went on to study music and ethnomusicology at Washington University, concentrating on early Delta blues. Bob is a slide and fingerstyle specialist, and he's gradually added Hawaiian, African, Indian, Japanese/Okinawan, and Caribbean styles to his mix.

Since his debut album in 1981, Bob has released 26 records including ten solo projects and a dozen or more collaborations. He is also a performing artist, a record producer, and an adjunct Professor at Macquarie University in Sydney, Australia. His 1993 publication, *The History And Artistry Of National Resonator Instruments*, is regarded as the definitive work in its field.

Can you describe the basic workings of resonator guitars? How do they differ from the conventional acoustic flat-top?

Resonator guitars were developed in the 1920s, before the invention of the electric guitar, to satisfy a general need for greater volume. The instruments work with a mechanical resonator, a spun aluminum cone, similar to the one found in the pickup head of a Victrola tone arm [in an old phonograph]. The cone resembles a loudspeaker cone exactly, and both were patented in 1926. The body of the instrument, usually metal, is more of a container/reflector for the resonator system than a vibrating object as with wood guitars.

For a full description of the workings of resonator guitars, I refer you to my book *The History And Artistry Of National Resonator Instruments*, which deals in great detail with this esoteric subject. In terms of performance and recording, Nationals are unique in having a huge dynamic range, which makes them very powerful instruments in performance, but sometimes challenging to record accurately.

I have noticed that you often play a tri-plate guitar. How do they differ sonically from the single-cone designs?

The tri-plate, or tricone, was the original resonator design. Three 6"-diameter cones resonate the sounds transmitted to them from the strings via a T-shaped cast-aluminum bridge. The single-cone guitar has one large cone, with a bridge-biscuit assembly transmitting from the apex of the cone. The later-developed Dobro inverted the cone and the sound is transmitted to the cone's perimeter via a "spider" bridge assembly. The sound of the tricone is definitely more complex and musical, while the single cone is more brash and punchy. The tricones have greater sustain, making them more useful for slide playing.

What are the constructional and tonal differences between the biscuit bridge and spider bridge guitars?

The way the sound reaches the single cone is critical to the character of the sound. It's difficult to describe in words, but the biscuit/cone resonator is more punchy and perhaps banjo-like, while the spider/cone assembly has a more country "twang." Both instruments share the quality of great potential "bark." Normally, Dobro [spider] guitars have a wood body, and single-cone Nationals are constructed of metal. However, both companies tried to imitate each other, so there are plenty of exceptions. Dobros are generally associated with bluegrass and country music, while Nationals are more often used for blues, Hawaiian, and jazz.

Does the diameter of the resonator have a big influence on tone?

Yes, but it is only one of several important factors. The resonator itself can vary in tone, depending on the quality of manufacture. The body-neck joint is also critical to tone, as is the final set-up, since slight changes in angles and pressures can change the tone substantially.

Do the vintage models sound different from the reissues?

Perhaps. There is definitely a factor of "playing-in" or "break-in" with the new Nationals, but I find that after a month of steady play, the new ones actually develop a better sound than the old ones. And, more importantly, the intonation is accurate on the new ones and usually pretty bad on the vintage Nationals. I have seen unplayed-condition vintage Nationals that also required a breaking-in period. The elements must all vibrate together.

When I record conventional flat-top acoustic guitars I expect to pick up low frequencies from the area near the bridge. The top-end sparkle occurs around the part where the neck joins the body. Is this also true of Nationals and Dobros?

It is somewhat the opposite with Nationals. The bass comes out of the f-holes or grilles in the upper bouts, as it is reflected sound off the back of the guitar. The cones produce most of the high-mid frequencies. There is additional higher treble

> **"With National resonator guitars, the bass comes out of the f-holes or grilles in the upper bouts – it is reflected sound off the back of the guitar. The cones produce most of the high-mid frequencies."**

at the upper bouts that a microphone will perceive. So in a sense, the upper bouts have bass, low-mid, and treble, "bracketing" the strong high-mid frequencies that are coming from the cone area.

Do resonator guitars have a wider frequency range and dynamic range than flat-tops?

Absolutely! Especially dynamic range – over 90dB under the hands of a man with normal strength. Super high harmonics are very audible, and yet there can be massive, warm, round bass recorded from the upper bout openings.

Where do you point the microphones when you are recording, and how close are they to one another?

Several different options are possible, and all of them would use condenser mikes. The first method is to put a large capsule mike six to 12 inches away from the upper bout, plus a small capsule six inchges away from the cone area. The second scheme would be similar to that, but adding one more large diaphragm mike, three to four feet away from the front of the guitar. Thirdly, I would suggest coincident miking with two matched condensers, vertically a foot in front of the guitar.And lastly you could take any of these three methods, and then add some monitors in the room to color the sound, and that way you would get more of a live house sound.

Do you record in mono or stereo?

Usually stereo, but I have no fear of mono.

Do you have any favorite microphones?

Large capsule Neumann mikes, and for the small capsules I like Neumann KM-150, KM-190, and KM-84 mikes, in that order.

Are you a fan of ribbon microphones?

For vocals, and for distant miking of guitars.

Do you look for particular acoustic characteristics in a studio live room? For instance live or dry, large or small, wood or stone?

> **"I like a big dynamic range. It is an important part of my aesthetic, and often dynamics are severely lacking in recordings these days."**

I prefer live rooms, and often a large room with high ceilings. However, I can get good sound in most situations except absolutely dead rooms. Personally, I like hearing a bit of the room in a recording – it makes it more like what recording means in the dictionary: recording something that happened.

Do you ever use ambient microphones?

I will often use ambient mikes to add more room tone, create part of a reverb sound, and to "blend" multiple musicians who are playing together in a room.

Do you often find yourself using EQ when recording resonator guitars?

I generally do not use EQ when recording, only when mixing. And for mixing, I use it fairly mildly, usually adding a little more in the "bark frequencies," 1k to 2kHz.

Do you like to use compressors or limiters when recording or mixing?

Never for the Nationals, never in live shows, sometimes for string bass and/or vocals. I like a big dynamic range. It is an important part of my aesthetic, and often dynamics are severely lacking in recordings these days.

Any thoughts on the analog versus digital debate?

Analog sounds five to ten per cent better to the right ears, in ideal conditions, with super-high-end audiophile playback gear, but digital has many other advantages, particularly with time, tape, and budgets. I have done plenty of both, and I feel that the playing, miking, engineering, and mixing have a much bigger effect than the difference between analog and digital.

LINDY FRALIN

Pickups are the crucial link between the vibrating strings on your guitar or bass and your amplifier. During the 1970s, musicians gradually became more aware that aftermarket replacement pickups could greatly enhance their instrument's tone and playability. There are now many companies offering everything from meticulous re-creations of the Gibson and Fender originals to ultra high-gain units, voiced for the contemporary rock player. To understand the function and performance of a range of types of pickups, it seems best to turn to an expert.

Lindy Fralin started making pickups some 20 years ago. As a player, he gradually taught himself the craft of guitar maintenance and started to experiment with pickup rewinding. By his own admission this was, more often than not, motivated by economic necessity. The word spread and Lindy found himself re-winding and repairing pickups for friends and other local musicians. Gradually his reputation and his business grew and Lindy Fralin Pickups is now one of the most prestigious pickup manufacturing companies in the US. In this interview, Lindy explains how pickups work and the complex interaction of the factors that combine to determine their sound. Lindy Fralin Pickups are based in Richmond, Virginia, and you can find more information about their own products on the company's website at www.fralinpickups.com.

Are you a player, Lindy?

Yeah, but now I only do about two jobs a month.

What guitars do you play?

I'm enjoying my '65 Gibson ES-125 with our P-90s and a Bigsby on it, but I was a Strat player forever. My band is pure rockabilly, and I wanted to make it different. I never liked P-90s until I learned to under-wind them. With all pickups, fewer turns of wire around the coil equals a higher fidelity. More turns gets to be thicker, more powerful, quicker to break up, and darker. I've always liked wound strings to sound clear and bright, so that's what made me a Fender guy for all those years.

How does a single coil pickup work?

With rod magnets, the lines of magnetic force go in a curve from north to south – basically in every direction at once. They repel each other, so the quickest way from north to south ends up being a C shape. If you put a coil in that field by wrapping a coil of wire around those magnets, a guitar string will actually move the magnetic field up and down with it as it vibrates. Once you have a magnetic field that is moving within a coil of wire it induces a current. It's called induction, and it's basically a representation of what the string is doing. Of course, it's only a representation at the point where the pickup is situated. That's why a neck pickup sounds different to a bridge pickup.

| *Interviews: Lindy Fralin*

So a pickup gets a different balance of harmonics to the fundamental depending on where it is placed?

Right. That's the simplest pickup, so I've just described the Fender style, but they are all based on that.

How does a humbucker differ from a single coil?

If you have two coils an inch apart you are basically picking up the string from two points an inch apart. Otherwise it's the same principle, but all the problems associated with humbuckers are not because of how they are wound, necessarily, but because you are picking up the string in two places.

Is this like the comb filtering you might experience when you combine a close mike with an ambient mike?

In a way, yes, and the same thing applies to a Strat when you have two pickups switched on. You will cancel the wavelength that is the distance between the two pickups or the two coils, because while the pickups are in phase, the string at only that one wavelength is moving towards one coil and away from the other. It's the physics of the string that causes this. In a humbucker it cancels extreme high-end.

Is this why people associate humbuckers with a darker sound?

Well, darker on the wound strings. The thing is that when it gets to the treble strings it's such high-end that your speakers can't reproduce it anyway. You are not missing it there, you are only missing that real high-end texture on the wound strings. The pickups are actually voiced to have a lot of treble, so that's why your treble strings are very bright on humbuckers.

There's a cancellation on a Strat with two pickups switched on. With the neck and the bridge two and a half inches apart, there is a midrange cancellation, so people call that the "out of phase position." The pickups are in phase; only the string is out of phase.

How do humbuckers "buck hum?"

They have two coils and one is wound clockwise and the other counterclockwise. They actually pick up the hum in the air as mirror images.

So their polarity is opposite?

Only to the hum, because you also put opposite magnet polarity on these coils. So to the guitar string it's actually double reversed. Any two coils with opposite windings and opposite magnet polarity – on a Strat or a Tele even – will function as a humbucking.

So only the hum is cancelled and none of the guitar signal?

That's true. Coils that are not exactly matched do not fully cancel hum.

Some manufacturers are deliberately winding each coil in their humbuckers differently to get more bite and cut. Does this work?

Yeah, we do that with our Unbucker pickup where we are deliberately mismatching the coils. We found that if you make the coil with the screw polepieces hotter, it actually sounds better, but they do hum. They are about 60 per cent quieter than a single coil.

A true 100 per cent humbucking pickup shouldn't even have screws in the one side and slugs in the other. You would actually have to count the turns, duplicate the induction and have the same polepieces. Only a Joe Barden is 99.9 per cent hum canceling; anything I make or Gibson makes is going to have around one per cent hum. But that's OK, because you can't hear it!

> **"A true humbucking pickup shouldn't even have screws in the one side and slugs in the other. You would actually have to count the turns, duplicate the induction and have the same polepieces."**

Humbuckers are thought to be louder than single coils. Is this something to do with the way the two coils interact?

It's actually because it's a very efficient design and, just like a P-90, much of the coil is close to the string. There are two physical properties of this type of pickup: the flatness and wideness of the coil. This makes them more sensitive to the string but also darker. If you have a tall coil like a Fender size and shape, you will have a brighter but slightly less efficient coil.

I always tell people that before they start adjusting polepieces, get the whole coil positioned right; even if you have to put shims underneath your P-90 or something, because those old dog-ears don't adjust for height. If you get the height exactly right and then adjust your polepieces you'll have the best output-to-noise ratio. The hum is not affected by how close the pickup is to the string, but the pickup volume is. However, if the magnetic pull on the string is too strong it can produce a funny, two-notes-at-once kind of sound. Your bass strings can sound out of tune as you go up the neck. Strat neck pickups on the bass side are the best example of this. If you hear this, the first thing to do is back off the neck pickup on the bass side. If it's still doing it, you'll have to adjust the other pickups. This is more prominent on smaller gauges of string.

Which factors in the construction of pickups influence the tone?

Everything at once influences the tone. The main things are capacitance, inductance, impedance, and something called reluctance. That is the resistance of a magnetic field to change. These combine, in a formula I've never even tried to use, to give you your output. What's so hard about winding coils and making pickups is that you want them to be good inductors and pick up what the magnetic field is doing – but they can't be good inductors because by definition inductors impede AC (alternating current). So you are balancing tension, the number of turns, and how much air is in the coil, to get the optimum output. It's extremely complex, and since I'm not an electrical engineer all we've ever done is a lot of trial and error for every pickup design. If you just try to add a thousand turns to a Strat pickup you've got to figure out what the new layering pattern and tension is going to be.

One of the hardest things about coil winding for us manufacturers is that because the diameter of both the wire and the insulation constantly changes, you have to continually monitor every pickup you wind if you want consistency. We have to stop at least five or six times for each coil to see how big it's getting – maybe make them tighter, looser, whatever. I'm sure we've all heard a hundred 6k Strat pickups, but they all sound different. If you do something wrong when winding a pickup it will end up missing bass, middle or highs; it won't be loud and it won't have a flat frequency response. If you do everything right, you have the loudest pickup that design is capable of, while maintaining a flat frequency response. That's our goal: to make each pickup as loud as we can with the fewest turns and without making a strong magnetic field.

People talk about different magnets, Alnico II, III, V, ceramic, and so on. How do different magnetic materials affect tone?

Each magnetic material has something called historicis, which is a curve of its resistance to change at each different frequency, because they resist change too. This is one of the factors that differentiates how different magnet materials behave, and sound. You know, it's not always so easy to have the magnetic field move just because a guitar string is moving. Which is probably why the weaker magnetic materials such as Alnico II and III are just as loud as Alnico V, even though they have half the gauss. I can't look at a historicis curve and tell you what a magnet will sound like; the only way is to go listen to them.

What do people mean when they talk about "ageing" magnets? Does it actually mean anything?

I have not actually found that it means a great deal. If a magnet is at 100 per cent strength it can have a little bit of a harsh high end, but the magnetizers we use don't actually charge to 100 per cent because I'm using the same magnets as Fender did. It's basically a C magnet. Big capacitor discharge machines are the way to get them to 100 per cent. We have never really had to deal with that.

I think that Seymour Duncan knows a lot more than me about this and strongly believes that after you have charged them to 100 per cent you have to knock them back a small percentage. I don't know how he does it, but I have my own method for discharging magnets if anybody ever wants it. I have only ever heard the pickup get a little bit weaker, I haven't heard an improvement in the tone. And the truth is that the half-life of Alnico V is 300,000 years so most of them out there haven't lost any of their magnetic field. If you leave them feeding back on top of a Marshall stack for 20 minutes they might loose something, but most of the vintage pickups we get coming into the shop aren't weaker.

How does wire gauge and material affect the sound?

We have never used anything but copper, so I don't know about aluminum and silver. I've heard people talk about it but I don't know what it would do. But you'd have to learn how to wind them all over again. The gauge of the copper is another one of those things. You want a wider gauge because it's a better inductor but you are not going to get enough turns. If you use a smaller gauge to get more turns, it has more resistance, which is a bad thing.

Somewhere along the line at Fender and Gibson, someone decided that 42 gauge was the optimum. All the pickups I have seen use somewhere between 38 and 44 gauge wire, but most of them use 42. That covers Fenders, Gibsons, Guilds; DeArmond loved 44 gauge. You get more turns with 44 but you get a higher resistance, which is why DeArmonds also had stronger magnets – because a higher resistance makes it darker and a stronger magnet makes it brighter. If we try to make a Strat pickup with a finer gauge wire, it doesn't sound exactly like a vintage Fender any more. It might sound good, it might even be an improvement to some people, but it changes things to do that. The reason you would go for a smaller gauge would be to fit more turns and more power.

What is meant by "scatter winding?"

I've talked about balancing impedance, inductance, capacitance, and reluctance, and one of the ways to get this to balance right is how much air is in the coils. So scatter winding would make a looser coil. The main thing is tension, and having the right amount of air in the coil is one way to manipulate these parameters.

Some of the vintage replica pickups are deliberately being left un-potted – in other words they have no wax potting. What are your views on this?

Well, I like to pot 'em because they squeal and we warranty our products for ten years. I don't want them to get corrosion, that's what kills most pickups – beer and sweat! There seems to be a lot of beer around guitars; I don't know why that is... We know that the potting is going to raise the capacitance by 1.5 per cent, so to get around the problem when we are designing a pickup and figuring out how to wind it, we deliberately make the capacitance 1.5 per cent lower so potting it brings it back to right. If you had a pickup that already had too much capacitance and you wax potted it, it would sound worse. If you had a pickup that didn't have enough capacitance, it would actually make it sound better. Higher capacitance makes a pickup sound darker.

> **"That's what kills most pickups – beer and sweat. There seems to be a lot of beer around guitars. I don't know why that is..."**

In the '60s and '70s there was a vogue for removing the covers from humbucking pickups. Does this actually have any influence on the tone?

Oh yes. Any metal cover raises the capacitance; it's the same as turning your tone knob down. It will darken the tone. As long as you know it's going to have a cover on it, you can still make a great sounding humbucker. You make it with not quite enough capacitance so that when the cover goes on, you have decent high end.

What is the purpose and effect of the metal plate that you get under the bridge pickup of a Telecaster?

It seems to raise the induction and pull the magnetic field down towards the coil more. It makes the pickup have more bass and appear louder. We've tried it with Strat pickups and it seems to give them about 10 per cent more bass. We call it the bass plate and we've been marketing it ever since. There was steel under any DeArmonds ever made and many Hofners had steel under them.

Many players go for more windings or stronger magnets when they are trying to get a rock sound. Are there any drawbacks?

They both have a downside. Not only does it get darker because of the higher resistance, but also another problem surfaces: the resonant peak shifts to a lower frequency. The resonant peak is the frequency at which your coil is most efficient. A Strat pickup with a 25-foot cable and a 250k pot has a resonant peak at 3.5k and that's a very pleasant place to have a lot of treble. If you over-wind the coil to 10k the resonant peak drops to around 2.2k. That's a very unpleasant place to have a lot of treble, so the manufacturer has to make it a darker pickup or it's going to be a real clicky sound. So you really have to redesign the pickup somewhat if you are going to wind them really hot.

Tube amps can accept a wide range of pickup impedances because you can plug in a 3k Danelectro pickup or a 2k Gretsch Hi-Lo'Tron and it sounds fine. Or you can put in a 30k EB-0 bass pickup or a 14k Gretsch DeArmond and they sound fine. They designed these pickups and made them sound good for what they were. The chances are that a DeArmond wouldn't sound good with any other type of wire but 44 gauge. As for Danelectros, I've tried to wind them hotter and they don't sound good. Too many of the reissues try to put them at 6k or 7k and they don't sound good with the smaller-gauge wire. Danelectro did it best. In my opinion, Fender did the Strats best too – when you try to wind them hotter they might make your single note solos sound better but will clog up the wound strings. The sparkle is no longer a sparkle; it's a little bit of a harsh treble.

These guys in the '50s really knew what they were doing and they pretty much had these designs well refined. That was also back when electronic engineers knew what coils were about. In this day and age, nobody needs to know about coils so it's becoming a lost art.

> **"These guys in the '50s really knew what they were doing, and they pretty much had these pickup designs well refined."**

Postscript

The future

The sad news is that much of the information in this book could one day be redundant. How can this be? We plug guitars into amps and we record them with microphones. That's the way it has always been, but things are changing. Let's be honest for a moment. Guitar amps are a pain in the ass to record. For a start they're too loud, so the neighbors complain. They rattle, they break down, their sound changes with temperature and different room acoustics. You need good quality microphones and microphone preamps to even come close to capturing "the sound." Plus you need a good knowledge of microphone placement and a lot of patience – and time really is money in a recording studio. Don't get me wrong, I love it all, I'm happy to put myself through it over and over again, but many engineers and producers are becoming more reluctant.

Dance music has changed many things, and among them is the willingness of record companies to allow groups to spend huge amounts of time and money in recording studios. A significant proportion of the records we hear in the charts are being made cheaply in private home studios that have been set up in back bedrooms, lofts and garages throughout the country. These days we call them "project" studios. We all have to remember that the music business is first and foremost a business. Can we really be surprised if record companies attempt to make quick bucks by releasing tracks that have arrived with them in a finished state? This involves less investment and risk, and record companies are motivated by profit, not quality.

Over the past few years many traditional recording studios have gone out of business. My prediction is that this trend is likely to continue. Technological advances in computing have made multitrack hard disc recording an affordable and practical proposition for the project studio owner. Programs such as Logic Audio, Cubase VST, and Pro Tools also provide a virtual mixing desk as part of the package. High quality mic amps, EQs and compressors are also available at reasonable prices. This is bad news for studios that try to provide a facility for live groups, programmed music, and mixing because the only area in which they can truly compete is live recording.

Many live recording studios have survived this far because we still need soundproofed, acoustically treated spaces to record drums and guitars. While this might remain true for drums, it is no longer true for guitars. Huge advances have been made over recent years in the area of digital modeling. Waveforms generated by musical instruments can be analyzed in minute detail and rebuilt by computers to create virtual musical instruments. Scientists have learned to focus on the "essential ingredients" of instruments and take advantage of the inherent "data reduction" in human hearing to ensure that computer power is not wasted by processing vast amounts of data which are inaudible to humans. This means that these modeled sounds can operate in real time on a single DSP chip, which is cheap to produce.

I first encountered digitally modeled sounds with the drum modules and bass modules produced by Novation. I guess that short, harmonically simple noises with a very narrow dynamic range (on or off) must have been the logical starting point for this type of technology. Now we can see much more sophisticated models in the recent generations of synthesizers. Often digital modeling technology is used to recreate the classic analogue machines of the '70s and early '80s. Nobody – to my knowledge – has produced a virtual '59 Les Paul or a virtual '63 Strat – yet. The focus of the digital modelers has been the sounds of great amplifiers from the past and present.

The most famous company in this field is Line 6 with their POD. Other companies such as Johnson, Zoom and Digitech also make similar products, and even classic names in amplification such as Fender and Vox have now joined in the game. These devices claim to mimic the sounds of Tweed and Blackface Fenders, Vox AC30s and AC15s and many of the classic Marshalls. In addition they emulate Mesa/Boogie Dual Rectifiers, Soldanos, Matchless, and Roland JC-120s. Many modelers have also analyzed the sounds of various speaker configurations. With one diminutive POD you can put your virtual AC15 through a vintage 4x12" Marshall cab or your Dual Rectifier through an early '50s Fender 1x12" or even a Leslie. You can do so without the hassle of impedance matching or the risk of blowing up your alnico Jensens. You can add effects such as delay, tremolo, reverb, chorus and flange, plus it has a built-in tuner and noise gate. Not bad for something that looks like a kidney bean – but does it work?

The short answer to that is "yes." I was recording an album in Spain with a large collection of amps. We had a tweed Fender Bassman, a Fender Champ, a Vox AC10 and AC30, a vintage 100W Hiwatt, a Marshall Plexiglas, a Roland JC-120 and a Dual Rectifier. Guess what – I still ended up using the pod on a few occasions. I was able to compare the simulations with the real things, and the digital models do come close to capturing the character of the originals. I was impressed by the way that the models responded in an amp-like manner. Play light or turn down and the sound cleans up, dig in and it starts to crunch. I'm not arguing that the digital models sound as good as the real thing or even that they sound good. My point is that they sound good enough. This means that producers and studio engineers – who might not share your sensibilities about tone – will want you to use them. The absolute accuracy of the digital models is relatively unimportant; these units provide usable, high quality sounds in a quick and convenient package.

It is possible to control units like the POD from a computer via MIDI, and there are even software versions of the unit. Amp Farm runs with Pro Tools and Guitar Port provides an interface between your guitar and the Internet. All the parameters of the various amp and speaker configurations come up on your computer screen. You get to see the top of a Vox amp with chickenhead knobs or a Marshall with round knobs, and you can even link the channels with a virtual patch cable!

Competition is heating up in this field. I'd like to think that companies would try to stay ahead by perfecting their digital models. My worst fear is that they will simply bring out products with even more amp models but no major improvement in quality. Let's face it: there are only a finite number of classic amps. What's next, the virtual Valvestate or the Vox AC10 with authentic microphonic valves and virtually shagged speakers? I can't wait.

So things are changing. There will always be a place for guitars and amps – live and in the studio – but digital modeling is here to stay. Guitarists tend to be a conservative bunch and are often slow to catch up with new ideas, but no musician with professional aspirations can ignore computers and technology any longer. The "project studio" is no longer the sole preserve of the dance crowd or the Hip Hop artists, but an increasingly important part of rock music in all its forms. A significant proportion of the recordings of the future will take place in home studios or project studios. They will be computer-based, and it is more than likely that bands will be expected to engineer themselves. Some producers are now booking studio time simply to record drums; they then finish guitars, bass and vocals in editing rooms with small vocal booths. I have often enjoyed the feel and sound of a demo tape performance so much that I have lifted it straight from a 4-track machine or the original hard disc recording and used it on a finished record. Hard disc editing makes this task relatively simple, so you never have to worry about re-capturing that moment of inspiration or that special sound ever again. We might even reach the point where session guitarists are able to work from home, linked to studios via the Internet.

Every era throws up some great stuff, and a whole load of dross. One of the most exciting aspects of sound engineering at this point is the opportunity to mix and match technology and equipment from different eras. We do this to enjoy the benefits and minimize the drawbacks of each. I might record a guitar with a '50s ribbon or tube microphone and run it through a '60s tube Telefunken V72 pre amp (my favorite). From there I might add a little '70s Roland Space Echo to the stew and record direct to hard disc via a state of the art 96K digital converter. All of these items, both vintage and modern, are relatively inexpensive. After this I might use a program like Logic Audio or Pro Tools to manipulate the sound by adding EQ or compression inside the computer. Sometimes I use "hyper draw" to add tremolo to the sound with super accurate timing for the track. Once I've got things the way I like them I like to dump everything down onto analog multitrack tape to provide a little tape compression and second-harmonic distortion (warmth), as well as a reliable backup.

Some musicians and recordists tend to believe that there is a "pure" or "right" way to make music. Lots of people cling to the notion of a golden era when guitars, amps, drums and bass combined to create "real" music. It's a lovely idea, but there never was a golden era and recording music was never that simple. I think that if a golden era exists, it has been going on since around 1952, and it is as great now as it was then. It's tragic to reach a point in one's life where everything stops and new ideas become a threat to a carefully constructed sense of reality, rather than a source of inspiration and fun. Try to listen with an open heart and a critical ear and don't be fooled into following the crowd. Things are going to become tougher in the recording industry and the professional musician of the future will need to have engineering and programming skills as well as instrumental prowess. Cherish the past and embrace the future – you'll be a happier person.

Glossary

A

AC Short for "alternating current," an electric current that can change the direction in which it flows. This is the type of electricity that flows from common domestic wall outlets (commonly 120V in the US, 230-240V in the UK). See also *DC*.

acoustic (1) Natural (non-electrically aided) sound produced by a musical instrument, or enhanced by the shape or construction of a room. (2) Guitarists' abbreviation for acoustic guitar.

acoustic lens Unlikely-looking set of slanted slats ("louvre plates") at front of PA horn to disperse high frequencies over a wide angle for good coverage. Rarely used in frontline PA now.

action Often used to describe only the height of the strings above the tops of the frets; thus "high action," "low action," "buzz-free action," etc. In fact, the term can refer to the entire playing feel of a given instrument; thus "good action," "easy action," etc.

active (active electronics, active circuit) Circuitry in some guitars that boosts signal and/or widens tonal range with necessary additional (usually battery) powering. Refers to a pickup or circuit that incorporates a preamp. See also *preamp*.

active crossover See *crossover*.

active powered Not necessarily amplified, but using (active) electronics to assist or improve functioning.

ADAT Multitrack digital audio tape.

ADSR Stands for attack, decay, sustain, release – the elements that make up a standard volume "envelope."

ADT Artificial (or automatic) double tracking. Used to reinforce an existing signal, for instance making one singer sound like two.

alder Medium weight hardwood commonly used for solid guitar bodies, like some made by Fender.

alnico (1) Magnet material used for pickups and speakers (generally of "vintage" design). Often called the "musical magnet," alnico is an alloy of aluminum, nickel, and cobalt. (2) Nickname for a single-coil Gibson pickup with flat-sided polepieces.
alternating current See *AC*.

ambience General sound quality or atmosphere created by a particular room or venue, or by signal processors designed to recreate acoustic qualities, for example reverb.

amp (1) Short for amplifier – could be a power amp or backline instrument amplifier or line amp. Any device for increasing the level of a signal. (2) Short for ampere – a unit of current, the symbol for which is I.

amplification Making a signal bigger (may refer to voltage, analogous to signal level and loudness, or current). Term for amps, speakers, and associated gear.

amplitude Academic term for size or magnitude – particularly of a signal voltage or level.

analog (UK: analogue) "Traditional" electronics, where soundwaves are turned into analogous electrical waves, not chopped up and processed mathematically as with digital audio.

analog-to-digital interface Converts analog sound into digital information (which will then need to be converted back to analog so that we can hear it). Modern converters can cope with sample rates ranging from 44.1kHz to 48k, 88.2k,

96k and 192k. Bit rates are generally 16 bit (consumer) or 24 bit (professional).

anode (plate) Part within a vacuum tube (UK: valve) that collects current.

antinode Point of maximum vibration amplitude of a vibrating guitar string.

anti-phase (1) Alias for the "cold" side (negative, or return wire) of a pair of balanced signal wires. (2) Signal source where the phase (or more correctly the polarity) has been reversed.

anti-surge "Delayed" fuse (body marked "T") that withstands brief current surges without breaking. Note that it doesn't prevent current surges.

array Group of speaker cabinets arranged to work in mutual support. In PA, often piled vertically or splayed out in one or two planes.

ash Medium to heavy hardwood commonly used for solid guitar bodies, for example some by Fender.

attack Speed at which a sound (or filter, or "envelope") reaches its maximum level. Percussive sounds, for example, usually have fast attacks, while smooth, liquid sounds have slow attacks (see also *ADSR*).

attenuate Reduce in strength.

attenuator Electronic circuitry that reduces level, usually in fixed steps of useful round-figure amounts, like -10dB, -20dB and so on. Also the knob or switch that controls such a setting.

audio energizing See *sonic maximization*.

aux Short for auxiliary – a mixer section and control which redirects part of a channel signal elsewhere (to add effects, or for monitoring, etc).

aux return Abbreviation of auxiliary return. Inputs on a mixer used for

adding back the signal from/with the FX.

aux send Abbreviation of auxiliary send. Output typically from a mixer to FX and other locations.

AWG American Wire Gauge. Designates the diameters of the conductors in many cables. Similar to British SWG, using a set of mainly even numbers between 0 and 40 instead of mm².

B+ Symbol used to indicate high voltage supply in an amplifier circuit schematic. Also "HT" (for High Tension), the latter particularly used in the UK.

baffle Front panel or baseboard of a speaker cabinet onto which direct-radiating drivers and smaller horn flares are mounted.

balance (1) Tonal "symmetry" of sound – correct amount of all frequencies present. (2) Old term for the mix – the blend of different vocal and instrumental sounds. (3) Left/right side equality, as in hi-fi usage.

balanced In a balanced instrument signal cable (lead, cord) a pair of identical insulated wires operate as the hot and cold signal conductors, while a separate ground/earth shield protects the audio signal from noise interference. Longer cable lengths can be used compared with unbalanced leads.

bandwidth (1) In analog terms, the frequency range over which some device or system usefully works, often measured in Hz and kHz. (2) In digital terms, the rate (measured in MHz or GHz) at which a processor can "clock" (push through) streams of data. bantam Solid, mini (phone/jack) plug

of high quality, used for dense patchbays on some mixing consoles.

bench repairs Fixes and maintenance done in a workshop rather than at a gig or on the road ("field" repairs).

bi-amp(ed) Any system using a two-way active crossover – which usually means that for each complete speaker unit, two separate amplifiers are used: one to drive the bass speaker, the other to drive the mid/high speaker.

bias Critical "tune-up" setting of an amp, tape machine, or other equipment, generally involving some auxiliary voltage or current that helps the circuitry to work properly.

biasing Setting the bias of the tubes (valves) within an amplifier for optimum performance. See *bias*.

BiFET "Hybrid" integrated circuit that uses J-FETs at the input stage but bipolar parts elsewhere (see *FET*).

bipolar Short for bipolar junction transistor (BJT) – the "ordinary" species of transistor, as opposed to the other major type, the field-effect transistor (see *transistor*, *FET*, *JFET*, *MOSFET*).

blackface Used to denote "vintage" Fender amps manufactured between approximately 1963 and 1967, so-called because of their black control panels. Also used to describe the sound produced by these amps. (Black control panels were occasionally returned to in later years, but any post-'67 Fender amps would not accurately be termed blackface.) See also *brownface*, *silverface*.

blade pickup (bar pickup) Pickup (humbucker or single-coil) that uses a long single blade polepiece for each coil, rather than the more usual individual polepieces for each string.

board Slang term for mixer.

bolt-on neck Describes a (usually solidbody) guitar with neck bolted rather than glued to the body. Typified by most Fender electric guitars. (In fact, such a neck is most often secured by screws.)

bottleneck Style of guitar playing using a metal or glass object to slide up and down the guitar strings instead of fretting individual notes. The broken-off neck of a bottle was originally used, hence the name.

bottles Slang term for tubes.

boutique amp High-end, generally handbuilt and handwired guitar amplifier produced usually in limited numbers by an independent craftsman.

BPM Beats per minute – the tempo of a piece of music.

braces (bracing) Wood structures beneath hollowbody guitar's front and back intended to enhance strength and tonal response.

Brazilian rosewood Hardwood derived from the tropical evergreen Dalbergia nigra and used to make some guitar bodies, necks, and fingerboards. Protected species; further exportation from Brazil banned.

bridge Unit on guitar body that holds the saddle(s). Sometimes also incorporates the anchor point for the strings.

bridge pickup Pickup placed nearest the bridge. At one time known as the lead or treble pickup.

brown (brown sound) Soft distortion produced by a guitar amp when run at slightly lower mains voltages than its specs require. (Derived from the term "brown-out," the partial loss of power to a city's supply grid – itself a contrast to "blackout," a total loss of power.)

brownface Used to denote Fender amps made between about 1960 and 1963; so-called because of their brown-colored control panels. See also *blackface*, *silverface*.

bug "Acoustic" pickup attached to double basses, electro-acoustic guitars.

bus/buss (1) In audio, a mix-buss is an elongated common point or "conduit" into which many signals can be "poured" (grouped) without overloading, and without risk of back-contamination. (In computers and the digital world, MIDI, SCSI and USB are examples of connections that have "bus" properties.) (2) In electrical systems, a bus is an elongated main distribution conductor (usually a solid bar) shared by several outgoing conductors.

C

cab Abbreviation of (speaker) cabinet, commonly used for enclosure containing drivers for one or more frequency ranges.

cable Speaker/instrument/power cord (lead). The sheathed connecting wires, with or without connectors.

Cannon See *XLR*.

cans Slang term for headphones.

capacitor (cap) Frequency-dependent electrical component. Within an electric guitar tone control, for example, it's used to filter high frequencies to ground (earth) making the sound progressively darker as it is turned down. Also used in guitar amps, and for filtering noise from power supplies by passing AC signal to ground.

capacitor mike Also commonly known (though not technically accurate) as a condenser mike. Generally high-quality, if relatively fragile, and requires phantom power to operate. Contains two thin metal plates, one of which (the diaphragm) is moved by soundwaves to create a

change in electric charge (capacitance). The modulating voltage is fed to a head-amp and transformer before being output as a high-level signal with low impedance.

capo (from capo tasto or capo dastro) Movable device that can be fitted over guitar's fingerboard behind any fret. It shortens the strings' length and therefore raises their pitch. Used to play in different keys but with familiar chord shapes.

capsule Guts of a microphone – its delicate inner workings, as opposed to robust casing designed for handling.

cardioid Description of heart-shaped response pattern of a unidirectional microphone (see *polar pattern*).

cascade Linking of two or more devices or circuits where the output of one feeds directly to input of the next.

cathode biased In a tube amp, an output stage which is biased according to the voltage drop across a resistor connected to the cathode of the power tube(s). Often considered a source of "vintage" tone, it is a feature of the tweed Fender Deluxe, the Vox AC30 and others. See also *fixed bias*.

CCW Counter-clockwise (UK: anti-clockwise). Usually means "turning down" a control knob.

cedar Evergreen conifer of the Mediterranean; the timber is used particularly in the making of classical guitar necks. In flat-top and other building the term often refers to "western red cedar," which is not a cedar at all but a North American thuya or arbor vitae.

center tap Output provided at the mid-point of a power supply or transformer, usually designated zero volts (0V).

ch Abbreviation for channel – could be of a splitter, mixer, crossover, power amp, etc.

channel Input on mixing desk, amp, or other gear, and/or controls relating to it.

channel separation Extent to which signals in separate channels are kept apart. Opposite of crosstalk – so if crosstalk is low, it means separation is high, and vice-versa.

charge Ability of elementary particles to attract or repel other particles, depending on whether their charge is negative or positive (electrons and protons are essentially microscopic magnets). The symbol for charge is Q, though it's measured in units called coulombs, the symbol for which is C. The charge (in a copper wire, for example) can be forced to move in a certain way by attaching the wire to a battery or some other kind of electrical pump. This process is known as electro-magnetic induction. The resulting flow of charge is called current.

chassis Steel or aluminum casing that houses the electronics of an amp, effects unit, etc.

chip Tiny slice of semiconductor material (usually silicon crystal) on which an integrated circuit (IC) is built (see *IC*).

choke Special type of inductor (coil) designed to work with audio or radio frequencies while also handling high DC currents – which would more normally degrade performance.

class A Term for an amplifier with output tubes set to operate throughout the full 360-degree cycle of the signal. Class A is sometimes considered "sweeter" sounding harmonically, but is less efficient power-wise than class AB. (The term is often incorrectly used to describe guitar amps which are in fact cathode-biased class AB circuits with no negative feedback, and therefore share some sonic characteristics with class A amps.) See *class AB*.

class AB Term for an amplifier with output tubes set to cut off alternately for a portion of the signal's 360-degree cycle, thereby sharing the load and increasing output efficiency. (In reality, this is the operating class of the majority of guitar amps, and certainly of many classics by Marshall, Fender, Mesa/Boogie, and others.) See *class A*.

class A-B Term for an amplifier that operates in Class A for most signal excursions, and in class B, with slightly lower fidelity, for occasional peaks.

class B Term for an amplifier that uses the least standby power but with acceptable performance.

clip Abrupt flattening (chopping off) of the peaks of a signal, when the equipment can go no further. It creates aggressive, hard sound; removes most sonic detail; hurts nearly everyone's ears; and can quickly blow drivers.

coil(s) Insulated wire wound around bobbin(s) in a pickup.

coil-split Usually describes a method to cut out one coil of a humbucking pickup, giving a slightly lower output and cleaner, more single-coil-like sound. Also known, incorrectly, as coil-tap.

coil-tap (tapped pickup) Pickup coil that has two or more live leads exiting at different percentages of the total wind, in order to provide multiple output levels and tones. Not to be confused with coil-split.

cold Negative, low, or return side of a balanced line, or balanced input/output.

coloration Tonal (frequency response) and timbral problems and aberrations, as well as ordinary distortion. Usually quite a complex effect caused by speakers and room acoustics, rather than, say, a gentle roll-off of treble.

comb filtering Partial phase cancellation that occurs when direct sound is combined with reflected sound. A series of evenly spaced "nulls" occurs when the extra distance traveled by the reflected sound is equal to a 180-degree phase shift.

combo Abbreviation of combination, meaning a combination in one cabinet of an instrument amplifier and speaker system.

comp-lim Short for compressor-limiter. A processor that can perform both compression and limiting.

components (1) Loudspeaker parts: drive-units, horns, adaptors, etc. (2) Electronic and electrical building-block items: diodes, coils, capacitors, relays, resistors, etc.

compression Squeezing the dynamic range by reducing peaks and troughs in sound level, making loud sounds quieter and/or quieter sounds louder. An effect often used on individual signals (tightening up vocals or basslines) or whole mixes (increasing the overall level without clipping/ distortion).

compressor Sound processor that can be set to smooth dynamic range and thus minimize sudden leaps in volume. Overall perceived loudness is in this way increased without "clipping."

concert pitch Standardized instrument tuning used in most Western music (at least since 1960) where the A above middle C has a fundamental frequency of 440Hz. This can be measured using an electronic tuner or checked against a tuning fork.

condenser mike Popularly used though technically less accurate name for a capacitor microphone.

conductor Something that allows electricity to pass easily through it (in other words it allows its electrons to move around freely from atom to atom), presenting low resistance.

Good conductors include metal and water.

conductor wires Wires attached to the start and finish of a pickup coil which take the output signal to the controls.

cone Front, moving part of a loudspeaker drive-unit – normally round, usually black, and made of papier-maché or plastic, or else silvery and made of metal foil. It vibrates very precisely to turn electrical signals back into soundwaves.

console Another name for mixer, console, board, or mixing desk.

control room Separate area in recording studio with monitor speakers, mixing desk (and production team).

cord (UK: lead) Cable to supply unit with power, to connect amps and speakers, or to connect instruments and amps.

coulomb (symbol: C) Unit of electric charge – one coulomb-per-second is a current of one ampere.

coupling Exchange of mechanical energy between an instrument's string(s) and soundboard.

CPS Cycles per second. Same as Hertz, the unit of frequency.

crossover (1) Unit that splits a signal into two or more complementary frequency ranges, for instance sending low frequency sounds to the bass drivers and remaining mid and trebly sounds to the mid and HF drivers. Active or electronic crossover uses powered electronics to provide refined filters and other signal processing capabilities, producing a better result than passive crossovers, which are simpler, and powered from signal itself. (2) Central region of a signal (as seen on an oscilloscope) where a

wave passes through zero and changes polarity (alternates). It is something that happens many tens, hundreds, or thousands of times a second with sound signals. Some circuits and equipment can develop distortion in this area. (3) Form or style of music that straddles genres.

crossover distortion Horribly graunchy distortion caused by bad or sick amplifier circuits. Has nothing to do with speaker crossovers.

crosstalk Signal leakage from one channel to others (as on a mixer). current Flow of electrons in an electrical circuit, measured in amps.

current draw Current taken by gear from the main power supply.

CW Clockwise. Usually equates to "turning up" a control knob.

cycle One whole wave or single vibration of a signal, from maximum in one direction, through zero, to maximum in the other, and back to zero. Can be audio, RF, or AC electrical. One cycle per second is expressed as 1Hz.

D

DAC Abbreviation for a digital-to-analog converter or interface.

DAT Digital audio tape.

dB Decibel. Unit of measure used to describe relative levels (of sound, voltages, etc), or absolute levels if used with certain suffixes that specify a reference point (see *dB SPL*, *dBu*, etc).

dB SPL Scale of sound pressure levels where 0dB SPL is the lower threshold of human hearing.

DC Direct current. In theory a rock-steady voltage, as from an ideal battery. In practice, it may vary in time (with ripple, noise, discharge) but should maintain a constant polarity. Tube (valve) amps use DC voltages for the vast portion of their internal operation.

DC resistance Direct current resistance. Meaurement (in ohms) often in pickup specs for relative output.

DDL Short for digital delay line. Signal processor that creates delay/echo FX.

decay Gradual drop in level of a sound or signal. For some sounds it starts as soon as the "attack" has peaked.

de-esser Dynamics processor that reduces sibilance on vocal signals, or compresses the HF part of a signal.

delay (1) Effect added to instrument or voice to create either a thick, doubled-up effect, or a more pronounced echo. (2) Unwanted processing delay in digital electronics, otherwise known as latency, which can be maddeningly long. Can also occur in analog electronics, but usually only on the edge of audibility as it's measured in millionths of a second.

desk See *board*.

DI Abbreviation of direct injection. Means of isolating, adjusting and balancing a line-level instrument signal (from keyboards, guitars, etc) so it can be connected to a recording mixer at a suitable level and without creating buzzes.

digital System of transmitting or storing information (including sound) as a series of numbers. Since 1980 has been gradually replacing "traditional" analog systems in many music-related applications, despite early concerns about loss of sound quality, particularly at extremes of frequency ranges, and problems with unwanted delays (latency). Advantages include accuracy, memory, and automation facilities, and a clean, low-hiss delivery.

digital modeling See *modeling amp*.

diode Electronic component used within some guitar amps as a solid-state rectifier to convert AC current to DC. Also occasionally used in solid-state overdrive circuits. See also *rectifier*.

direct injection See *DI*.

directivity (1) Angular sound dispersion of a drive unit or whole cab that usually must be specified (in degrees horizontal and vertical) at different frequencies. (2) Map of "reception strength" for a mike or pickup device. In all cases the change in sound level is progressive, so the line is drawn usually where the level has dropped by 6dB (that is by 50 per cent).

dissipation Power lost as heat.

distortion (1) Corruption or deviation from the original, preceding, or intended signal, however introduced into the system. Sometimes used deliberately to create harsher, grittier, or sweeter and more compressed sound. (2) "Fuzz" effect deliberately created by using an FX unit (usually on electric guitar).

dog-ear Nickname for some P-90 pickups, derived from the shape of the mounting lugs on the cover. See also *soap-bar*.

drain (1) Another name for the bare wire that makes connection with the foil shield inside some signal cables. (2) One of two main terminals on a MOSFET. (3) Slang for an earthing/grounding point or terminal.

dreadnought Large flat-top acoustic guitar designed by Frank H. Martin and Harry Hunt and named for a type of large British battleship. Now used to describe any acoustic of this body style.

dry Slang for signal without reverb (or any other effect). Consequent opposite is "wet".

DSP Digital signal processing. The digital engine behind digital crossovers, processors, and FX.

duct tape (UK: gaffer tape) Very adhesive cloth tape used for sticking down cables, fixing microphone stands, eliminating rattling noises, and silencing hostages. Generally recognized as one of the few things holding the music industry together.

dust cap Slang term for the domed center of a loudspeaker driver.

dynamic mike Common, rugged, versatile, low-cost kind of mike that uses "dynamo" (motor) principles. (Not related to signal dynamics.) It's also known as a moving-coil mike because a small coil inside is vibrated by soundwaves and, thanks to electro-magnetic induction, creates an electrical signal.

dynamic range Difference in dBs between the maximum output level before clip (say +20dBu) and the noise floor, where signals disappear (say -80dBu). In this example it's 100dB.

dynamics Expression in music using a range of volume (intensity) shifts.

earth See *ground*.

earth loop See *ground loop*.

ebony Dense, black hardwood used for guitar fingerboards and bridges.

E-Bow Electronic handheld device to induce guitar string vibration and thus

sustain notes (indefinitely if needed).

echo Repetitions of a signal, with gradual reduction in volume, recreating the reflective acoustics of, for example, a large cave, canyon, or stone building.

effects (effects units, FX) Generic term for audio processing devices such as distortions, delays, reverbs, flangers, phasers, harmonizers, and so on.

effects loop Connections from and back to mixer or guitar amp that allow FX to operate on selected signals.

electret mike Lesser type of capacitor mike. Doesn't require phantom power, but uses a battery.

electric Guitarists' shorthand/slang for electric guitar.

electro-acoustic (electro) Acoustic guitar with built-in pickup, usually of piezo-electric type. The guitar usually has a preamp and includes volume and tone controls.

electron tube See *tube*.

EQ See *equalization*.

equalization (EQ) Filters, resonators, and other devices (either analog electronic circuits or digital realisations) that alter tone/tonal/timbral qualities by cutting and/or boosting certain frequencies. Simplest are just treble and bass controls with limited adjustment, operating at fixed frequencies (mixers usually have at least three, with a mid control); more complex are variable parametric units. (See also 'graphic').

European spruce Sometimes called German spruce, picea abies tends to come from the Balkans. Spruce originally meant "from Prussia." Used for some acoustic guitar soundboards.

F

fader Slider volume control, mainly on mixers. Used rather than rotary knobs to enable several to be moved at once.

fan-strutting Wooden struts beneath lower soundboard of guitar, arranged approximately in the shape of an open fan.

feedback Howling noise produced by leakage of the output of an amplification system back into its input, typically a guitar's pickup(s). Jimi did it best.

female Connector designed to receive the pins/prongs of a "male" plug.

FET Field effect transistor. May be J-FET or MOSFET type. See *transistor*.

figure 8 Visual analogue of mike response pattern where its pickup sensitivity is the same at the front as at the back, but lower at the two sides.

fill Speaker used to "fill" an area with sound that wouldn't be covered otherwise.

filter Circuit or digital process that allows parts of a signal at certain frequencies to pass unchanged while rejecting or reducing others.

filter cap Component in power supply circuit that allows AC ripple voltage remaining after rectification to drain off to ground while blocking DC voltage.

fixed bias In guitar amps, a technique for biasing output tubes using a pot to adjust negative voltage on the tube's grid as compared to its cathode. (The name is somewhat misleading as "fixed-bias" amps generally have a bias which is adjustable, whereas cathode-biased amps are set and non-adjustable.) See *cathode biased*.

flat-top Acoustic guitar with flat top (as opposed to arched) and usually with a round soundhole.

14-fret Refers to the point at which a type of flat-top acoustic guitar's neck joins the body (and not the total number of frets).

frequency Number of cycles of a sound or electrical (or any) vibration occurring per unit of time; the perceived pitch of a sound. In music, what we hear as pitch is partly "frequency sensation". See also *Hertz*.

frequency response How sound (acoustic) and signal (electrical) levels vary across the audible range of frequencies, and beyond.

FX Shorthand for effects. Also known more formally as signal processors – boxes that can be used creatively and artistically to alter sound.

G

gaffer tape See *duct tape*.

gain Amount of increase or change in signal level. When dBs are used, increased gain is shown as +dB; reduction is shown –dB; and no change as 0dB.

gain structure "Map" of gains showing by how much levels are boosted and/or cut through a mixer, and the cumulative results for typical fader positions.

gate (1) Sound-dynamics processing device that can "clean up" signal feeds by muting the feed when the required signal is absent or too small to be useful (for muting low-level background noise, say, during quiet passages). Can be triggered by the required signal or others. Can also be used to create sound effects. (2) Any signal that triggers another device.

gauge Outer diameter of guitar string, always measured in thousandths of an inch (.009", .042" etc). Strings are supplied in particular gauges and/or in sets of matched gauges. Guitar fretwire is also offered in different gauges, or sizes.

gig Live musical event, man.

graphic Short for graphic equaliser. Type of EQ device with individual faders (from four or five to 30 or more) for adjusting the levels of various pre-determined frequency bands. The physical fader positions result in a visual "graphic" representation of the adjustments made.

greenback Describes a particularly desirable Celestion 12" guitar-amp speaker that had a green magnet-cover.

ground (UK etc: earth) Connection between an electrical circuit or device and the ground. A common neutral reference point in an electrical circuit. All electrical components (and shielding) within electric guitars, amplifiers, signal processors, etc, must be linked to earth as the guitar's pickups and electrics are susceptible to noise interference.

ground loop (earth loop) Problem caused by circular or multiple-looped connection of ground conductors. If two or more pieces of grounded equipment are cabled together result can be audible mains hum or buzzing.

ground wire Wire connected from guitar's vibrato, bridge, tailpiece, switch, pickup cover, grounding plate, etc, to ground.

grounding plate Metal baseplate of guitar pickup connected to ground (earth).

group (1) Bunch of channels or signals brought together on a mixer for easier collective manipulation. (2) Fader that controls such a group. (3) Band of musicians/performers, and not a cross word between them.

grunge tuning Tuning all strings down one half step (one semitone) for a fatter sound.

H

hard-disc recording Method of recording to the hard-disc of a computer using specialist software (Pro Tools, Logic Audio, Cakewalk, etc) or specialist hardware (Otari Radar, etc).

harmonic(s) (1) In sonic terms, part of any instrument's overall voice. Spurious added timbres or notes that are often musically related (by intervals) to the sounds causing them. (1) In guitar terms, ringing, high-pitched note produced by touching (rather than fretting) strategic points on string(s) while plucked, most noticeably at the fifth, seventh and 12th fret.

harmonic distortion "Ordinary" distortion occurring in analog (audio) electronics, speakers, and mikes, involving the generation of harmonics.

Hertz (Hz) Cycles per second (CPS), the unit of frequency. (Named after Heinrich Hertz, 19th-century German physicist and pioneer of signal transmission using radio waves.) There is a direct relationship between Hertz and audible pitch: the higher the fundamental frequency of a note, the higher its pitch. So 440Hz is the fundamental frequency of the note A (above middle C) at "concert pitch", while an A an octave higher has a fundamental frequency of 880Hz (double). See *octave*.

HF High frequency (treble, top end).

In sonic terms, usually refers to the frequency range above about 5kHz.

hi-fi Abbreviation of high fidelity. Sound systems with negligible distortion levels and extremely low noise that often treat the owner to flashing lights, exotic features, and designer aesthetics – none of which improves the sound quality, but can still cost a fortune.

high-end (up-market, upscale) High- or higher-cost kit, usually aimed at those seeking the best.

high-Z High impedance. Includes low-grade mikes, pickups, etc. Worth avoiding; if not, connect with short low-capacitance cable. (See *Z*).

hiss White noise, or any random noise where high frequencies dominate.

hot (1) In electrical connections, means live. (2) Used generally to mean powerful, as in "hot pickup."

hot-rodding Making modifications to a guitar, usually its pickups and/or electronics.

hot spot Area in space where an instrument sounds good.

HT Symbol denoting high voltage in amplifier circuits (short for High Tension) and particularly used in the UK. See *B+*.

hum Low-frequency noise, usually associated with AC power frequency interference (around 50/60Hz).

humbucker (humbucking) Noise-canceling twin-coil guitar pickup. Typically the two coils have opposite magnetic polarity and are wired together electrically out-of-phase to produce a sound that we call in-phase. See also *phase*.

hybrid (1) Any piece of gear that combines two or more systems of any kind. (2) Guitar that combines

"traditional" magnetic electric pickups with "acoustic"-sounding piezo-electric pickups.

I

impedance Electrical resistance to the flow of alternating current, measured in Ohms (Ω). A few electric guitars have low-impedance circuits or pickups to match the inputs of recording equipment; the vast majority are high impedance. Impedance matching is important to avoid loss of signal and tone. Also commonly encountered with speakers, where it is important to match a speaker's (or speaker cab's) impedance to that of the amplifier's speaker output (commonly 4Ω, 8Ω or 16Ω).

in-between sound Legendary tone achieved on older Fender Strats fitted with three-way Centralab switch by jamming the switch between settings so that pairs of pickups operate at once. Made easier from early '80s when Fender began fitting five-way versions of the switch to new Strats, a quarter of a century after the original launch.

Indian rosewood Hardwood from tropical evergreen tree, known as East Indian rosewood or Dalbergia latifolia. Used for acoustic guitar bodies, fingerboards, or necks, especially now that Brazilian rosewood is not easily available.

inductance Property met by alternating current flowing in a wire, especially when concentrated in a coil. Involves storage of magnetic energy. Inductance is the opposite of capacitance.

inductor Generic name for a coil.

input channel Strip generally found en-masse on the left portion of a mixer and dealing with individual sound sources rather than groups.

input impedance Loading presented at inputs of signal-handling equipment.

insulation Plastic, cloth or tape wrap, or sheath (non-conductive), around an electrical wire, designed to prevent wire(s) coming into contact with other components and thus shorting the circuit.

integrated circuit Entire circuit of many different electronic parts etched in layers on a pin-head-sized piece of silicon (or other semiconductor).

intonation State of a guitar so that it is as in-tune with itself as physically possible. Usually dependent on setting each string's speaking length by adjusting the point at which the strings cross the bridge saddle, known as intonation adjustment. Some bridges allow more adjustment than others, and therefore greater possibilities for accurate intonation.

J

jack (UK: jack socket) Mono or stereo connecting socket, usually $\frac{1}{4}$" (6.5mm), used to feed guitar's output signal to amplification. (Also in UK an abbreviation of "jackplug", the connector for insertion in such sockets. Also "mini-jacks" appear on some portable and low-tech gear. Jacks in general are not liked by sound engineers because of unreliability and general unsuitability.

jack socket See *jack*.

J-FET Junction field-effect transistor. Unlike a MOSFET, not used for power handling, but as a specialist type of transistor in mixers, pre-amps, radio-mike circuits, etc, either as a discrete part or hidden in the inputs of some widely used ICs.

jumbo Large-bodied flat-top acoustic

guitar. Also a name for special extra-wide, extra-high frets on guitar fingerboard.

K

k Short for kilo. As a prefix it means one thousand, as in kW (1,000 watts), kHz (1,000 hertz), kΩ (1,000 ohms).

key Trigger input of a gate, used for sophisticated triggering. May be frequency-sensitive and level-sensitive.

knee Usually refers to a compressor's compression ratio. For example, hard-knee compression kicks in more dramatically, while soft-knee is smoother in effect.

L

lacquer (UK: nitro-cellulose) Type of guitar finish used commonly in the '50s and '60s but now rarely seen on production guitars.

laminated Joined together in layers; in guitars, usually refers to wood (bodies, necks) or plastic (pickguards).

lavalier Miniature suspended (or clip-on) type of microphone.

lead (1) Shorthand for lead guitar. The main guitar within a group; the one that plays most of the solos and/or riffs. (2) UK term for cord; see *cable*, *cord*.

level Amplitude of a signal; in sound terms, usually equates to volume, intensity, and higher dB figures.

LF Low frequency (bass), usually meaning below 500Hz, down to 20Hz.

limiter Dynamics processor, unit, or circuitry that largely prevents a signal going above a preset level.

linearity Academic term for absence of distortion in audio circuitry. Parts and circuits that cause distortion are said to be non-linear.

live room Acoustically-treated space within a recording studio where the music is performed. It should be acoustically isolated from the outside world and from the control room.

load (1) Something that absorbs electrical power, or into which an electronic signal source is driven (for example, a speaker, or a mixer's input seen by a mike). (2) Total impedance of the several speakers connected to a power amp, etc. (3) Energy consumption of equipment, represented by the current draw at the power intake.

log Short for logarithmic, as used in mathematics and for calculating dBs.

low-pass filter (LPF) Circuit to filter out frequencies above the cut-off frequency, allowing those below to pass through. Potential complement to a high-pass filter.

loudspeaker (speaker, LS) Transducer that converts electrical signals into acoustic soundwaves (in effect, the reverse of a microphone). Term refers either to the complete speaker unit (including cabinet/case) or only the drive-units, or drivers and horns, depending on context.

low-end (down-market, bargain, budget) Low- or lower-cost kit, often aimed at beginners and players on restricted budget.

LPF See *low-pass filter*.

M

m Short for milli, a thousandth part. Used as a prefix, as in mA (milliampere, a thousandth of an amp), mV (a thousandth of a volt).

M Short for Mega, a million. Used as a prefix, as in MHz (megahertz, a million hertz).

mahogany Very stable, medium-weight hardwood favored by most guitar makers for necks and by many for solid bodies.

mains UK term for AC power, as delivered by the electricity supplier to wall outlets in homes, venues, etc.

maple Hard, heavy wood, often displaying extreme figure patterns prized by guitar makers. Varying kinds of figure give rise to visual nicknames: quilted, tigerstripe, curly, flame, etc.

master volume/tone (1) In amplification, a master volume control governs the output level – or operating level of the power section – when partnered with a gain, drive, or volume control that governs the level of the individual preamp(s). (2) On a guitar, a control that affects all pickups equally.

mastering Final process of "polishing" studio mixes to create a production master. It can involve equalization, compression, limiting, and sonic maximization.

MF Short for mid frequency. Wide-ranging term that can cover sound frequencies between around 500Hz to 5kHz (and is often further subdivided into "high-mid," "low-mid," etc).

micro (μ) A millionth part. Used for describing very small electronic component values.

microfarad See *Farad*.

microphonic (1) Used of a guitar pickup, this means one that is inclined to squeal unpleasantly, usually due to incomplete wax saturation, to loose coil windings, or to insecure mountings that create so-called microphonic feedback. (2) Used of a tube, results in a metallic rattling sound set off by vibration from a cranked-up amp.

mid(s) Abbreviation of mid-range.

mid-band Middle of human hearing range, where the ear is most sensitive, typically 500Hz to 5kHz and centering on 1.5kHz or so.

MIDI Musical Instrument Digital Interface. Industry standard for communication of control signals and data between electronic musical gear.

MIDI port MIDI connection socket.

mid-range Refers to middle-band sound frequencies.

mixer Mixing desk, board, or console, where all sound signals are collected and processed, as required. Anything from four channels to several dozen, depending on the size of musical line-up and/or the studio.

mod Abbreviation for modification. Any change or after-market customization made to an instrument or piece of gear.

modeling amp Guitar amplifier using digital technology (occasionally analog solid-state circuitry) to emulate, or model, the sounds of classic tube amps.

monitors (1) Speakers in studio control room for listening to recordings. (2) Specialised speakers pointed at artist(s) to "monitor" performances.

mono Abbreviation of monophonic. Originates from the Greek for "single sound." In sound reproduction, all musical information in a monophonic system is relayed through a single speaker, regardless of its original location in a stereo field.

moving-coil mike See *dynamic*.

multi-track Popularized in the 1950s by Les Paul and now ubiquitous, the multi-track tape machine allows the user to record on individual tracks without erasing previous recordings, so that musical pieces can be built up one or more tracks at a time.

musicality Term meaning "easy to hear" used by musicians before it was taken over by gearheads to describe the sound quality of equipment.

N

Nashville tuning Replacing some of the lowest strings of a guitar with strings tuned an octave higher in order to fill out recorded rhythm parts.

neck pickup Guitar pickup placed nearest the neck. At one time known as the rhythm or bass pickup.

negative feedback See *feedback*.

node Any point of zero vibration amplitude of a vibrating guitar string.

noise Any undesirable sound such as mains hum or interference.

noise-canceling Type of guitar pickup with two coils wired together to cancel noise, often called humbucking. Any arrangement of pickups or pickup coils that achieves this.

noise-gate See *gate*.

non-linear See *linearity*.

nut Bone, metal, or (now usually) synthetic slotted guide bar over which a guitar's strings pass to reach the tuners and which determines string height and spacing at the headstock end of neck.

octave (1) Interval (change of frequency) with a ratio of 2:1 or 1:2. When a sound's frequency is doubled, it and the pitch heard go up by one octave, and when it's halved, it and the pitch drop an octave. Two octaves upwards means a quadrupling (x4) of frequency. Like dBs, this is a ratiometric scale (steps of x2 rather than +2) that suits humanwhen the polarity (or 'phasing') of a signal conflicts with (and tries to cancel) another signal, causing partial or full cancellation if combined. See 'polarity'. sound perception. (2) Musically, a distance of 12 semitones.

ohm (Ω) Unit of electrical resistance and/or impedance.

open back Speaker cabinet with no airtight panel at the rear, thus leaving the speaker magnets exposed. Most commonly seen with combo amps.

open tuning Tuning the guitar to a chord or altered chord, often for slide playing.

oscilloscope (scope) Short for cathode ray oscilloscope. Important visual-based test tool that shows all kinds of signals and waves, from DC and audio to RF waves, on a screen. Analog types work in real time, digital types don't and are inferior for non-steady music-type waveforms.

out of phase (1) State when polarity or phasing of a signal conflicts with (and tries to cancel) another signal, causing partial or full cancellation if combined. See 'polarity'. (2) On electric guitars, audible result of the electrical linking of two coils or two pickups in either series or parallel in such a way as to provide at least partial cancellation of the signal. Usually the low frequencies are cancelled so that the resulting sound is thin, lacking in warmth, and often quite brittle. To create an audible result that is in-phase (for example of two coils within a humbucker) the coils must be linked electrically out-of-phase. Phase relationship also depends on polarity of the magnets. See also *humbucker*.

pad Switchable attenuator, used to drop ("pad out") excess level.

PAF Gibson pickup with Patent Applied For decal (sticker) on base, originally fixed to the first Gibson humbucker.

pan Left and right speaker output "balance" control on a mixer.

pan pot Short for panoramic control potentiometer. Knob fader that rotates between two paths, apportioning signals to the left and right.

parametric Short for parametric equaliser. EQ device that allows the most precise control over a sound's tonal quality, through three main adjustable parameters: gain (boost/cut); frequency; and Q (which controls the breadth of the affected frequency range).

parallel Electrical circuit that has all the positive points joined together and all the negative points joined together. If we consider that a single-coil guitar pickup has a positive (live, hot) and negative (ground, earth) output, when for example two single-coil pickups on a Stratocaster (position two and four on a five-way switch) are selected together, they are linked in parallel. Can also apply to the parallel linking of resistors or capacitors in a circuit, etc. See also *series*.

passive Normal, unboosted, non-powered circuit.

Patent Applied For *See* PAF. Also slang term for amplifier turned up to maximum.

P Bass Common abbreviation for Fender's Precision Bass and similar models.

PCB Printed circuit board. Thin insulating sheet covered with conducting interconnections and electronic components that all solid-state and even most tube-based circuitry is built upon. Employed in majority of guitar amplifiers, other than those that employ expensive hand-wired designs.

peak (1) Highest value. The transitory peak level of a signal (seen as wave's tip on oscilloscope) as opposed to the highest "RMS" value, which is averaged out over time. These can differ by a factor of 1.5 to ten times in sound signals. (2) Highest point of a frequency response or EQ curve, where boost is greatest.

peak limiting Academic term for clipping.

peaking out See *clipping*.

pentode Tube containing five functional elements. Most output tubes in guitar amplifiers are pentodes. Also see *triode*.

PFL Pre-fade(r) listen. Button on mixer that enables selected channel's signal to be monitored, regardless of whether the channel's fader is up or down.

phantom power 48-volt DC power from the mixer or mike splitter provided to a suitable mike.

phase Timing of two signals relative to one another, expressed in degrees. A complete waveform cycle of a particular frequency is 360 degrees, so if two identical signals at the same frequency are 180 degrees out-of-phase, they'll cancel each other out. Can be compared to but shouldn't be confused with polarity. See also *out of phase*.

phasiness Describes the highly-colored sound from two or more speaker cabs interacting to create an unpleasantly spikey "comb filtered" response (so-called because the frequency response is seen to have numerous close-spaced peaks and troughs, like a comb's teeth).

phone plug (UK: jackplug) Plug with a quarter-inch diameter barrel.

phono plug See *RCA plug*.

pick (plectrum, flat pick) Small piece of (usually) plastic or metal – and in olden times tortoiseshell – that is used to pluck or strum a guitar's strings.

pickguard (UK: scratchplate) Protective panel raised above or fitted flush to a guitar's body.

piezo pickup (piezo-electric pickup) "Acoustic" guitar pickup that senses string and body movement. "Piezo-loaded saddles" are bridge saddles with an integral piezo elelment.

pink noise Random noise (sounds like a waterfall) similar in character to music, with most of the power in the low end. Used technically for endurance-testing of amplifiers and speakers.

pitch Frequency of a note. Perceived "lowness" or "highness" of a sound.

plectrum See *pick*.

P-90 Model name for early Gibson single-coil pickup.

point-to-point Method of constructing hand-wired amplifier circuits where individual components are connected directly to one another without the use of a circuit board.

polarity (1) Opposing negative or positive "halves" that all analog and some digital signals have. (2) Arbitrary labelling of opposite sides (180 degrees different) of balanced signal and also speaker connections as "hot" and "cold" and "+" and "−" Commonly called phase, but true phase (shifts) can assume any value in degrees, while polarity only "knows" 0 (zero) and 180 degrees. A full cycle, from positive to negative and back again, happens over 360 degrees, so if two identical signals have opposite polarities they will be exactly 180 degrees out of step with one another – which has the same effect as being directly "out-of-phase", in other words they'll cancel one another out. This is why polarity and phase are often used synonymously, though they're only interchangeable when the signals are musically simple, such as sine waves. (3) The magnetic polarity of a guitar pickup refers to the north or south orientation of the magnetic field as presented to the strings.
polar pattern/diagram/plot Nothing to do with signal polarity; this is the 3D response pattern of a speaker or mike in the horizontal or vertical plane.

polepieces Non-magnetic (but magnetically conductive) polepieces are used to control, concentrate, and/or shape a guitar pickup's magnetic field. Can be either adjustable (screw) or non-adjustable (slug) as in an original Gibson humbucker. Magnetic polepieces are those where the magnet itself is aimed directly at the strings, as in an original Stratocaster single-coil.

popshield See *windshield*.

pot Short for potentiometer. (1) Variable electrical resistor that alters voltage by a spindle turning on an electrically resistive track and used for guitar volume and tone controls, etc. Most variable controls (volume knobs, etc) on analog gear use pots. Technically not the knob itself, though often erroneously used as such.

power (symbol: P) Rate at which energy is expended, wasted, transferred, or absorbed, measured in watts, and defined in electrical terms as voltage multiplied by current (V×I).

power amp Output stage of a guitar amplifier that converts preamp signal to signal capable of driving a speaker. In a tube amp, this is where the big tubes live.

power supply Electrical circuit that converts power AC voltage into DC voltage at the required level.

PPM (1) Peak program meter. Original and best peak reading "needle meter," rather oddly scaled 0 to 7, though others exist with own specifications and dB scales. (2) Parts per million. Used when measuring distortion, noise, or other signal contamination.

preamp Short for pre-amplifier. (1) Circuit designed to boost low-level signals to a standard level and EQ them before they're sent towards the power amp (hence "pre-amplifier") for full amplification. (2) Guitar circuit usually powered by battery that converts the pickup's output from high to low impedance (preamp/buffer) and can increase the output signal and boost or cut specific frequencies for tonal effect. Also, the first gain stage in a guitar amp, which generally also includes the EQ circuitry and any overdrive-generating stages.

pre-fade(r) Signal feed taken from a mixer before the volume fader.

pressed top Arched top (usually laminated) of hollowbody guitar made by machine-pressing rather than hand-carving.

project studio Recording studio or programming room set up in a garage, spare bedroom, loft, etc. Usually based on a hard-disc recording system plus a small selection of effects units.

proximity effect (1) In microphones,

the bass boost and popping that occur when you get up close. (2) In closely-spaced speaker cables, high current peaks that cause the cable's resistance to increase dynamically.

pull/push pot Combination guitar-circuit component offering the functions of both a volume/tone pot and a mini-toggle (usually of DPDT type) switch. See also *push-pull*.

push-pull Using two identical power devices (in power amps) or drive-units (in cabs) working oppositely, meaning 180 degrees "out-of-phase" with one another. Done to provide more power and/or lower distortion. The most common power amp format in guitar amps that contain more than one output tube. In a push-pull driver the diaphragm is attracted to one side at the same time as being repelled by the other, producing a more linear, less distorted response. See also *pull/push pot.*

Q "Sharpness" of a bell type (frequency-specific) equalizer, corresponding to the resonant frequency of a resonator. High Q (stronger filter resonance) reduces the affected signal to a narrow frequency range around a selected point; low Q (less filter resonance) means the affected range is wider around the central, peak point.

quarter-inch (phone plug; UK: jackplug) Term derived from diameter of commonly-used plug/connector. May be mono (TS, tip & sleeve connections) or stereo (TRS, tip, ring & sleeve). In the metric world, that would be 6.35mm.

quarter-sawn Wood cut on radius of tree so that "rings" are perpendicular to

the surface of the plank. Structurally preferable to flat-sawn wood for guitar building.

rackmount Gear that's designed to be fitted into standard 19"-wide racks.

RCA plug/jack (UK: phono plug) Named for US company that first developed it in late 1930s, specifically for VHF (RF) use. Long superseded technically, it's still a budget recording-gear fave, though shunned by pros.

rectifier Diode (solid-state or tube) dedicated to converting AC power to DC, as it passes current in a forward direction only.

resistance Impediment to the flow of electrical current through a wire in a DC circuit (or soundwaves through the air or other material). In AC circuits it is combined with reactance to create impedance. Can be calculated by dividing the voltage across a device by the current running through it ($R = V \div I$).

resistor Electrical component which introduces a known value of resistance (measured in ohms) to the electrical flow in a circuit.

resonance (1) Vibration (intentional or otherwise) of anything in the musical environment that can have an impact on what an audience ultimately hears. Natural, sustaining oscillation can occur in musical instruments, speakers, cabs, and rooms, and in circuits (such as EQs). Also synthesised by drum machines, keyboards, synths, etc. Desirable in musical instruments; sometimes desirable (a bit) in EQs and rooms;

undesirable almost everywhere else.

resonant frequency Frequency at which any object vibrates most with the least stimulation.

resonator Generic term for guitar that has metal resonator(s) in its body, designed to increase volume.

retrofit Any component added to an instrument or piece of gear after it leaves the place where it was made (retrofit pickup, vibrato, tuner, etc) and (usually) one that can be fitted directly with no alterations to the original.

reverb (reverberation) (1) Natural reflections of sound off hard surfaces, creating a room's distinctive acoustic ambience. (2) Same effect imitated electronically, generally by the installation of a spring unit in guitar amps, or digitally in pedals and studio effects units.

rhythm section Instruments that provide rhythmic backing to a piece of music. Usually means at least the drums (and/or percussion) and bassline, but may also include chordal guitar, piano. Originally a jazz term; now used elsewhere too.

ribbon mike Uses a piece of very fine (ribbon-like) metal foil suspended in a magnetic field. Good at capturing nuances of sound, especially vocals, but its delicacy makes it less than ideal for knockabout or outdoor gigs.

ripple Sawtooth wave with buzzy sound and 100/120Hz fundamental frequency. Occurs in most AC/DC power supplies.

RMS Root-mean-square. True average measurement of an ever-changing music signal, be it expressed in volts, amperes, dB, etc. Simple averaging of a complex signal gives wrong results.

rosewood Variegated hardwood traditionally used for acoustic guitar backs, sides, and fingerboards. Brazilian or Rio is most highly prized; Indian more common.

rumble Low-frequency vibration and noise, usually physical or mechanical rather than electronic, such as traffic, trains, thunder, air-conditioning fans.

S

sag Slight drop in power supply of a guitar amplifier (particularly noticeable in designs comprising tube rectifiers) when a powerful note or chord is played, producing a compression-like softening and squeezing of the signal.

saturation (1) When a sound system is driven into compression and/or clipping. (2) When transistors reach their "end stops," passing the most current that can be forced. (3) When a magnetic core (inside inductors, transformers) is likewise "flooded out".

scallop Gentle sloping of sides of acoustic guitar's internal bracing for lightness and tonal modification. Also describes mid-'80s fad for scooping out guitar fingerboard between frets, allegedly to assist speedy playing. Very nice fried.

schematic (diagram, plan) Electronic circuit drawing.

scratch test To verify if a pickup on a guitar plugged into an amp is working by gently rubbing ("scratching") the tip of a screwdriver on the pickup's polepieces and listening for sound.

semi-acoustic (semi-solid, semi) Electric guitar with wholly or partly hollow thin body. Originally referred specifically to an electric guitar with a solid wooden block running down the center of thinline body, such as Gibson's ES-335.

sensitivity Amount of input voltage needed to achieve a given output level. Low sensitivity means more volts are needed. For speakers (only), sensitivity is also a partial measure of efficiency.

separation (1) Sonic/electrical isolation between, say, left and right stereo signal paths, or adjacent mixer channels, to minimize "crosstalk." (2) Physical separation of instruments and performers, to minimize "spill."

series Electrical linkage of positive and negative points within an electrical circuit with additive effect – for example, the two pickup coils within a guitar's series-wired humbucker. In this instance, the total resistance of a series-wired humbucker is the sum of the resistance of each coil. Parallel linkage of the same two coils results in the resistance being one quarter of the sum total. Generally, the higher the resistance, the "darker" the resulting tone. Also applies to method of linkage of capacitors or resistors within an amplifier or other electrical circuit. See *parallel*.

set neck (glued neck, glued-in neck, fixed neck) Type of guitar neck/body joint popularized by Gibson that permanently sets the two main components together, usually by gluing.

shock-mount Device for reducing the transmission of shock and vibration, in an amp, etc. Generally a section of rubber with threaded (metal) couplings attached to each end.

sibilance Harsh, high-frequency distortion, especially on vocals (sounds like bad lisping), often due to poor mike technique, mike placement, or mixing. Also caused by HF driver's distortion, or after mike-diaphragm damage.

signal Transmitted electrical information – for example between control circuits, or guitar and amplifier. The transmission is usually achieved by means of a connecting wire or cord (lead).

silverface Fender guitar amps with silver control panels, generally produced between 1968 and the late '70s and considered somewhat inferior tonally to earlier "blackface" versions, though often still very good amps by today's standards. See also *blackface*, *brownface*.

single-coil Original guitar pickup type with a single coil of wire that is wrapped around (a) magnet(s).

single-ended Amplifier in which the power tube – usually just one – operates through the entire cycle of the signal. Such amps are necessarily, therefore, class A. Classic examples include the Fender Champ and the Vox AC4.

sitka spruce (picea sitchensis) Large conifer, originally from North America, popularly used for soundboards on acoustic guitars, especially by US makers.

slide Metal or glass tube worn over a guitarist's finger to produce glissando effects. Also, the style of playing using these effects; thus, "Did Lowell like to play slide?" See also *bottleneck*.

soapbar Nickname for variant of P-90 pickup with cover that has no mounting "ears". See *dog-ear*.

solid-state Where all the active (amplifying, rectifying) components of a circuit are solid (transistors, chips, etc).

sonic maximization Computer process designed to increase the apparent loudness of music, often applied at mixing stage.It identifies transient peaks and attenuates them by a user-defined amount; the overall level of the music is then boosted back to the digital maximum. Part of current obsession with loudness over quality.

S/PDIF Sony/Philips standard for a digital connection on CD players, etc, using either ordinary RCA (phono) or superior Canare (BNC) connectors.

speaker See *loudspeaker*.

speaking length Sounding length of a guitar's string: the part running from the nut down to the bridge saddle.

spike Another name for transient.

spill/spillage Unwanted external sounds picked-up by a microphone.

SPL Sound pressure level (in deciBels). Measure of sound intensity, analogous to the voltage level of the signal.

splitter (box) Dividing device that ideally isolates signals going off to different places, with minimal interaction.

spruce Soft, light hardwood used for the soundboard on many acoustic guitars.

stereo Short for stereophonic. (1) Using left and right channels to reproduce improved dimensional sound (nearer to 3D at best) rather than single-channel mono(phonic). (2) Any two-channel equipment, whether used for left-and-right signals or not.

string length Sounding length of string, measured from nut to bridge saddle.

subsonic Frequencies below normal audibility (less than about 20Hz). Widely used in dance music.

sustain (1) Length of time a guitar string vibrates. (2) Purposeful elongation of a musical sound, either by playing technique or electronic processing.

synthesizer Electronic instrument for sound creation, using analog techniques (oscillators, filters, amplifiers) or digital techniques (FM or harmonic synthesis, sample-plus-synthesis etc). Preset synthesizers offer a selection of pre-programmed sounds which cannot be varied; programmable types allow the user also to vary and store new sounds. Guitar synthesizers at first attempted to build much of the required circuitry into the guitar itself, but the trend is to synth-access systems.

T

tapped pickup See *coil-tap*.

THD Total harmonic distortion.

timbre Tone quality, or "color," or "flavor" of a sound.

top (soundboard, plate) Vibrating face of (usually acoustic) guitar.

tracking up Recording multiple takes of the same musical part to create a "big" sound. Often used with power chords, backing vocals, and acoustic guitars.

tranny Short for "transistorized." Nickname given to solid-state circuitry or equipment.

transducer Unit that converts one form of energy to another. For example, a microphone changes soundwaves into electrical signals; a speaker does the reverse. For guitars, sometimes used generically for piezo-electric pickups, but technically applies to any type of pickup, loudspeaker, etc. See *piezo pickup*.

transformer Fundamental electrical/electronic component. It can change voltages and impedances up or down, and provides isolation, balanced connections, etc, without affecting frequency – as used in an AC adaptor, which transforms high-voltage AC mains current into low-voltage DC for powering some electrical gear. Also used in mikes and DI boxes to create balanced signal, and in preamps to unbalance the signal after its journey along the cable. Also, this is sometimes used as a general term for power supply.

transient Sudden, steep, shortlived change or burst in any signal or waveform, musical or otherwise.

transistor Basic semiconductor component that can amplify signals. Invented '40s as smaller, more reliable alternative to tube. Two main types: bi-polar junction transistor (BJT); field-effect transistor (FET or MOSFET).

treble-bleed cap Simple guitar circuit where capacitor (sometimes plus additional resistor) is attached to volume control pot and thus retains high frequencies when the volume control is turned down.

treble pickup See *bridge pickup*.

tremolo (tremolo arm, tremolo system, trem) Musical definition of tremolo is the rapid repetition of a note or notes. (1) Erroneous but much-used term for vibrato device/system. (2) Fender amplifier effect: regular variation in the sound's volume.

triode Tube containing three functional elements, and most common in the preamp circuits of guitar amplifiers in the form of "dual triodes," tubes which contain two triodes in a single glass bottle.

tube (UK: valve) Abbreviation of electron(ic) vacuum tube. In a guitar amp, a tube amplifies the input signal by regulating the flow of electrons.

tweed Linen material used primarily by Fender (but also some other makers) to cover guitar cases and amplifier cabinets, originally in the '50s. Now generally used to define an amp from that period (such as a '59 Bassman), or the sonic characteristics produced by such amps, or the emulation of such characteristics in modern amps.

tweeter High-frequency speaker.

12-fret Refers to the point at which a type of flat-top acoustic guitar's neck joins the body (and not the total number of frets).

twisted pair Audio cable pair arranged (by twisting) to reject hum and RF noise fields when used with balanced outputs and inputs.

U (1U, 2U, 3U, etc) Standardized measurement of rack-unit height: 1U = 1 3/4″ (44.45mm).

unbalanced (1) Single-sided circuit or connection, usually as in a cable/cord that has a sole central signal wire and uses the ground shield to double as the second signal wire. (2) Disabled balanced circuit.

unity gain What goes in comes out at the same level. A gain of x1 – in other words no change.

V

valve Short for "thermionic valve." British term for electron tube. See *tube*.

V-FET Old term for a MOSFET transistor.

VHF Very high frequency. Could be RF or audio above 10kHz. Frequencies in this band used for radio-mikes.

vibrato (arm, slush lever, trem, tremolo, tremolo arm, vibrato bridge, vibrato system, wang bar, whammy) Guitar bridge and/or tailpiece which alters the pitch of the strings when the attached arm is moved. Vibrato is the technically correct term because it means a regular variation in pitch. Also refers to similar-sounding electronic effect in an amp.

volt (V) Unit of electrical "pressure" or

electromotive force/energy. Voltage equals current multiplied by resistance (V = IR) for DC circuits.

voltage Amount of energy carried by a charge as it flows in a circuit or wire.

VU Volume unit. Swing-needle meter responding to average signal levels, ignoring peaks and spikes but giving a good idea of subjective loudness.

Watt (symbol: W) Unit of electrical power. Commonly defines output of guitar amps, power-handling capabilities of speakers, etc. Technically, the rate that energy is transferred (or work is done) over time, equal to a certain amount of horsepower, or joules per second. Named for James Watt, British steam-power pioneer.

wavelength Distance between identical points on a wave cycle.

western red cedar Not a cedar at all, but Thuya plicata, the North American arbor vitae, a conifer. First used as a guitar soundboard material by classical maker José Ramírez III and now used by many classical (and some flat-top) builders.

wet Sound with an effect added (especially reverb). See also *dry*.

white noise Naturally-produced random noise. Sounds more trebly and/or hissy than pink noise.

windshield (popshield) Protective cover, built into most stage mikes or may be a removable (spongy) accessory. It will transmit most sound while preventing damage and unwanted noise such as wind and explosive breath from close-up vocal action.

wolf note (wolf tone, dead note) Note with a sound unpleasantly different from or less resonant than those around it. Much affected by instrument construction, and can be indicative of a minor flaw in a guitar

X

X-brace Pattern of acoustic guitar's internal bracing in an X shape.

XLR (XLR3, Cannon) Three-pin plug or jack (socket) named for its connections (eXternal, Live, Return). The standard audio connector for mike, line, and many speaker-level jobs.

Y

Y-lead splitter (or combiner) cord/cable. Most common type is female XLR to two male XLRs, to drive two inputs, but may also consist of quarter-inch connectors.

Z Symbol for impedance. Why? Impedance is measured in ohms, for which the symbol is Ω, or omega, the last letter of the Greek alphabet. And the last letter of the English alphabet is Z.

zero level This doesn't in fact mean "nothing." Rather, it is a starting-point – which can be arbitrary or standardized – from which the levels above it and below it are measured.

On the CD

THE RECORDINGS

Most of the recordings for this CD were made in the author's kitchen. Apologies in advance to all those readers with bat-like hearing who will certainly detect the occasional truck, refrigerator click, and passing aircraft. I hope you will agree that it all adds to the atmosphere. Other recordings were made by Javier Ortiz at Estudio Brazil in Madrid, Spain.

No attempt has been made to enhance these recordings using equalization, compression, or any other studio trickery. The intention is to provide the reader with raw sounds directly from the microphone that most effectively demonstrate the various techniques described in the text.

All the recordings at the author's house were made with a pair of Telefunken/Siemens V72 tube microphone preamps. Signals were sent to hard-disc via Apogee analog-to-digital converters. At Estudio Brazil, Javier used the microphone preamps in his Harrison console, and Apogee analog-to-digital converters.

Unless otherwise noted, all instruments were played by Rod Fogg (see page 176).

TRACKS ON THE CD

Illustrating chapter 1

TRACK 1. A sine wave.
TRACK 2. The harmonic series, starting with a guitar's open A-string.
TRACK 3. A square wave.

Illustrating chapter 2

These three tracks were recorded using a 1962 Fender Stratocaster (fiesta red) through a 1962 Vox AC-10 (copper-top). All microphones were placed slightly off the center of the speaker.

TRACK 4. Shure SM57 moving-coil microphone.
TRACK 5. Neumann U67 tube microphone.
TRACK 6. Coles 4038 ribbon microphone.

The next three tracks illustrate the effect of microphone position. This time the same Strat is played through a '50s tweed Fender Deluxe with a slightly distorting 12 speaker. The microphone used was a Shure SM57.

TRACK 7. Microphone pointed directly into the center.
TRACK 8. Microphone halfway between center and edge.
TRACK 9. Microphone at edge.
TRACK 10. Neumann U67 mike sweeping from the edge of the speaker to the center and back again. Listen for the high-frequency change in the hiss. It's quite dramatic when you consider that the microphone is only traveling five inches.

The next five tracks feature a high-gain distorted guitar sound close miked with a U67 and an SM57 placed together, firing directly at the center of a speaker cone. An Eggle guitar in dropped-D tuning with a Seymour Duncan humbucker was played through a Soldano preamp and a Mesa/Boogie power amp. A Marshall cabinet was used with two vintage 30W Celestion speakers. These five tracks were recorded by Javier Ortiz at Estudio Brazil in Madrid, Spain.

TRACK 11. Close microphones only.
Track 12. Close microphones combined with ambient microphone placed 20 feet in front of the cabinet and 15 feet in the air.
TRACK 13. Close microphones combined with ambient microphone placed 30 feet away from the cabinet in a corner.
TRACK 14. Close microphones combined with ambient microphone placed 10 feet away from the cabinet and directly in front.
TRACK 15. As 14, but time adjusted to minimize "comb filtering" effect.

Illustrating chapter 3

For the next two examples, Rod Fogg played his 1965 Fender Strat (sunburst) through the Vox AC-10.

TRACK 16. A Shure SM57 and a Neumann U67 are placed as close together as possible at an equal distance from a single speaker on the AC-10. First you will hear the SM57, then the U67, and last both microphones combined.
TRACK 17. A Shure SM57 and a Neumann U67 are placed at equal distances from individual speakers on the AC-10. You will hear the SM57 on its own with the U67 gradually fading in with opposite polarity. At the point

of maximum cancellation, the polarity of the Neumann is switched back and you can hear the two microphones together.

The next three tracks were recorded using the '62 fiesta red Strat through the '62 copper-top Vox AC-10. All microphones were placed slightly off the center of the speaker.

TRACK 18. Shure SM57 in front of speaker and slightly off-center.

TRACK 19. Neumann U67 firing into the back of the cabinet. Note the warm roundness in the low and low mid frequencies and the lack of high end.

TRACK 20. Front and rear microphones together. The combined sound is fatter and more three-dimensional than that from the front microphone alone.

Illustrating chapter 5

All electric bass tracks feature Rod Fogg's late-'70s Fender Jazz Bass. Direct sounds were recorded through a Ridge Farm Gas Cooker tube DI box. Bass amp was a silverface Fender 135 Bassman with a matching speaker cabinet. All electric basses recorded by Javier Ortiz at Estudio Brazil in Madrid, Spain.

TRACK 21. DI sound.

TRACK 22. AKG D112 microphone. Note uneven quality in low mids. Close.

TRACK 23. Neumann U47 FET condenser microphone. Close.

TRACK 24. AKG D112 and Neumann U47 FET combined. Close.

TRACK 25. Neumann U47 one foot away from the cabinet.

TRACK 26. Neumann U47 two feet away from the cabinet.

TRACK 27. Neumann U47 three feet away from the cabinet.

TRACK 28. Neumann U47 as boundary mike. Lots of very low frequencies.

TRACK 29. Neumann U47 three feet away from the cabinet with wood panel.

TRACK 30. DI and U47 mixed together.

TRACK 31. DI and U47 combination, with filtered bass mixed in.

TRACK 32. Neumann U47 (close) with Neve 2252 compressor, deliberately over-compressed to exaggerate the effect. Listen to the squashed attack at the front of notes.

The following double-bass tracks were played by Rod Fogg on a French instrument made in the 1850s.

TRACK 33. Neumann U47 FET below bridge, two feet in front. Pointed up towards the bridge.

TRACK 34. Neumann U47 FET level with bridge, two feet in front.

TRACK 35. Neumann U47 FET level with bridge, two feet in front, mixed with Neumann KM84 near fingers of left hand.

TRACK 36. Pair of Neumann KM 84s on a stereo bar directly opposite bridge, around one foot away. Panned hard left and right.

Illustrating chapter 6

The next three tracks feature the red Stratocaster played through a silverface Fender Deluxe amplifier with a Coles 4038 microphone. These tracks are designed to demonstrate the sound of various reverb devices. This is where the author gets to have a go at playing.

TRACK 37. With the tube stereo EMT plate reverb at Estudio Brazil.

TRACK 38. Roland Space Echo spring reverb.

TRACK 39. Digital reverb effect with a computer plug-in. Notice how the effect and the dry guitar seem to exist separately, whereas the plate reverb integrates to become part of the overall sound.

TRACK 40. Back to Rod Fogg playing a 1963 Gretsch Tennessean through a '50s tweed Fender Deluxe. We added a little slapback tape echo using a Roland Space Echo RE-201 to give it a Chet Atkins vibe.

TRACK 41. Bruce Knapp playing the red Strat through an original Ibanez Tube Screamer and the tweed Fender Deluxe, miked with a Neumann U67. Here the playing has been reversed to demonstrate the sound of backwards guitar. A little reverb has been added.

TRACK 42. Javier quickly programmed up a drum part on an old Roland 909 drum machine with a couple of trigger beats. The author recorded two tracks of feedback with Javier's 1958 anodized-'guard Fender Jazzmaster and blackface Fender Bassman amp, and his Big Muff fuzz box. We put the guitar tracks through a couple of noise gates and triggered them from the drum machine. You can use real drums to create this effect too.

Illustrating chapter 7

The following acoustic guitar pieces were recorded with a nuvistor AKG C28 microphone at the bridge and an Andy Lawrence tube Type B near the neck. Both were placed about 18 inches away from the guitar's soundboard (top). The signals from the two mikes are panned at 10 o'clock and 2 o'clock.

TRACK 43. In this example you get to hear each microphone individually. First is the Andy Lawrence, then the AKG, and finally they are combined.

The next four examples demonstrate just how drastically a guitar's body size and shape can influence the sound. Rod Fogg plays a piece of his own called 'Remembrance' on four different guitars. Mike positions and preamps were not adjusted while these four guitars were being recorded. Decide which one you like best: in situations like this it's down to artistic considerations. Rod was torn between the gentle Froggy Bottom and the ethereal 000. In the end he settled for the 000, but maybe he was just being nice to the guy who built it.

TRACK 44. Martin D-35 dreadnought (new). Check out the huge but woolly bottom end. To be honest, this test is a little unfair on the D-35 because this type of guitar is not really designed for fingerstyle playing.

TRACK 45. Lowden L-32 built in 1979 by George Lowden himself. This guitar has the low end of the D-35 but retains clarity and focus throughout.

TRACK 46. Martin 000-28 built from a Factory Kit by the author. This guitar was completed two weeks before the recording. You can hear that it is slightly immature, with a lot of high-frequency content but a lack of bass. A week after this recording had been completed it had gained another half an octave in the bottom end. New guitars change fast.

TRACK 47. Froggy Bottom 00-size, 12th fret neck/body join. This guitar was handmade in Vermont in 1996 and sounds really sweet and warm.

Four different stereo microphone techniques are heard next. A pair of Neumann KM84s were used with the Froggy Bottom acoustic. If you can switch your monitoring system or hi-fi to mono, check out each technique's mono compatibility.

TRACK 48. Spaced stereo, microphones 24 inches from the soundboard. To my ears this sounds spacious but a little vague.

TRACK 49. Coincident pair, microphones 24 inches from the soundboard. Note the more solid central image.

TRACK 50. Mid-and-side with a Neumann KM84 and a U67 in figure 8 format. Notice how this technique provides a wide and ambient sound.

TRACK 51. Dummy head technique using a real head. Rod Fogg is facing into the corner too, Robert Johnson style. Rod commented that this had an "old" sound and was well suited to the piece. Beware however that dummy-head techniques often display poor mono compatibility.

TRACK 52. A demonstration of the various tones produced by different gauges of plectrum. Note how the thin plectrum is clear but slappy. The thick hard plectrum has a rounder sound in the low mids but is less transparent. It also produces a metallic click against the string. The pointed tortoiseshell plectrum seems to combine the best qualities of each.

The next eight examples indicate how you can achieve various textures when tracking-up acoustic guitars. The microphones used are the Andy Lawrence Type B and the AKG C28.

TRACK 53. Martin D-35 on its own panned to the center.

TRACK 54. Martin D-35 with the 000-28 Martin kit. Hard left and right.

TRACK 55. Martin D35 with 000-28 Martin kit played with capo. Hard left and right. This one has a mandolin-type effect.

TRACK 56. Martin 000-28 kit in Nashville tuning. On its own, panned to the center.

TRACK 57. Martin D-35 with 000-28 Martin kit in Nashville tuning. Hard left and right.

TRACK 58. Martin D-35 with 000-28 Martin kit hard left and right. Martin 000-28 kit in Nashville tuning, panned center.

TRACK 59. Martin D-35 with 000-28 Martin kit played with capo, hard left and right. Martin 000-28 kit in Nashville tuning panned center.

TRACK 60. Martin D-35 with 12-string Washburn. Hard left and right.

TRACK 61. The author grappling with a National steel guitar and a brass slide, desperately trying to get a usable take before the circulation in his legs was cut off. A Coles 4038 was used near the f-holes for the bottom-end and a Beyer 160 near the resonator for the top-end. National steels are possibly the butchest guitars in the world.

Illustrating chapter 8

Here is a distorted guitar using a combination of amplifiers: the Soldano preamp and Mesa/Boogie power amp, plus the Vox AC-10 (blue-top). Javier Ortiz used a Neumann U67 and a Shure SM57 on the former and a Neumann Geffel UM57 and a Coles 4038 on the latter. Ambient microphones were placed slightly above the amplifiers, around 15 feet away.

TRACK 62. Both amps recorded without ambience. Hard left and hard right.

TRACK 63. Both amps recorded with ambience. Hard left and hard right. Each ambient microphone panned to opposite side of mix from the amplifier of source.

See page 176 for information about the pieces played for the various tracks.

Index

Acknowledgements

AUTHOR'S THANKS

Love and gratitude to my wife Ruby, my son Danny, and my parents for putting up with my musical obsessions over so many years. Thanks to my uncle, Professor John Elliot, who first suggested that I should write this book, to Dave Hunter for his huge contribution and the loan of some great guitars, and to Rod Fogg for playing them. Thanks also to: Javier Ortiz at Estudios Brazil in Madrid, Spain; Oz and the crew at FX Rentals in London; Andy Lawrence; Juanma Mas; Chandler Guitars in Kew, London; David Nathan, for his contribution to the impedance section; and to Norman Hall for making me listen.

This book is dedicated to my friend Frank Tovey (aka Fad Gadget) 1956-2002, for all the good times we had.

Jacket picture of author by Steve Bray.

FURTHER READING

We consulted the following books during research for this book.

William R. Cumpiano & Jonathan D. Natelson *Guitar Making* (Chronicle 1993)

Ralph Denyer *The Guitar Handbook* (Pan 1982)

Richard Kaufman *Enhanced Sound* (Tab 1988)

Alec Nisbett *The Use Of Microphones* (Focal 1989)

Aspen Pittman *The Tube Amp Book* (Groove Tubes 1995)

A.A. Strassenburg & Arnold Adolph *The Guitar: A Module On Wave Motion And Sound* (McGraw-Hill 1976)

John Watkinson *The Art Of Sound Reproduction* (Focal 1998)

Tom Wheeler *American Guitars* (Harper & Row 1982)

We also consulted various issues of the following magazines: *EQ*; *Guitar Player*; *Guitarist*; *Sound On Sound* (internet archive); *Studio Sound*; *The Guitar Magazine*.

MUSIC ON THE CD

Find your CD in the book's inside back cover, opposite.

Tracks 4, 5, 6, 18, 19, 20: 'Cayenne' (Fogg).

Tracks 7, 8, 9: 'A Wing And A Prayer' (Fogg).

Tracks 11, 12, 13, 14, 15, 62, 63: 'Drop Death' (Fogg).

Tracks 16, 17: 'Lager Supernova' (Fogg).

Tracks 21, 22, 23, 24, 25, 26, 27, 28, 29, 30, 31, 32: 'Da Da' (Fogg).

Tracks 33, 34, 35, 36: 'Trouble Bass' (Fogg).

Tracks 37, 38, 39: 'Twin Phreaks' (Price).

Tracks 40, 48, 49, 50, 5: 'Chetty Chetty Bang Bang' (Fogg).

Track 41: 'Flip Side' (Knapp).

Track 42: 'Rubia' (Ortiz/Price).

Track 43: 'Three-Chord Wander' (Fogg).

Tracks 44, 45, 46, 47: 'Remembrance' (Fogg).

Track 52: 'Different Strokes' (Fogg).

Tracks 53, 54, 55, 56, 57, 58, 59, 60: 'You've Got Rhythm' (Fogg/Price).

Track 61: 'Polka Hall Blues' (Price).

All music copyright Jazznik 2002.

Rod Fogg became guitar obsessed as a teenager and now plays guitar and bass in and around London, England. His self-penned CD, *A Cool Move*, was released during 2002 on Jazznik (*jazznik.co.uk*); his own website, for downloads and transcriptions, is *rodfogg.com*.

For more detailed information about all the CD tracks see pages 170-172.